Troubadours & Troublemakers

The Evolution of American Protest Music

This work is dedicated to my students:
past, present and future.

For Dad

Contents:

Introduction: Page 7

Chapter One: Page 11
From Settlement to Westward Expansion: The Origin of American Protest Songs

Chapter Two: Page 37
Slave Songs: The Root of Contemporary American Popular Protest Music

Chapter Three: Page 57
Abolitionists & Soldiers: The Rise of Militant Protest Songs

Chapter Four: Page 93
The Industrial Revolution: Singing Their Way to Unionism

Chapter Five: Page 119
Labor & Radical Politics: The Music of Ralph Chaplin, Joe Hill & the IWW

Chapter Six: Page 151
Woody Guthrie, Pete Seeger & the Songs of Patriotic Radicalism

Chapter Seven: Page 169
Pete Seeger: The Johnny Appleseed of Protest Music

Chapter Eight: Page 189
Bob Dylan & the 1960s: The Birth of Protest Rock

Chapter Nine: Page 211
Phil Ochs & the Protest Songs of American Youth

Chapter Ten: Page 231
Rock'n'roll: A New Vehicle for Protest Songs

Chapter Eleven: Page 261
John Lennon: A Minstrel of Radical Protest

Conclusions: Page 281
Protest Traditions Popularized

Acknowledgements: Page 287

Appendix: Page 289
Slave Song List

Bibliography: Page 295

Song Index: Page 316

Introduction

From an early age I knew I was lucky to live in a nation where liberty and the freedom of thought, expression and music was part of our cultural fabric. My parents always taught me the value of freedom and responsibility and music was always a part of our home growing up. We had all kinds of music floating through the house; everything from classical and jazz to blues and rock'n'roll. I don't remember the first time I heard a protest song. It could have been my brother playing a copy of the Beatles' "Revolution;" or it could have been my mother listening to Billie Holliday singing "Strange Fruit." I do know now however, that I grew up listening to protest music and I didn't even realize it.

Songs with stories and messages of protest make up much of our folk and pop songs. Many of the stories of our folk songs have changed through oral tradition and the art of storytelling but they all still retain elements of truth and protest. Our songs are a cultural record of our exceptional experience as a nation and they tell the many stories of our country and its history; the good and the bad. When we examine our songs we examine ourselves and how we came to be. When we examine our protest songs, we examine the dark side of ourselves and the flaws our nation needs to repair to be better.

Serge Denisoff, one of the most prolific and knowledgeable writers on the history and development of American protest music, formulated research guidelines for categorizing protest songs within American culture. Denisoff designed six main classifications of what he called "magnetic" protest songs: they attract outside support, promote solidarity among the group, recruit new members, reinforce the value system of its participants, point out issues to protest and invoke possible solutions. Denisoff wrote that the protest songs written and performed in the sixties diverged from addressing the six elements of what he also called "propaganda songs." I believe, however, that American protest music, throughout its entire history, has contained all or most of the categories identified by Denisoff. I believe protest songs of the rock era did follow Denisoff's six categories and directly used the traditions created by earlier musical troubadours and troublemakers.

As we examine the songs identified in this book we will find elements of almost all of Denisoff's categories. His first two categories were attracting outside support and promoting solidarity. Music is a form of communication like no other in the human experience. The act of making music in a group, like singing along with musicians, or even clapping your hands with the music, is a form of communication that goes beyond words or language. It is a sharing of an emotional groove that puts all participants in an emotive connection. This form of communication automatically complies with Denisoff's categories of attracting outside support and promoting solidarity among the group.

Denisoff's third classification was to recruit new members. Music is a verbal form of communication that attracts attention and in the process recruits new members. The very nature of music causes curiosity. When music is heard, whether it comes from a voice or an instrument, the immediate reaction is to listen. If the music is good, or the words are interesting, it may encourage you to listen more and find out what the song is about. This act of performing music publically so others can listen satisfies Denisoff's recruit new members' category.

The remaining three classifications, reinforce the value system of its participants, point out issues to protest and invoke possible solutions depend on the words and presentation of the music. I intend to show, through a chronological and biographical examination of the people and events that made topical music throughout history that the use of songs to protest social, political and economic injustice falls within Denisoff's categories.

Our story begins in chapter one where we examine the protest songs of settlers, revolutionaries, migrants, forty-niners and cowboys. In chapter two we see how the protest songs of slaves helped create American traditions in the evolution of protest singing in the United States. Chapter three continues with the songs of abolitionists and soldiers during the civil war. Chapter four begins the story of labor organizing which is continued in chapter five with Ralph Chaplin, Joe Hill and the IWW. In chapters six and seven we explore the contributions of Woody Guthrie and Pete Seeger from the days of the Great Depression to the McCarthyism of the 1950s. In chapters eight and nine we explore the protest music of the 1960s through two artists: Bob Dylan and Phil Ochs. Our examination continues with chapter ten where we survey the many rock-protest songs from the 1960s, especially the protest artists and songs of the Monterey Pop Festival and Woodstock. In chapter eleven we examine the politics and protest songs of John Lennon. The book concludes with a survey of contemporary artists who are carrying on the tradition of singing protest songs with new forms of music.

Although this book is not a comprehensive examination of every protest song ever written in the United States, it was my intention to provide examples of protest songs that show a *link in a chain* of topical singing in the evolution of American protest music. I must admit that the songs chosen for this work are those which attracted my attention and maintained my interest. It is my hope that this book will inspire you to do your own research and listen to the wide variety of protest music available in American culture.

It would not have been possible for me to write this book without the collectors that have made protest songs available to the general public. Just like the singers, writers and performers analyzed in this work, collectors like Joyce L. Kornbluh, Archie Green, Richard A. Reuss, John & Alan Lomax, John Greenway and Serge Denisoff, dedicated large portions of their adult lives to the collection, analysis and dissemination of American protest music. These people also deserve the title of troubadours and troublemakers, for it is their work that I build upon with all the words that follow.

I feel compelled to note why the second half of this book is almost completely devoid of lyrics. The corporations that hold the copyrights to the songs in these chapters demanded a licensing payment that would have been impossible for me to provide. For economic reasons, I decided to remove all copyrighted material from this book. Many of the song lyrics that are discussed in this text can be found on various webpages on-line. All lyrics included in this collection, except where noted, are in the public domain.

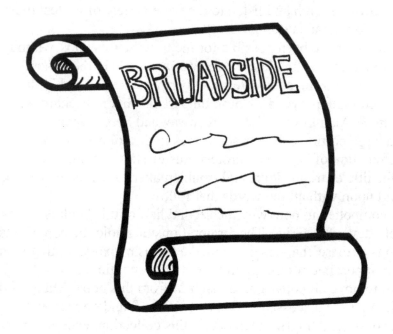

Chapter One:
From Settlement to the Westward Expansion: The Origin of American Protest Songs

Let us pause in life's pleasures
And count its many tears
While we sup sorrow with the poor
There's a song that will linger
Forever in our ears
Oh hard times come again no more

Stephen Collins Foster

As the early immigrants from Western Europe began to settle and prosper they remembered their ballad and broadside traditions and wrote new songs to fit their current conditions. As settlers created a new nation and moved west on the American continent; they endured harsh weather conditions, long hours working on the farm or in the mine, new diseases, attacks from Native Americans, and the bigotry of their fellow Americans. These settlers, revolutionaries, migrants, farmers, 49ers, Indian fighters, immigrants, anti-Mormons and cowboys who created protest songs to address their new conditions were some of the first troubadours and troublemakers in American history.

Some of the earliest songs in the American colonies were ballads brought over from England and Scotland and, over time, turned into American folk songs. People sang them to their children and passed on the songs from generation to generation; from Europe to America. According to Gordon Hall Gerould in The Ballad of Tradition, "The popular ballad…had no real existence save when held in memory and sung by those who have learned it from the lips of others."

One such song was "Barbara Allen," a Scottish ballad probably written in the mid-sixteenth century. Listed as number 84 in the Francis Child collection of British ballads, it was widely recognized as a love song. There have been at least 198 lyrical versions of the song and at least "four basic tunes" used as accompanying music. The ballad's story is a protest against societal or family expectations; it expressed the dread of unrequited love. At the end of the song, Barbara Allen, who refused to return the love of William, died herself full of sad regret.

> She on her deathbed as she lay
> Begged to be buried by him
> And sore repented o every day
> That she did ever deny him

"Barbara Allen" (or Barbary Allen, Barbry Ellen etc.) has been recorded by many musicians in the past one hundred years including Bradley Kincaid, Merle Travis, Pete Seeger, Joan Baez, Jean Richie, Dolly Parton, Emmylou Harris and Bob Dylan. Folk songs like "Barbara Allen" gave Bob Dylan the encouragement to be a singer and writer of socially relevant topical songs. According to Dylan, "the folk songs showed me the way. They showed me that songs can say something human. Without 'Barbara Allen' there'd be no 'Girl From the North Country'."

Along with traditional ballads, European settlers also brought with them the Broadside Ballad. Printed on a piece of parchment, these songs would be set to old tunes that were easily recognized by many colonists. Other Broadsides were actually stories that were passed down through oral tradition and then picked up by someone and printed for sale and distribution. These Broadsides were used in the American colonies to protest the tyranny of the British King during the American Revolution, against the American government during the Sedition Act crisis of 1798, opposing John Adams' re-election of 1800, and to protest the British again during the War of 1812.

When the friction between the American Colonies and Britain increased in the 1760s and 1770s a number of topical songs were written to protest the autocratic empire. One such song was "Free America," written in 1770 by Dr. Joseph Warren. (Dr. Warren was also involved in helping Paul Revere in his famous ride warning of the British advancement toward Lexington and Concord.) The song clearly blames Britain for tyrannical behavior and called on those who believe in liberty to join the fight for freedom against all the European monarchies.

> That Seat of Science Athens, and Earth's great Mistress Rome
> Where now are all their Glories, we scarce can find their Tomb
> Then guard your Rights, Americans! nor stoop to lawless Sway
> Oppose, oppose, oppose, oppose, -- my brave America
>
> Proud Albion bow'd to Caesar, and num'rous Lords before
> To Picts, to Danes, to Normans, and many Masters more

But we can boast Americans! we never fell a Prey
Huzza, huzza, huzza, huzza, for brave America

We led fair Freedom hither, when lo the Desart smil'd
A paradise of pleasure, was open'd in the Wild
Your Harvest, bold Americans! no power shall snatch away
Huzza, huzza, huzza, huzza, for brave America

Torn from a World of Tyrants, beneath this western Sky
We form'd a new Dominion, a Land of liberty
The World shall own their masters here, then hasten on the Day
Huzza, huzza, huzza, huzza, for brave America

God bless this maiden Climate, and thro' her vast Domain
Let Hosts of Heroes cluster, who scorn to wear a Chain
And blast the venal Sycophant, who dares our Rights betray
Preserve, preserve, preserve, preserve my brave America

Lift up your Heads my Heroes! and swear with proud Disdain
The Wretch that would enslave you, shall spread his Snares in vain
Should Europe empty all her force, wou'd meet them in Array
And shout, and shout, and shout, and shout, for brave America

Some future Day shall crown us, the Masters of the Main
And giving Laws and Freedom, to subject France and Spain
When all the Isles o'er Ocean spread shall tremble and obey
Their Lords, their Lords, their Lords
Their Lords of brave America

"The Rich Lady Over the Sea" was written in the midst of the taxation crisis following the Tea Act of 1773. The main complaint of the colonists was that these taxes were being imposed without their consent or input. Colonial legislators had been running their own legal and economic affairs for years until the end of the French and Indian War in 1763. After that costly conflict, the British parliament began to impose a system of taxes that the colonists opposed. The mother in this song is Britain and the daughter is the American colonies.

There was a rich lady lived over the sea
And she was an island queen
Her daughter lived off in the new country
With an ocean of water between (x3)

The old lady's pockets were filled with gold
Yet never contented was she

So she ordered her daughter to pay her a tax
Of thru pence a pound on the tea (x3)

"Oh mother, dear mother," the daughter replied
"I'll not do the thing that you ask
"I'm willing to pay a fair price for the tea
But never a thru penny tax (x3)

"You shall!" cried the mother, and reddened with rage
"For you're my own daughter you see
"And it's only proper that daughter should pay
Her mother a tax on the tea (x3)

She ordered her servant to come up to her
And to wrap up a package of tea
And eager for three pence a pound she put in
Enough for a large family (x3)

The tea was conveyed to her daughter's own door
All down by the Oceanside
But the bouncing girl poured out every pound
On the dark and the boiling tide (x3)

And then she called out to the island queen
"Oh mother, dear mother," called she
"Your tea you may have when 'tis steeped enough
But NEVER a tax from me
But NEVER a tax from me
But NEVER a tax from me"

During the War for American Independence an old Irish song was adapted by the soldiers with new lyrics that protested the war. "Johnny Has Gone for a Soldier" was sung from the perspective of a grieving mother who has lost her son to the war and wants to know if he is dead or alive.

Oh I wish I were on yon green hill
There I'd sit and cry my fill
And every tear would turn a mill
For my Johnny has gone for a soldier

I'll sell my clock; I'll sell my reel
I'll sell my only spinning wheel
To buy my love a sword of steel
Johnny has gone for a soldier

I'll dye my petticoat; I'll dye it red
And round the world I'll bake my bread
Till I find my love alive or dead
My Johnny has gone for a soldier

"Hail Columbia" was written in 1798, sixteen years after the United States won its independence from Britain and during a time the newly formed American government was under the control of those who called themselves Federalists. They passed laws that punished people who criticized their efforts to fight an undeclared Quasi-War against France. This was one of the first songs written in protest against the new American republic.

Hail Columbia, happy land!
Hail, ye heroes, heaven-born band
Who fought and bled in freedom's cause
And when the storm of war was gone
Enjoyed the peace your valor won
Let independence be our boast
Ever mindful what it cost
Ever grateful for the prize
Let its altar reach the skies

Firm, united let us be
Rallying round our liberty
As a band of brothers joined
Peace and safety we shall find...

Another early protest song put to print in the emerging American Republic was "Jefferson and Liberty." The song comes from the election of 1800 but was changed many times. Most famously by Lincoln's presidential campaign that changed it to "Lincoln and Liberty." The song was another protest against the Alien and Sedition Acts passed by the Federalists in 1798 and 1799.

The gloomy night before us flies
The reign of terror now is o'er
Its gags inquisitors and spies
Herds of harpies are no more

Rejoice, Columbia's sons, rejoice
To tyrants never bend the knee
But join with heart and soul
And voice for Jefferson and liberty

15

No lording here, with gorging jaws
Shall wring from industry the food
Nor fiery bigots holy laws
Lay waste our fields and streets in blood

Here strangers from a thousand shores
Compelled by tyranny to roam
Shall find, amidst abundant stories
A nobler and happier home

Here Art shall lift her laurelled head
Wealth Industry and peace divine
And where dark pathless forests spread
Rich fields and lofty cities shine

From Europe's wants and woes remote
A friendly waste of waves between
Here plenty cheers the humblest cot
And smiles on every village green

Here free as air, expanded space
To every soul and sect shall be
That sacred privilege of our race
The worship of the deity

Let foes to freedom dread the name
But should they touch the sacred tree
Twice fifty thousand swords would flame
For Jefferson and liberty

From Georgia to Lake Champlain
From seas to Mississippi's shore
Ye sons of freedom loud proclaim
"The reign of terror is no more"

Another song from the campaign of 1800 was collected by John Greenway in American Folksongs of Protest. It was called "Every Man His Own Politician" and perpetuated the image created by the Jeffersonians that John Adams and the Federalists represented the rich and powerful. This Broadside clearly calls for the masses to turn out the aristocrats and monarchists for the good of the people.

Let every man of Adam's line
In social contact freely join
To extirpate monarchic power

That kings may plague the earth no more

As pow'r results from you alone
Ne'er trust it on a single throne
Longs oft betray their sacred trust
And crush their subjects in the dust

Nor yet confide in men of show
Aristocrats reduce you low
Nobles, at best, are fickle things
And oft, far worse than cruel kings

Nobles combine in secret fraud
Tho in pretense for public good
To frame a law the most unjust
And sink the people down to dust

When laws are fram'd, the poor must lie
Distrust beneath the nobles' eye
Unpity'd there, to waste their breath
In fruitless prayers 'till by death

A year is long enough to prove
A servant's wisdom, faith and love
Release him from temptation then
And change the post to other men

Now is the prime important hour
The people may improve their pow'r
To stop aristocratic force
And walk in reason's peaceful course.

Choose all your servants once a year
Will strict reserve and nicest care
And if they once abuse their place
Reward them with deserv'd disgrace

During the War of 1812 (also known as the Second War for American Independence) there were many songs with protest messages that became very popular in America. I have chosen three for this collection. The first of these was "Parliament of England." Most of the song is a listing of the many ships that fought and defeated the British in the battles for the Great Lakes. The first, second and last verses contain the most direct message of protest.

Ye Parliament of England
Ye Lords and Commons too
Consider well what you're about
What you're about to do
For you're to war with Yankees
And I'm sure you'll rue the day
You roused the Sons of Liberty
In North America

You first confined our commerce
And said our ships shan't trade
You next impressed our seamen
And used them as your slaves
You then insulted Rodgers
While plying o'er the main
And had we not declared war
You'd have done it o'er again…

Grant us free trade and commerce
Don't you impress our men
Give up all claims to Canada
Then we'll make peace again
Then England we'll respect you
And treat you as a friend
Respect our flag and citizens
Then all these wars will end

The second song was "Patriotic Diggers" written by Samuel Woodworth. This song was a rallying cry to the Philadelphia community to volunteer and help reinforce the city against British invasion. It was a protest against the tyranny of the British Empire. Johnny Bull was the symbol of the British Empire just like Uncle Sam became the symbol of the United States.

Johnny Bull beware, keep a proper distance
Else we'll make you stare at our firm resistance
Let alone the lads who are freedom tasting
Recollect our dads gave you once a basting

Pick-axe, shovel, spade, crow-bar, hoe and barrow
Better not invade, Yankees have the marrow
To protect our rights 'against your flint and triggers
See on yonder heights our patriotic diggers
Men of every age, color, rank, profession

Ardently engaged, labor in succession

Grandeur leaves her towers, poverty her hovel
Here to join their powers with the hoe and shovel
Here the merchant toils with the patriotic sawyer
There the laborer smiles, near him sweats the lawyer

Scholars leave their schools with patriotic teachers
Farmers seize their tools, headed by their preachers
How they break the soil - brewers, butchers, bakers
Here the doctors toil, there the undertakers

Bright Apollo's sons leave their pipe and tabor
Mid the roar of guns join the martial labor
Round the embattled plain in sweet concord rally
And in freedom's strain sing the foes finale

Plumbers, founders, dyers, tinmen, turners, shavers
Sweepers, clerks, and criers, jewelers and engravers
Clothiers, drapers, players, cartmen, hatters, tailor
Gaugers, sealers, weighers, carpenters and sailors

Better not invade, don't forget the spirit
Which our dads displayed and their sons inherit
If you still advance, friendly caution slighting
You may get by chance a bellyful of fighting!

Also written by Samuel Woodworth, the third song of the War of 1812 was "The Hunters of Kentucky." Fifteen days after the peace treaty was signed between the British and the United States the two armies fought a battle in New Orleans. This battle gave birth to an American hero, Andrew Jackson and a popular patriotic protest song.

Ye gentlemen and ladies fair, who grace this famous city
Just listen, if you've time to spare, while I rehearse a ditty
And for the opportunity conceive yourselves quite lucky
For 'tis not often that you see a hunter from Kentucky
Oh, Kentucky! The hunters of Kentucky.

We are a hardy free-born race, each man to fear a stranger
Whatever the game we join in chase, despising toil and danger
And if a daring foe annoys, whatever his strength and forces
We'll show him that Kentucky boys are alligator horses

I suppose you've read it in the prints, how Packenham attempted
To make old Hickory Jackson wince, but soon his schemes repented
For we with rifles ready cocked, thought such occasion lucky
And soon around the general flocked the hunters of Kentucky

You've heard, I suppose, how New Orleans is famed for wealth & beauty
There's girls of every hue it seems, from snowy white to sooty
So Packenham he made his brags, if he in fight was lucky
He'd have their girls and cotton bags in spite of old Kentucky

But Jackson he was wide awake, and wasn't scared at trifles
For well he knew what aim we take with our Kentucky rifles
So he led us down to Cyprus swamp, the ground was low and mucky
There stood John Bull in martial pomp, and here was old Kentucky

A bank was raised to hide our breast, not that we thought of dying
But then we always like to rest unless the game is flying
Behind it stood our little force, none wished it to be greater
For every man was half a horse and half an alligator

They did not let our patience tire, before they showed their faces
We did not choose to waist our fire, so snugly kept our places
But when so near to see them wink, we thought it time to stop 'em
And 'twould have done you good I think, to see Kentuckians drop 'em

They found at last 'twas vain to fight, where lead was all their booty
And so they wisely took to flight, and left us all our beauty
And now if danger ever annoys, remember what our trade is
Just send for us Kentucky boys, and we'll protect your ladies

Following the War of 1812 there were a number of songs that
contained themes of protest. There were songs against debtor prison
like "The Charlestown Land Shark" and even songs about the Dorr
Rebellion in Rhode Island in the 1840s. Two such numbers were
"Rhode Island Algerines' Appeal to John Davis" and "Landholders
Victory." "The Wayfaring Stranger," written in the first decade of the
19th century, was originally intended as a religious song, but over time
became a standard folk song protesting the loneliness of those who are
away from their homes because of work or war.

I'm just a poor wayfaring stranger
I'm traveling through this world of woe
Yet there's no sickness, toil nor danger
In that bright land to which I go

20

I'm going there to see my mother/father
I'm going there no more to roam
I'm just a-going over Jordan
I'm just a-going over home

I know dark clouds will gather 'round me
I know my way is rough and steep
Yet golden fields lie just before me
Where God's redeemed shall ever sleep

I'm going there to see my father/mother
She/he said he'd/she'd meet me when I come
I'm only going over Jordan
I'm only going over home

I want to wear a crown of glory
When I get home to that good land
I want to shout salvation's story
In concert with the blood-washed band

I'm going there to meet my Savior
To sing his praise forever more
I'm just a-going over Jordan
I'm just a-going over home

As Americans continued to move west they not only brought singing traditions with them, they also made up new songs to fit their situation. There were many songs that protested the hard life migrants endured on the ever expanding American frontier. One such song was the "Wisconsin Immigrant." This was written about those settlers who intended to go on to California but ended up staying behind in Wisconsin.

Since times are so hard, I've thought, my true heart
Of leaving my oxen, my plough, and my cart
And away to Wisconsin, a journey we'd go
To double our fortune as other folks do
While here I must labor each day in the field
And the winter consumes all the summer doth yield

Oh husband, I've noticed with sorrowful heart
You've neglected your oxen, your plough, and your cart
Your sheep are disordered; at random they run
And your new Sunday suit is now every day on

Oh, stay on the farm and you'll suffer no loss
For the stone that keeps rolling will gather no moss

Oh wife, let's go; oh, don't let us wait
Oh, I long to be there; oh, I long to be great
While you some rich lady - and who knows but I
Some governor may be before that I die?
While here I must labor each day in the field
And the winter consumes all the summer doth yield

Oh husband, remember that land is to clear
Which will cost you the labor of many a year
Where horses, sheep, cattle, and hogs are to buy
And you'll scarcely get settled before you must die
Oh, stay on the farm and you'll suffer no loss
For the stone that keeps rolling will gather no moss

Oh wife, let's go; oh, don't let us stay
I will buy me a farm that is cleared by the way
Where horses, sheep, cattle, and hogs are not dear
And we'll feast on fat buffalo half of the year
While here I must labor each day in the field
And the winter consumes all the summer doth yield

Oh husband, remember that land of delight
Is surrounded by Indians who murder by night
Your house they will plunder and burn to the ground
While your wife and your children lie murdered around
Oh, stay on the farm, and you'll suffer no loss
For the stone that keeps rolling will gather no moss

Now wife, you've convinced me; I'll argue no more
I never had thought of your dying before
I love my dear children, although they are small
But you, my dear wife, are more precious than all
We'll stay on the farm, and suffer no loss
For the stone that keeps rolling will gather no moss

Farmers on open plains had many hardships they openly sang about. One such song of protest was "The Farmer is the Man." It was probably written in the 1870s or 80s by a supporter of the Grangers, Greenbacks, or Populists. It was a protest against all those who seemed more concerned with lawyers, butchers or cooks. The song reminded the listener that without farmers working the land, people living in urban areas would have no food and the society would collapse.

When the farmer comes to town
With his wagon broken down
The farmer is the man who feeds them all
If you'll only look and see
I am sure you will agree
The farmer is the man who feeds them all

The farmer is the man
The farmer is the man
Lives on credit till the fall
Then they take him by the hand
And they lead him from the land
And the middleman's the man who gets it all

When the lawyer hangs around
While the butcher cuts a pound
The farmer is the man who feeds them all
And the preacher and the cook
Go a-strolling down the brook
The farmer is the man who feeds them all

When the banker says he's broke
And the merchant's up in smoke
The farmer is the man who feeds them all
It would put them to the test
If the farmer took a rest
The farmer is the man who feeds them all

One of the most difficult aspects of farming is the harsh and unpredictable environment. Drought, extreme temperatures and insects can be devastating to the farmer's crop. "The Boll Weevil" song expressed protest against a little insect that can destroy an entire farm. These bugs got into everything, including cloths and food. Years later Woody Guthrie would be performing this song in New York City! This particular version was written in a slave dialect and contains a word that is offensive in contemporary speech (which we will examine in chapter two), but holds powerful historical and cultural meaning.

Oh, de boll weevil am a little black bug
Come from Mexico, dey say
Come all de way to Texas

23

Jus' a-lookin' foh a place to stay
Jus' a-lookin' foh a home, jus' a-lookin' foh a home

De first time I seen de boll weevil
He was a-settin' on de square
De next time I seen de boll weevil
He had all of his family dere...

De farmer say to de weevil
"What make yo' head so red?"
De weevil say to de farmer
"It's a wondah I ain't dead...

De farmer take de boll weevil
An' he put him in de hot san'
De weevil say: "Dis is mighty hot
But I'll stan' it like a man
Dis'll be my home, it'll be my home"

De farmer take de boll weevil
An' he put him in a lump of ice
De boll weevil say to de farmer
"Dis is mighty cool and nice...

De farmer take de boll weevil
An' he put him in de fire
De boll weevil say to de farmer
"Here I are, here I are

De boll weevil say to de farmer
"You better leave me alone
I done eat all yo' cotton
Now I'm goin' to start on yo' corn
I'll have a home, I'll have a home"

De merchant got half de cotton
De boll weevil got de res'
Didn't leave de farmer's wife
But one old cotton dress
An' it's full of holes, it's full of holes.

De farmer say to de merchant
"We's in an awful fix
De boll weevil et all de cotton up
An' lef' us only sticks

We's got no home, we's got no home"

De farmer say to de merchant
"We ain't made but only one bale
And befoh we'll give yo' dat one
We'll fight and go to jail
We'll have a home, we'll have a home"

De cap'n say to de missus
"What d' you t'ink o' dat?
De boll weevil done make a nes'
In my bes' Sunday hat
Goin' to have a home, goin' to have a home"

An' if anybody should ax you
Who it was dat make dis song
Jus' tell 'em 'twas a big buck niggah
Wid a paih o' blue duckin's on
Ain' got no home, ain' got no home

One of the reasons American migrants spread west was the search for gold. In January 1848 James W. Marshall and John Sutter found gold in a stream near their saw mill in Coloma, California. When President Polk found out about the find, he proclaimed in his State of the Union Address: "The explorations already made warrant the belief that the supply is very large and that gold is found at various places in an extensive district of (our) country." Once the word spread across the nation that gold was discovered in California, migrants from all walks of life dropped their livelihood and made the rush west. As the opening to the song "Seeking the Elephant" exclaims:

When I left the states for gold
Everything I had I sold
A stove and bed, a fat old sow
Sixteen chickens and a cow

These migrants became famously known as the "forty-niners." There were many songs written for these prospectors. One song called "The Days of Forty-nine" was a protest against all the good men who died in the early days of the California Gold Rush. Another was "The Good Old Days of 50, '1 and '2" that continued the same theme and sang: "And now I wander on alone… But I'll ne'er forget those dear old friends." A song called "Life in California" actually had the following

25

chorus: "But I'm a used up man, a perfect used up man. And if ever I get home again, I'll stay there if I can." The first two lines of a song "California As It Is" sums up the feeling of the prospector once he realized his situation: "I've been to California and I haven't got a dime, I've lost my health, my strength, my hope, and I have lost my time."

"When I Went Off to Prospect" was a song written by John A. Stone that expressed the true prospecting opportunities to the multitudes that went west to get rich quick in California. There may have been gold in the west, but with all the thousands of prospectors looking for the same riches, there just wasn't enough to go around.

When I got there, the mining ground
Was staked and claimed for miles around
And not a bed was to be found
When I went off to prospect

The town was crowded full of folks
Which made me think 'twas not a hoax
At my expense they cracked their jokes
When I was nearly starving…

Now all I got for running about
Was two black eyes, and bloody snout
And that's the way it did turn out
When I went off to prospect

And now I'm loafing around dead broke
My pistol and tools are all in soak
And whisky bills at me they poke
But I'll make it right in the morning

As we conclude our examination of the protest music of the gold prospector we need to look at one more song. "The Lousy Miner" clearly is protesting the awful condition of the poor migrant who expected to get rich and return home with bags of money. Instead, all they got were pains cause by hunger and the loss of missed loved ones.

It's four long years since I reached this land
In search of gold among the rocks and sand
And yet I'm poor, when the truth is told
I'm a lousy miner, I'm a lousy miner
In search of shining gold

26

I've lived on swine till I grunt and squeal
No one can tell how my bowels feel
With flapjacks swimming round in grease
When will my troubles cease

I was covered with lice coming on the boat
I threw away my fancy swallow-tail coat
And now they crawl up and down my back
A pile is all I lack

My sweetheart vowed she'd wait for me
Till I returned, now don't you see
She's married now, so I am told, left her
In search of shining gold

O land of gold, you did me deceive
And I intend you my bones to leave
So farewell home, now my friends grow cold
In search of shining gold

Songwriter Jessy Hutchinson Jr. of the famous Hutchinson Family Singers (who we will discuss in chapter three) wrote a song for these migrants protesting their conditions and even ending with a condemnation of slavery. "Ho! For California!" can be considered partly patriotic and partly protest.

We've formed our band, and we're all well manned
To journey afar to the Promised Land
Where the golden ore is rich in store
On the banks of the Sacramento shore

As off we roam through the dark sea foam
We'll ne'er forget kind friends at home
But memory kind shall bring to mind
The love of those we left behind

Oh don't you cry, nor heave a sigh
For we'll all come back again by and by
Don't breathe a fear, nor shed a tear
But patiently wait for about two year...

Oh the land we'll save for the bold and brave
Have determined there never shall breathe a slave
Let foes recoil, for the sons of toil
Shall make California God's Free Soil

Some migrants traveled to California via boat and had a difficult journey around Cape Horn. Written by John A Stone and put to the melody of "Dearest Mae," "Coming Around the Horn" was a description of the challenging journey around the southern tip of South America. The third, fourth and fifth verses are the most vivid in their protest of the conditions on the ship.

> We all were owners of the ship, and soon began to growl
> Because we hadn't ham and eggs, and now and then a fowl
> We told the captain what to do, as him we had to pay
> The captain swore that he was the boss, and we should him obey
>
> We lived like hogs, penned up up to fat, our vessel was small
> We had a "duff" but once a month, and twice a day a squall
> A meeting now and then was held, which kicked up quite a stink
> The captain damned us fore and aft, and wished the box would stink
>
> Off Cape Horn, where we lay becalmed, kind Providence seems to frown
> We had to stand up night and day, none of us dared sit down
> For some had half a dozen boils, 'twas awful, sure's you're born
> But some would try it on the sly, and got pricked by the horn

One of the greatest fears migrants had when crossing the plains were confrontations with American Indians. From the perspective of these Native Americans, it was the migrants that were invading their territory. They had lived, hunted, and thrived on these plains for hundreds (if not thousands) of years. From the migrants perspective the American Indians were nothing but savages who were harming their fellow countrymen only trying to make their way to a new home. "Sioux Indians" is a traditional song that has been passed down through oral tradition and eventually ended up being recorded in the 1950s by Pete Seeger. (More on Seeger in chapter six and seven.)

> I'll sing you a song, though it may be a sad one
> Of trials and troubles and where first begun
> I left my dear family, my friends and my home
> To cross the wide mountains and deserts to roam
>
> I crossed the Missouri and joined a large train
> Which bore us over mountains, through valley and plain
> And often of an evening a-huntin' we'd go
> To shoot the fleet antelope and wild buffalo

We heard of Sioux Indians all out on the plains
A-killing poor drivers and burning their trains
A-killing poor drivers with arrows and bows
When captured by Indians no mercy they'd show

We traveled three weeks till we come to the Platte
A-pitching our tents at the head of the flat
We spread down our blankets on the green shady ground
Where the mules and the horses were grazing around

While taking refreshment, we heard a loud yell
The whoops of Sioux Indians come up from the dell
We sprang to our rifles with a flash in each eye
And says our brave leader, "We'll fight till we die"

They made a bold dash and they come near our train
The arrows fell around us like showers of rain
But with our long rifles we fed them hot lead
Till a-many a brave warrior around us lay dead

We shot their bold chief at the head of their band
He died like a warrior with his bow in his hand
When they saw their brave chief lie dead in his gore
They whooped and they yelled and we saw them no more

In our little band there were just twenty four
And of the Sioux Indians five hundred or more
We fought them with courage, we spoke not a word
The whoop of Sioux Indians was all could be heard

We hooked up our horses and started our train
Three more bloody battles this trip on the plain
And in our last battle three of our brave boys fell
And we left them to rest in the green shady dell

Immigrants also had many songs of protest in the early days of the
United States. Some of the earliest immigrants were the Irish. Except
for the African slaves, stolen from their country and brought to America
in chains, the Irish had it the hardest in the early American republic.
One song that describes their fight against prejudice and discrimination
was "No Irish Need Apply." It was based on the ever heard refrain an
Irish immigrant confronted when applying for a job. I have included
here the first four verses which include the strongest messages of
protest.

I'm a decent boy, just landed from the town of Ballyfad
I want a situation: yes, I want it mighty bad
I saw a place advertised. "It's the thing," says I
But the dirty spalpeen ended with: "No Irish need apply"
Whoo! says I; but that's an insult -- though to get the place I'll try
So, I want to see the black guard with his no Irish need apply

Well, I started off to find the house; I got there mighty soon
There I found the old chap seated: he was reading the TRIBUNE
I told him what I came for, when he in a rage did fly
"No!" Says he, "you are a Paddy, and no Irish need apply!"
Then I felt my dander rising, and I'd like to black his eye
For to tell an Irish Gentleman: "No Irish need apply!"

Well I couldn't stand it longer: so, a hold of him I took
And I gave him such a welting as he'd get at Donnybrook
He hollered: "Millia murther!" And to get away did try
And swore he'd never write again: "No Irish need apply!"
He made a big apology; I bid him then good-bye
Saying: "When next you want a beating, write:
"No Irish need apply!"

Sure, I've heard that in America it always is the plan
That an Irishman is just as good as any other man
A home and hospitality they never will deny
The stranger near or ever say: "No Irish need apply"
But some black sheep are in the flock: a dirty lot, say I
A decent man will never write: "No Irish need apply!"

The Mormons had to deal with a tremendous amount of
discrimination and persecution because of their creation of a new
American religion. Founded by Joseph Smith as the Church of Latter
Day Saints of Jesus Christ (also known as the L.D.S. Church or
Mormon Church), the Mormons were rejected by other Christian sects
in the United States. Following the murder of Joseph Smith in Carthage
Illinois, Brigham Young took up leadership and led a group of latter
day saints on a westward trek to the Great Salt Lake in modern day
Utah. Even in Utah the Mormons had to deal with hatred and
harassment. At one point in the late 1850s, the pressure was so bad that
the Mormons of Cedar City responded with violence. The incident was
eventually put to verse in the 1870s and has now passed into oral
tradition with the original author unknown. From the verses included

below, the "Mountain Meadows Massacre" clearly places the blame for the murders in the hands of the Mormon Church itself.

Come all you sons of liberty, unto my rhyme give ear
'Tis of the bloody massacree you presently shall hear
In splendor o'er the mountains some thirty wagons came
They were awaited by a wicked band, oh Utah, bear the blame!

In Indian colors all wrapped in shame this bloody crew was seen
To flock around this little train all on the meadows green
They were attacked in the morning as they were on their way
They forthwith corralled their wagons and fought in blood array

Till came the captain of the band, he surely did deceive
Saying, "If you will give up your arms we'll surely let you live."
When once they had given up their arms, thinking their lives to save
The words were broken among the rest which sent them to their graves.

When once they had given up their arms they started for Cedar City
They rushed on them in Indian style, oh what a human pity!
They melted down with one accord like wax before the flame,
Both men and women, old and young, oh Utah! where's thy shame?

Both men and women, old and young, a-rolling in their gore
And such an awful sight and scene was ne'er beheld before
Their property was divided among this bloody crew
And Uncle Sam is bound to see this bloody matter through.

The soldiers will be stationed throughout this Utah land
All for to find those murderers out and bring them to his hands.
By order from their president, this bloody deed was done
He was the leader of the Mormon Church, his name was Brigham Young.

The Mormon Church has taken responsibility for what took place in September 1857. The official website of the L.D.S. Church reads the following:

> What was done here long ago by members of our Church represents a terrible and inexcusable departure from Christian teaching and conduct. We cannot change what happened, but we can remember and honor those who were killed here. We express profound regret for the massacre carried out in this valley 150 years ago today and for the undue and untold suffering experienced by

31

the victims then and by their relatives to the present
time.

Other westerners had to deal with different forms of hardships. One
job an American could take out west was as a Buffalo Skinner. This
occupation was so difficult that a song was created to protest the
working conditions. It was passed into oral tradition eventually taking
its place as a permanent part of American musical folklore. Below are
three verses that were collected by John and Alan Lomax in the 1930s
and published in their collection Cowboy Songs.

> He fed us on such sorry chuck, I wished myself most dead
> It was old jerked beef, croton coffee and sour bread
> Pease River's as salty as hell fire, the water I never could go
> O God! I wished I had never come to the range of the buffalo

> Our meat it was buffalo hump and iron wedge bread
> And all we had to sleep on was a buffalo robe for a bed
> The fleas and gray-backs worked on us, O boys, it was not slow
> I tell you there's no worse hell on earth than the range of the buffalo

> Our hearts were cased with buffalo hocks,
> Our souls were cased with steel
> And the hardships of that summer would nearly make us reel
> While skinning the damned old stinkers, our lives they had no show
> For the Indians watched to pick us off on the hills of Mexico

Another protest song about the cowboys called "Cowboy's Life is a
Dreary, Dreary Life." It shattered the romantic image of a cowboy on
the open plains playing his harmonica and enjoying a beautiful sunset.
The facts were completely different from the myth. Cowboys were
lonely, cold, hungry and in constant danger from wolves, Indians,
disease and outlaws. There are different versions of this song. One
version is printed in Irwin Silber's collection: Songs of the American
West. I have included here a version I found on-line. Some of the words
may be different, but the message is the same.

> A cowboy's life is a dreary, dreary life
> Some say it's free from care
> Rounding up the cattle from morning till night
> In the middle of the prairie so bare

Half-past four, the noisy cook will roar
"Whoop-a-whoop-a-hey!"
Slowly you will rise with sleepy-feeling eyes
The sweet, dreamy night passed away

The greener lad he thinks it's play
He'll soon peter out on a cold rainy day
With his big bell spurs and his Spanish hoss
He'll swear to you he was once a boss

The cowboy's life is a dreary, dreary life
He's driven through the heat and cold
While the rich man's a-sleeping on his velvet couch
Dreaming of his silver and gold

Spring-time sets in, double trouble will begin
The weather is so fierce and cold
Clothes are wet and frozen to our necks
The cattle we can scarcely hold

The cowboy's life is a dreary one
He works all day to the setting of the sun
And then his day's work is not done
For there's his night herd to go on

The wolves and owls with their terrifying howls
Will disturb us in our midnight dream
As we lie on our slickers on a cold, rainy night
Way over on the Pecos stream

You are speaking of your farms, you are speaking of your charms
You are speaking of your silver and gold
But a cowboy's life is a dreary, dreary life
He's driven through the heat and cold

Some folks say that we are free from care
Free from all other harm
But we round up the cattle from morning till night
Way over on the prairie so dry

I used to run about, now I stay at home
Take care of my wife and child
Nevermore to roam, always stay at home
Take care of my wife and child

33

Half-past four the noisy cook will roar
"Hurrah, boys! she's breaking day!"
Slowly we will rise and wipe our sleepy eyes
The sweet, dreamy night passed away

The cowboy not only lived a dreary life, they also lived a lonely life. When out on the plains they were all alone. Even if they work with other cowboys guiding the herd, they might only have limited contact with other people for days at a time. Many of these cowboys also had loved ones back home that they missed. This little number expressed the lonely conditions of the cowboy.

I struck the trail in seventy-nine,
The herd strung out behind me;
As I jogged along my mind ran back
For the gal I left behind me.
That sweet little gal, that true little gal,
The gal I left behind me!

If ever I get off the trail
And the Indians they don't find me,
I'll make my way straight back again
To the gal I left behind me.
That sweet little gal, that true little gal,
The gal I left behind me!

The wind did blow, the rain did flow,
The hail did fall and blind me;
I thought of that gal, that sweet little gal,
That gal I'd left behind me!
That sweet little gal, that true little gal,
The gal I left behind me!

She wrote ahead to the place I said,
I was always glad to find it.
She says, "I am true, when you get through
Right back here you will find me."
That sweet little gal, that true little gal,
The gal I left behind me!

When we sold out I took the train,
I knew where I would find her;
When I got back we had a smack
And that was no gol-darned liar.

That sweet little gal, that true little gal,
The gal I left behind me!

There have been many songs of, for, and about the cowboy. "Bury Me Not On The Lone Prairie" speaks volumes about the desire of the cowboy to be laid to rest back in civilization and not on the wild frontier. "The Cowboy's Dream" was about the cowboys who died on the plains from either disease, fever, or even American Indian attacks. But I think "Poor Lonesome Cowboy" expresses it all:

I ain't got no father…
I ain't got no mother…
I ain't got no sister…
I ain't got no brother…
I ain't got no sweetheart…

I'm a poor lonesome cowboy
And a long way from home

Protest songs have been a part of the American tradition ever since the first settlers arrived on the eastern shores of the continent. Whether it was a protest against hard living conditions, the effects of a tyrannical government, racism, the horrors of war, the difficulties of hard work, fear of Indians, hatred of Mormons, or the loneliness of the cowboy; songs have been used by people to express themselves, point out injustice and call people to their cause. In the preceding pages we have sampled only a small portion of those early American songs that exhibited traits of protest. In the next chapter we move on to songs that not only opposed the evils and conditions of slavery, but also set the traditions and precedents of many musical elements that are found in contemporary American popular and protest music.

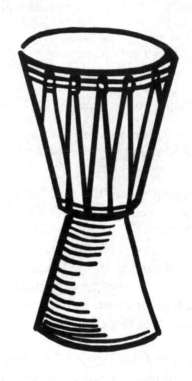

Chapter Two:
Slave Songs: The Root of Contemporary American Popular Protest Music

Oh, nobody knows the trouble I've seen
Nobody knows but Jesus
Nobody knows the trouble I've seen
Gloria Hallelujah

Traditional

Twenty first century contemporary American popular music was created through a process of cultural diffusion over five centuries of Euro/African civilization on the American continent. Contemporary music in our popular culture is a derivative of many different styles of music, a diverse heritage, and a controversial history. In fact, we can trace many of the stylistic elements of contemporary popular music, including the singing of protest songs, directly to the singing slaves of antebellum America. Within America's "peculiar institution," slaves created specific traditions of singing songs that have been kept alive by all kinds of artists immersed in America's rich musical heritage. Once slave music (or spirituals) were accepted as a legitimate form of music and recognized as a profitable form of entertainment, it spread throughout the academic and musical worlds.

There are a number of specific elements that this chapter will examine. We begin by looking at the early acceptance of this music as a legitimate form of American culture that deserved academic study. We continue by examining the drum and banjo that have become instrumental components of American music. The use of double entendre as a form of political and social expression is then examined which has been used by jazz, blues and rock musicians throughout the 19th and 20th centuries. Our examination continues with a look at the N-word in the music of the slaves and contemporary American culture from blues to hip hop. Finally, we examine the use of songs that directly protest injustice. While not overly prevalent in the songs of slaves because of fear of reprisal and punishment, protest songs certainly did exist. This use of direct protest was later used by workers and activists in the one hundred and fifty years following the end of slavery in America. The fact that these musical and cultural elements of the singing slaves endured and became a major cornerstone of popular music, speaks to the strength of the musical culture of the African American. It was the singing slaves who were some of our first troubadours and troublemakers in the evolution of American protest music.

Any study of American music would be incomplete without understanding the songs of the African slave in America. This music was not only a collective cry for justice, it also influenced the music of an entire nation. W.E.B. DuBois described slave songs as "not simply… the sole American music, but as the most beautiful expression of human experience born this side of the seas.... And the greatest gift of the Negro people." In his autobiography, Frederick Douglass described how the slaves would create spirituals. "They would compose and sing as they went along, consulting neither time nor tune. The thought that came up, came out, if not in the word, in the sound; and as frequently in the one as in the other. They would sometimes sing the most pathetic sentiment in the most rapturous tone, and the most rapturous sentiment in the most pathetic tone." These songs were beautiful and sorrowful. They were influenced by the conditions of slavery, traditions of the past and evolved through improvisation.

Improvisation was required from the slave. Brought to America in a ship crammed full of people from different tribes and languages, the slave had to adapt to completely new surroundings. Once reaching his or her destination, the slave would be purchased and completely owned by another individual who would direct the slave's entire life. This slave had to adopt a new set of cultural norms, including language, religion and traditions. In this new environment, the slave was required to be improvisational in order to survive. Part of that improvisation came out in the form of music, singing and dancing. This improvisation continued in the following centuries with the blues and jazz artists, the rock'n'rollers and the rappers. While improvisation was required of the slave in antebellum America to survive, in our modern era, improvisation is one of the most cherished traits of our music, whether it is blues, jazz, rock or hip hop.

Immediately following the Civil War scholarly collections of slave music began to appear in print. In one such collection, Slave Songs of the United States, William Allen and his fellow editors concluded that this new American music was "partly composed under the influence of association with the whites, (and) partly actually imitated from their music." While acknowledging the obvious influence from Christian hymns and European ballads, Allen and his fellow editors also concluded that the slave music "appears to be original in the best sense of the word, and the more we examine the subject, the more genuine it appears to us to be."

Slave spirituals received the commercial recognition they deserved not long after the Civil War. African American schools like the Hampton Normal and Agricultural Institute used "the singing of racial music (as) a part of the life of the school… (and were) given full freedom to expand and develop…." At Fisk University slave music was taken to a whole new level. In 1866 the treasurer of the school organized some of the students into a singing group. George L. White first created the group to raise money by traveling through the country singing European choral music. At first the endeavor failed. It wasn't until they started singing slave spirituals that the money flowed in. Many of the singers at first were hesitant about singing the songs of their parents from the plantations. They preferred to leave that part of their past behind them and sing those songs in private. Eventually, however, they added some plantation spirituals such as "Steal Away" and "The Graveyard," or the marching song "John Brown's Body" to their performance repertoire. Whenever the singers finished a spiritual, the crowds wanted more. In the words of Fisk Jubilee Singer Ella Sheppard, "the land rang with our slave songs." An important part of this experience was that this was quite possibly the first time that a white audience was exposed to African American slave music in a non-minstrelsy format. White America had heard some of this music before; it was either at a minstrel show (which approached African American musical culture with ridicule) or in the past on a southern plantation.

The study of slave songs became even more legitimate in 1888 when the American Folklore Society began to seriously examine antebellum slave music. This Harvard University affiliated organization began what has become an ongoing study. Ever since then, slave songs have been accepted as American "folk music." This recognition continued with various magazines from 1914 through the 1930s that acknowledged "negro music" as "the only American folk music…." Some of these journals included Musical America, Music Student, Current History, Annals of the American Academia and The Musical Courier.

Twentieth Century musicologists have solidified slave spirituals as a valuable anthropological study. Harold Courlander wrote in Negro Folk Music USA that "the Negro folk music idiom is an integral and

39

somewhat separate phenomenon and has a character completely its own." In other words, this music is a combination of different styles and types that created a unique music the world had never heard. In Negro Slave Songs, Dr Miles Mark Fisher wrote that there are five different cultural influences that contributed to the creation of African American slave songs. The first is the strong tradition of using rhythm. The second was the influx of Irish and Scottish folk songs that were heard throughout the backcountry during the 1830s and 1840s. The third influence began approximately in the mid-1750s in Virginia when Presbyterian Minister Samuel Davies introduced religious hymns to some slaves that set off the wave of spiritual singing. The fourth category of influence on slave music were the songs created in colonial America especially in the northern colonies of Massachusetts, New Amsterdam and Pennsylvania. And finally, the fifth element of influence Fisher attributes to the creation of slave songs were the important events that affected the consciousness of the slaves such as slave rebellions or severe punishment from their masters.

Today there is no doubting the value of studying slave songs as an important part of American culture. There have been hundreds of books written on the subject, thousands of recordings made of slave songs, and who knows how many lectures have been presented on the beauty, relevance and historic nature of slave songs. (See the Appendix for a slave song list and the bibliography for a selection of slave song collections and recordings.)

Today the drum is easily recognized as an integral part of many genres of American music. From jazz to rock and soul to hip-hop, the drum can be heard as the main instrument or a major accompaniment in most modern American musical styles. This was not so until the unwilling slave brought it from Africa. The Native Americans (American Indians) used the drum, but the interaction between the red and white peoples in America was intermittent, thus limiting the cultural diffusion. The daily interaction between the black and white races in the British colonies in America was much greater and therefore the cross pollination of culture had a greater impact.

The drum played an integral part in African culture. It was used at almost all ceremonies, and for long distance communication. Some examples of its uses in Africa were as a warning of an approaching fire, the announcement of someone's death or warning of a stranger's approach. One drum from Africa actually had a name that identified it as a communication device. It was translated to mean the "talking drum" (ntumpane) and was made from the skin of an elephant's ear. The cultural significance, usage, and tradition of the "talking drum" were transported to America.

There are examples of Africans singing songs and banging their drum on their journey to the shores of America. Slave ship Captain Theodore Canot was part of the triangular trade of slaves and molasses. He experienced the drum first hand and wrote about it in his journal. "During the afternoons of serene weather, men, women, girls, and boys are allowed a while on deck to unite in African melodies which they always enhanced by (an) extemporaneous Tom-tom on the bottom of a tub or tin kettle." The Africans came to America with melodies, rhythms, and even instruments.

This tradition of using the drum to communicate and celebrate survived the journey through the middle passage and caused fear in the minds of slave masters, as it was used by slaves to communicate with other plantations. Eventually many southern communities banned the drum because of its use in slave rebellions. The following account is from the Stono Rebellion. "Several Negroes joined them, they calling out liberty, marched on with colors displayed and two drums beating, pursuing all the white people they met with, killing man woman and child." The response of the slave masters was to ban the drum. This slave code only succeeded in forcing the slaves to create and adopt a new way of providing rhythm. They began to use their voice, feet and hands to maintain the beat in their songs. The drum of course never disappeared. Making something illegal doesn't eliminate it; it only adds a level of mystery and danger. It survived in places like Congo Square in New Orleans and become one of the main instruments of jazz. The drum continued to be a major instrument of rock'n'roll and all of its offshoots. Some of the greatest musicians of the twentieth century were drummers. Famous jazz artists such as Max Roach, Gene Krupa, Tony Williams, Elvin Jones, Joe Morello and Buddy Rich were drummers. Rockers such as Neil Peart of Rush, John Bonham of Led Zeppelin, Keith Moon of the Who, Ginger Baker of Cream, Mick Fleetwood of Fleetwood Mac and Phil Collins of Genesis were all drummers. The drum has become a major component of most American popular music.

Another instrument that the Africans brought with them from their homeland was the Banjo. Thomas Jefferson first noted it in his Notes on the State of Virginia, calling it a Banjar. Referring to the slaves on his plantation, Jefferson wrote, "The instrument proper to them is the Banjar, which they brought wither from Africa...." The Rev. Jonathan

Boucher noted it even earlier when he wrote <u>Boucher's Glossary of Archaic and Provincial Words</u>. He penned: "The favorite and almost only instrument in use among the slaves there was a bandore; or, as they pronounced the word, banjer. Its body was a large hallow gourd, with a long handle attached to it, strung with catgut, and played on with the fingers."

The knowledge of this instrument was passed onto white America through plantation music and minstrelsy. It gained popularity in the latter half of the 19th Century and turned up as the main instrument of folk singer and political activist, Pete Seeger. The banjo was even the major element of Steve Martin's comedy act in the 1970s. The Banjo can be seen in more contemporary times as the main instrument of Bluegrass revival bands and such outfits like String Cheese Incident, Bella Fleck and the Fleck Tones, Mumford & Sons, the Avett Brothers, Trampled by Turtles and Carolina Chocolate Drops. There are hundreds of organizations, clubs and bands that are devoted exclusively to the instrument. Some of these groups have names like the Jazz'n Banjos, Jubilee Banjo Band, Gulf Coast Banjo Band, Banjo Rascals, and Bill Bailey Banjos.

Another key element of most slave spirituals that has permeated American music ever since colonial America was the use of double entendre. It was necessary to keep the masters off guard, since the slaves were encouraged (and even expected) to sing while they worked. It was a way the master could keep track of his slaves in the fields and allow a forman or leader to keep them in time – thus working faster and more efficient. It was also thought that a singing slave was a happy slave. What the slaves knew, and what the white man didn't know, was that they were singing for themselves and not for the master.

They purposefully kept the meaning of the songs to themselves, cleverly hiding the true meaning behind some other obvious context. Religion was the most common theme in this musical phenomenon. Frederick Douglass acknowledged that the song's specific words didn't reflect its true meaning to the slave. Douglass used the song, "O' Canaan" as an example of this. He wrote that "O'Cannan" may really be about escaping to Canada and not the biblical story of the Israelites and Canaan. An escaped slave himself, Douglass wrote: "a keen observer may have detected Canada in our repeated singing of: O' Canaan, Sweet Canaan, I am bound for the land of Canaan."

Another double entendre song that has survived and flourished in American popular culture is "Swing Low, Sweet Chariot." The song was inspired by the Prophet Elijah being taken to heaven by a chariot. But the hidden meaning is about the desire for freedom. Instead of thinking about the Jordan River, the slave was imagining the Ohio River; instead of Elijah's chariot, it was the Underground Railroad; instead of heaven being the end of the journey, it was the north and freedom.

> Swing low, sweet chariot, Comin' for to carry me home
> I look'd over Jordan an' what did I see
> Comin' for to carry me home
> A band of angles comin' after me
> Comin' for to carry me home
> If you get there before I do
> Comin' for to carry me home
> Tell all my friends I'm comin' there too.

"Swing Low Sweet Chariot" has been recorded in almost every genre of American music. B.B. King brought us a blues version; Bill Monroe picked up the pace with bluegrass; Louis Armstrong interpreted the song with his Dixieland Jazz; Tommy Dorsey and Bennie Goodman gave us something to swing to; and while the band Acoustix gave the world a smooth jazz interpretation, Beyoncé sang her heart out in an a cappella R&B version. One of the more culturally trans-missive recordings was made live in Bethel New York in 1969 when Joan Baez performed this song to a quarter of a million Hippies at Woodstock. Even guitar legend Eric Clapton used the sounds of Jamaica and gave the world a reggae version in the mid-seventies while UB40 recorded their own take of this very old song.

Still popular in American music is another double entendre spiritual: "Go Down Moses." The song uses the biblical story of Moses in Egypt to exclaim their own prayers for liberation from the clutches of slavery in America. Most whites who heard the song recognized the biblical story, but when the slaves sang, they identified themselves with the Israelites and wished for their own liberator. The song calls "for a like deliverance from the hand of the white Pharaoh." When the slaves sang about Moses, they were thinking of Harriet Tubman or Peg Leg Joe; when they sang about "way down" in Egypt they were thinking of the Deep South; when they were singing about the Pharaoh they were thinking about their master or the President of the United States. Some believe that Nat Turner was either the author of this song or its inspiration. Turner was seen as Moses going to the white "Pharaoh" to free his people. This song also has the distinction of being the first slave spiritual to be written down.

Here are the complete lyrics to what some would consider the longest enduring and most popular slave song in American history.

When Israel was in Egypt land, Let my people go
Oppressed so hard they could not stand, Let my people go

Go down Moses, Way down in Egypt land
Tell ol' Pharaoh, Let my people go

This Spoke the Lord, bold Moses Said
If not, I'll smite your first born dead.

No More shall they in bondage toil
Let them come out of Egypt's Spoil

The Lord told Moses what to do
To lead the Hebrew children through

O come along Moses, you'll not get lost
Stretch out your rod and come across

As Israel stood by the water side
At God's command it did divide

When they reached the other shore
They sang a song of triumph o'er

Pharaoh said he's go across
But Pharaoh and his host were lost

O let us all from bondage flee
And let us all in Christ be free

You need not always weep mourn
And wear these slav'ry chains forlorn

Your foes shall not before you stand
And you'll possess fair Canaan's land

The amazing thing about this song is it's prophesy regarding America. In the line "If not, I'll smite your first born dead," the singing slave could be singing about the future in America. During the four bloody years of the Civil War from 1861 to 1865, a half a million

Americans from both the north and south died in a conflict that some say could have been avoided. Because of slavery, the first born in many houses in America were sent off to war to come home in a box or be buried without any identification. Just like in Egypt, the first born son from many American households were dead.

"Go Down Moses" has continued in American culture in many different genres. Guitar Frang created for us a blues version; Ralph Stanley sang country a cappella while Coda gave us a more pop a cappella interpretation. Moses danced into Egypt with the Magic Swing Band, Elvis rocked it out and Louis Armstrong recorded it in his own jazz style.

Another slave song that had hidden meanings and was important to the hope of the slave was "Follow the Drinking Gourd." For many slaves, escape to the north was the only way to freedom. Rebellion and resistance at home would result in death or more repression, and the stories of reprisal and punishment were well known among the slaves. Because of this reality, escape was the only reasonable course of action and the Underground Railroad was the communication network that could pull it off. While not an exact map of escape, the primary purpose of the song was to deliver a guide to slaves contemplating such action. When singing the line: "follow the drinking gourd," the masters took the phrase literally to mean a hollowed out gourd used for drinking. The slaves, on the other hand, were thinking of the Big Dipper constellation. In the first verse the runaway is told when and how to escape. "When the sun comes back" is after the winter solstice when the sun rises higher and higher. The singing slave is then told to find the "old man" who "is waiting" to help in the escape. This "old man" is represented by a man named Peg Leg Joe who could be played by any member of the Underground Railroad.

When the sun comes back and the first quail calls,
Follow the drinking gourd,
For the old man is waiting for to carry you to freedom,
If you follow the drinking gourd

The next verse tells the escapee to follow the Tombigbee River north from the Gulf of Mexico to Tennessee. The freedom seeker would then have to follow the dead trees and charcoal drawings of a peg leg foot made to lead him to the next destination.

> The riverbank will make a very good road,
> The dead trees show you the way,
> Left foot, peg foot traveling on,
> Follow the drinking gourd

The next river the slave would have to reach is the Tennessee River where he could follow toward Kentucky.

> The river ends between two hills,
> Follow the drinking gourd,
> There's another river on the other side,
> Follow the drinking gourd

The final verse describes the last leg in the journey. The meeting of the two rivers described in the song is best crossed in the winter. If the slave begins his escape as the song indicates (a couple of months after the winter solstice), it will take about a year to reach this point in the journey. At this time he can cross parts of the Ohio River because it's frozen and a conductor in the Underground Railroad would meet the runaway slave and help him get to a safe location in one of the northern states or Canada.

> Where the great big river meets the little river,
> Follow the drinking gourd
> The old man is a-waiting for to carry you to freedom,
> If you follow the drinking gourd

"The Drinking Gourd" has also been recorded many times in the Twentieth Century. In the late 1940s the Weavers recorded the first commercially released version that became popular. Other folk singers like New Christy Minstrels continued to perform the song years later; Taj Mahal sang the blues while Shore Grass approached the spiritual with a country flair; John Coltrane and Wynton Marsalis contributed their jazz interpretations while Jorma Koukonen and Hot Tuna recorded some jam rock. This song has also made it overseas with Spiritual Kvintet singing in Czech and the Motor Totemist Guild recording a Cambodian/Laotian interpretation in English.

The songs of the Twentieth Century and today may not be a literal map to freedom, but music is still used as a guide to a better life free of conformity or fear. Music can enliven, encourage and even guide people's lives. Christian rock for example takes its pride from having a moral message about the life and teachings of Jesus Christ. Songs call people to action like Neil Young's "Ohio" released in the midst of student protests of President's Nixon's policy of invading Cambodia. Aretha Franklin instilled pride in a whole generation of black women in America with her rendition of "Respect." Rappers NWA helped African Americans find a voice of solidarity in a culture that traditionally repressed the rights of black Americans with songs like "Express Yourself."

Just like the songs of protest and empowerment, songs with double entendre did not end with the singing slaves. Jazz artists used the concept with songs like "Black and Blue" where the singer could be complaining about police brutality or domestic violence. Blues artists sang songs like "Terraplane Blues" which could be about his car or his woman. The song "Little Red Rooster" could be about a farm animal or a body part. Pete Seeger's "King Henry" seems to about a king in some far away time, but in actuality is about President Lyndon Johnson and the Vietnam War. Grace Slick's "White Rabbit" was about the novel Alice in Wonderland, but in reality was also a call to experiment with drugs. Bob Dylan's "Rainy Day Women #12 & 35" seemed to be about getting high, getting drunk, or being stoned to death, but in reality it was Bob Dylan's reaction to being booed at Newport in 1965 and the negative reaction he received during his subsequent tour with The Band. While the double meanings in these songs were not necessarily political in nature, the fact that this type of song creation survived in America is a testament to its cultural power.

Another part of contemporary popular music derived from slave songs is the use of expletives. There have been movements to limit, ban and label songs that have lyrics that are offensive. A group represented by Tipper Gore in the 1990s succeeded in getting record companies and retailers to label recordings that contained offensive lyrics. The N-word has been a major target of this attempt at censorship. In an article in the National Post May 11, 2002, Robert Fulford wrote "Even in the censorious atmosphere of public education, nigger stands alone. It retains a terrifying grip on the imagination."

This word has been seen in American literature from science fiction to political prose. Below is only a selection of literary classics where the N-word is used: Uncle Tom's Cabin by Harriet Beecher Stow, Huckleberry Finn, Adventures of Tom Sawyer, and Life on the Mississippi by Mark Twain, Nigger of the Narcissus by Joseph Conrad, Adventure by Jack London, Mr. Higginbotham's Catastrophe by Nathaniel Hawthorne, Ar'n't I a Woman? by Sojourner Truth, The

Gold-Bug by Edgar Allan Poe, The Martian Chronicles by Ray Bradbury, and Gone with the Wind by Margaret Mitchell.

The history of the N-word has evolved over time through American culture. It was derived from the term negro that was also used by Europeans to describe people they saw in India, Australia, and Polynesia. It was used in the south as a derogatory term against people with African heritage until the mid-19th Century when its use began to change. It was at this time that the main target of this term, American blacks, began to co-op the word in their own vernacular. This new usage spread throughout black communities in the United States during the first and second Great Migrations ending up in the northern states and the west coast. This term, which was being used by some as a term of endearment, was adopted by urban blacks and ended up in the songs of jazz, rock, funk, soul and hip hop musicians.

The use of the N-word is prevalent in many titles of popular songs. A search in iTunes for songs with the N-word in the title will return over 150 songs available for purchase. There are at least fourteen different styles of music that contained nigger in the title. There was a classical number titled "Crazy Nigger" by Lester Donahue and a blues song called "Running in the Nigger Night" by The Kofma Bandit. Also listed was the jazz artist Sandra Weckert with "No Vietcong ever called me a Nigger"; Admiral Tibbe with a reggae song called "Old Nigger"; Earl Johnson and his Bluegrass songs "Nigger on the Woodpile" and "Nigger in the Cotton Patch"; Lord Melody with a calypso song called "Hi Nigger"; John Lennon and Yoko Ono and their rock song "Woman is the Nigger of the World"; a Punk band the Oblivions had "Nigger Rich"; Funk artists Sly and the Family Stone recorded "Don't Call Me Nigger Whitey"; and a hard rock band named the Anti-Heroes had a song called "I'm a Rock and Roll Nigger." This is only a sampling of the different genres of songs with titles using that word.

The music of NWA and Public Enemy are well known specifically for their controversial lyrics that use expletives and the N-word. NWA's songs that use the word (nigga or niggaz) include the big hits "Straight Outta Compton," "Appetite for Destruction," "Real Niggaz," and "Real Niggaz Don't Die." Public Enemy recorded songs with the word such as "Welcome to the Terrordome," "War at 33 1/3," "Anti-Nigger Machine," and "I Don't Wanna Be Called Yo Niga."

In the summer of 2008 the rap artist Nas put out an album he wanted to simply call "Nigger." Starting in the fall of 2007, it was rumored to have track titles like "You a Nigger Too" and "I'm Black."

Along with these songs and the proposed title, the album created controversy before it was even released. Nas was quoted saying about the controversy: "You ain't got no business worrying about what the word 'nigger' is or acting like you know what my album is about without talking to me. Whether you in the NAACP or you Jesse Jackson." Because of public outcry, and at the insistence of his record company, Def Jam, Nas changed the name of the album. Officially listed as an untitled album, most fans refer to it as "Nigger." Nas said following its release: "The people will always know what the real title of this album is, and what to call it." The official title may not be the N-word, but those who purchased it certainly don't call it Untitled.

The use of the N-word is nothing new in American songs. Early slave songs included the word in many instances and this continued into the post-Civil War era. One song was sung in parts of Tennessee, Arkansas and along the Mississippi River. Here the black man is assumed to be guilty because of who he is. If you were a black man, you were guilty of whatever you were suspected of doing. It was the color of your skin that determined your guilt.

> O some tell me that a nigger won't steal
> But I've seen a nigger in my cornfield
> O run, nigger, run, for the patrol will catch you
> O run, nigger, run, for 'tis almost day

Here is another post-Civil War song that showed the continued drive to move north, in which slaves believed to be the land of opportunity.

> Abe Lincoln treed the nigger
> With the gun and the trigger
> And I ain't going to get whipped any more
> I got my ticket
> Leaving the thicket
> And I'm a-heading for the golden shore

Here is another song from the reconstruction era that illustrated the new reality of the African American, where they get substandard food, housing and clothing.

> I went to Atlanta, Never been there befo'
> White folks eat de apple, Nigger wait fo co'…
> I went to Charleston, Never been there befo'
> White folks sleep on feather bead, Nigger on de flo'

I went to Raleigh, Never been there befo'
White folks wear de fancy suit, Nigger over-o'

Another song written in the post-Civil war period used the N-word in the final verse. Written by Billy Reeves in 1869, "Shew Fly Don't Bother Me" was intended as a comic song and dance number, but I include it here because of the use of the N-word.

If I sleep in the sun this nigger knows
If I sleep in the sun this nigger knows
If I sleep in the sun this nigger knows
A fly come sting him on the nose

I feel, I feel, I feel
That's what my mother said
Whenever this nigger goes to sleep
He must cover up his head

Some of these post-emancipation songs used the word in the process of self-ridicule as a cover for their distrust of the white man. The following two songs, "Nigger Be A Nigger" and "Oh, It's Hard To Be A Nigger", collected in John Greenway's 1953 American Folksongs of Protest, used this process to a startling effect.

Nigger be a nigger whatever you do
Ties red rag round de toe of his shoe
Jerk his vest on over his coat
Snatch his vest on over his coat
Snatch his britches up round his throat
God make a nigger, make 'im in de night
Make 'im in a hurry an forgot to paint 'im white
White man goes to college, Nigger goes to fiel'
White man learns to read an' write, Nigger learns to steal
Oh, it's hard to be a nigger!
Oh, it's hard to be a nigger!
'Cause a nigger don't get no show
I went walking one fine day; I met Mis' Chickie upon my way
Oh, her tail was long and her feathers were blue
Caw, caw, Missis Chickie, I'm on to you
Oh, it's hard to be a nigger!
Oh, it's hard to be a nigger!
And you can't get your money when it's due

This late 19th Century verse exhibits the bitterness of the African American regarding their economic and social condition where they do not even get what they have properly won or earned. The song allows the singer to use any city as a point of reference.

> Nigger and white man, Playin' Seven Up
> Nigger win de money, Skeered to pick it up
> Aught for Aught, And figger for figger
> All for de white man, Nothin for de nigger
> Went down to _____, Never been there before
> White folk on the leather bed, Nigger on the floor
> Nigger plow de cotton, Nigger pick it out
> White man pockets money, Nigger does without.

Here is another rendition of the same song that was collected by John Lomax in the early 1930s. This song evolved and combined with other songs to create something new. The use of the N-word remained throughout this process.

> Well, it makes no difference, How you make out your time
> White man sho' to bring a, Nigger out behin'
> Ain't it hard, ain't it hard?
> Ain't it hard to be a nigger? nigger? nigger?
> Ain't it hard, ain't it hard?
> For you can't get yo' money when it's due
> Lemme tell you, white man, Lemme tell you, honey
> Nigger makes de cotton, White folks get de money
> Ef you work all de week, An' work all de time
> White man sho' to bring a, Nigger out behin'
> Ef a nigger gits 'rested, An' can't pay his fine
> They sho' sen' him out, To the country gang
> Naught's a naught, Figger's a figger
> Figger fer de white man, Naught fer de nigger

The following verse is a fragment from an early 20th Century song that used the N-word. It showed the limited opportunities available for the African American. Most black Americans were limited to the service professions, such as cooks and domestic servants. The only avenue out of these dead-end jobs were acting and dancing in variety shows known as Minstrels. This next song clearly has the feel of vaudeville and minstrelsy.

Oh little nigger baby
Black face and shiny eyes
Better than po' white trash
In the sweet bye and bye
Black face born that way, brains all in his feet
That's the song of the little nigger baby
Down on Market Street...

Americans have different opinions about the use of the N-word. Our view of the word and how it affects us is based on our background and experiences. People that live in different communities have different experiences with that word. In one family it may be a swear word, while in others it may be a term of endearment. The important thing to remember is that all words have power, meaning and history. Understanding the history of words is part of understanding our own history: the good, bad, and the regrettable.

The use of songs as a direct protest against living or working conditions is another legacy of the American slave. They had to work long hours without sufficient nutrition, rest or proper exercise. W.E.B. Dubois described these songs as "the music of an unhappy people, of the children of disappointment; they tell of death and suffering and unvoiced longing toward a truer world...." Two specific slave songs that were a direct attack upon their condition were "Many Thousands Gone" and "Oh, Freedom."

"Many Thousands Gone" (also known as "No More Auction Block") was a song that protested the meager rations slaves received on many southern plantations. The peck of corn is symbolic of the slaves' daily food ration. When they sang "no more, no more," the slaves were expressing faith that one day a time will come when there is plenty of food to eat, and no more master's lash. William Allen, collector of southern slave songs, found a reference to the origin of this song in a speech given by J. Miller McKim, in Philadelphia, July 9, 1862. When asked where the song came from, Prince Rivers responded "Dey make 'em, sah... I'll tell you, its dis way. My master call me up, and order me a short peck of corn and a hundred lash. My friends see it, and is sorry for me. When dey come to de praise-meeting dat night dey sing about it. Some's very good singers and know how; and dey work it in – work it in, you know, till they get it right; and dat's de way."

No more peck o' corn for me
No more, no more
No more peck o' corn for me
Man-y thousand go(ne)
No more drivers' lash for me…
No more pint o' salt for me …
No more hundred lash for me…
No more mistress call for me….

This song was still being sung by Americans in the twentieth century. There are acoustic folk-style versions by Bob Dylan and Pete Seeger, blues interpretations from people like Matthew Sabatella and soul renditions recorded by groups like Sweet Honey in the Rock.

Another slave song of direct protest that was remembered and passed on while going through contemporary changes is "Oh Freedom." This song was passed on through the twentieth century as the sound track of the civil rights movement. Its call-and-response musical format allowed for easy adaptability to contemporary circumstances. The song was perfect for marches, strikes and sit-ins. There are recordings of people singing "Oh' Pritchett" (the Albany Police Chief in Georgia), or "Oh' Wallace" (the four-term governor of Alabama). Groups ranging from the Freedom Singers and Resurrection Singers, to the folk icon Pete Seeger (who made it a staple at his concerts), sang this song throughout the 1940s, 50s, and 60s. It was originally sung on the plantations as a cry for freedom, moving to the civil rights movement as a call for justice, and then into music festivals of the sixties as a reminder of the promise of America.

O freedom, O freedom, O freedom over me over me
And before I'd be a slave, I'd be buried in my grave
And go home to my lord and be free

No more mournin'…
No more weepin'…
No more misery…
No more conformin'…
No more violence.…

The songs of the African slaves in America were a major part of the evolution of music, especially protest music. They created traditions that were followed by generations of troubadours and troublemakers. The drum and banjo have become standard instruments in many popular and protest bands; the double entendre is still used to hide the messages within songs; the N-word is still used for shock value to attract attention and inspire cultural solidarity; and lyrical verse used to directly attack an injustice is heard every day on pop radio. It was the singing slaves who were the main inspiration for all of these practices. In the next chapter we will investigate the music created by the abolitionists who opposed slavery and the soldiers from the north and south who joined or were drafted into the army to fight in regards to slavery. The abolitionists and soldiers sang their way through the bloodiest war in American history.

Chapter Three:
Abolitionists & Soldiers:
The Rise of Militant Protest Songs

No other war in American history has produced
such a great variety of songs, nor such quality.

Irwin Silber

The existence of slavery not only created new musical traditions
and styles, it also affected the musical culture of the entire nation. The
abolition movement, which expanded in the 1830s and 40s, was
significant to the development of protest music in the culture of the
white northern elite. After the Civil War came in April of 1861, protest
singing was heard and sung by the soldiers who came from all walks of
life and from all corners of the continent. Northerners from different
states were interacting and exchanging songs as southerners were doing
the same. As the soldiers sang their songs of protest, many were
introduced to the songs of the opposing side in this devastating War
Between the States.

By the early 1830's, abolitionists were singing and collecting protest
songs in the struggle against slavery. William Lloyd Garrison was one
such abolitionist. Following his release from a Baltimore prison for
libel because of his abolitionist writings in The Genius of Universal
Emancipation, Garrison moved back to Boston and founded his own
newspaper in 1830 called The Liberator. After establishing the New
England Abolitionist Society in 1831 and the American Antislavery
Society in 1833, Garrison compiled a collection of antislavery songs.
Published in 1834, it was titled: A Selection of Anti-Slavery Hymns, for
the Use of Friends of Emancipation. The songs were written by
Garrison and others, and became the first of three songbooks. These
collections became known as the "Garrisonian Hymnbooks" and
contributed to the growing abolitionist movement in the northern
United States. Garrison considered these collections "an experiment"
and envisioned a much larger book containing many additional songs.

The second and most popular of all the Garrisonian songbooks was
known as Freedom's Lyre. Many different types of groups used the
songbooks: religious groups, abolitionist organizations, and community

festival organizers. It contained 291 songs and poems that were more direct and revolutionary than Garrison's first publication.

One song example clearly placed the blame of slavery on those who fail to see its injustice. It called on those with religious faith to destroy the enemies of freedom and liberate the enslaved. It warned those who defend human bondage that the wrath of God will be upon them with pain and suffering.

Judges, who rule the world by laws
Will ye despise the righteous cause
When vile oppression wastes the land
Dare ye condemn the righteous poor
And let rich despots live secure
While gold and greatness bribe your hands

Thus shall the vengeance of the lord
Safety to all th'oppress'd afford
And they who hear shall join and say
Sure there's a God that rules on high
A God that hears the bondmen cry
And will their sufferings well repay

In the twenty years following Garrison's first publication, many other books were printed by organizations and individuals with the same abolition theme. Some of these hymnbooks were even more political than Garrison's original and a few songs even made direct comments about political parties and specific slavery issues.

One of the earliest abolitionist political campaign songs was written for John C. Fremont, the famous commanding soldier in the Mexican American War. He was responsible for leading a force across the Great Plains into California and becoming the first military governor of California before it became a state in 1850. In 1854 Fremont ran for president and the following song was written for his failed presidential campaign. The Buchaniers in the song are the supporters of James Buchannan who ran and won on the Democratic (and proslavery) ticket. I have included here four verses and the chorus.

YE friends of freedom rally now
And push the cause along
We have a glorious candidate
A platform broad and strong
"Free Speech, Free Press, Free Soil, Free Men

Fremont," we have no fears
With such a battlecry, but that
We'll beat the Buchaniers

We'll give 'em Jessie
We'll give 'em Jessie
We'll give 'em Jessie
When we rally at the polls….

Where'er clear heads and gallant hearts
Are wanted, foremost he
And ever true, in word and deed
He's proved to Liberty
Survey him every way you will
The NOBLE MAN appears
So shout Fremont and Liberty
Down with the Buchaniers

Then rally, rally every man
Who values Liberty
Who would not see our fair land given
To blighting Slavery

Our cause, "Free Speech, Free Press, Free Soil
Free Men," So now three cheers
For the People's Candidate, FREMONT
Who frights the Buchaniers

Another song popular among those who opposed slavery was "The Abolitionist Song." This number was probably written in the 1850s set to a popular tune "Old Hundred." It was usually sung during abolitionist rallies throughout the north before the eruption of the Civil War.

We ask not that the slave should lie
As lies his master, at his ease
Beneath a silken canopy
Or in the shade of blooming trees

We ask not eye for eye, that all
Who forge the chain and ply the whip
Should feel their torture, while the thrall
Should wield the scourge of mastership

We mourn not that the man should toil
'Tis nature's need, 'tis God's decree

59

But let the hand that tills the soil
Be, like the wind that fans it, free

Abolitionism grew in the United States with the help of the Hutchinson Family Singers. The singing family originated from New Hampshire and came from a strict puritan background. They were already a popular topical singing group who performed songs of protest addressing issues such as temperance with the numbers "King Alcohol" and "Cold Water." In the years preceding the Civil War, they were concerned with three great causes: temperance, women's suffrage, and abolition.

It was apparent that they would be an inspiration to people battling slavery when they attended an abolition meeting in January 1843, at Boston's Faneuil Hall. It was reported that when the Hutchinson family sang their songs, they "made the thousands at Faneuil Hall spring to their feet simultaneously... and echo the anti-slavery appeal...."

Their audience did not always receive the protest songs favorably, however. At first, the singing family was afraid that the more controversial material would harm their popularity and upset what they called their "paying audiences." The impending national crisis over slavery, however, convinced the Hutchinson's to include anti-slavery songs at every performance. The controversial topics of their songs did create problems that followed them to many appearances. The attendees were split on whether they wanted to hear the popular material or the political songs. At some performances audiences actually hissed and booed the singing family. Other performances saw people walking out of the concert in disgust. And in some cases there were even fist fights outside the hall.

One of their most popular anti-slavery songs was written to the tune of "Old Dan Tucker" a popular minstrel song attributed to Daniel D. Emmett. "Get Off the Track" (also known as "Clear the Track") was written in 1844 by Jesse Hutchinson as a warning to the nation that a powerful force of change was coming. In this period of American history the locomotive was a symbol of economic growth, industrialization, and western expansion. The singing family fed off the public's view of a powerful locomotive to represent emancipation. The song warned people of all trades that the power of emancipation was as inevitable as the next train coming into the station. Accompanying the sheet music and lyrics was a drawing of a train with the words "Immediate Emancipation" painted on its sides above the windows.

Ho! the car emancipation
Rides majestic through our nation
Bearing on its train the story
LIBERTY! a nation's glory

Roll it along! roll it along!
Roll it along! roll it along!
Roll it along! through the nation
Freedom's car, Emancipation

Men of various predilections
Frightened, run in all directions
Merchants, Editors, Physicians
Lawyers, Priests, and Politicians

Get out the way, every station
Clear the track, Emancipation
Roll it along thro' the Nation
Freedom's Car, Emancipation

Another song of protest the Singing Hutchinsons performed was
"My Country." It was a direct attack against the institution of slavery
using the tune of the popular and patriotic song "America." The song
clearly asks the listener to weep for the nation; because slavery is a
betrayal of liberty and freedom clearly promised to all in the
Declaration of Independence.

My Country, 'tis for thee
Dark land of slavery
For thee I weep
'Land where the slave has sighed
And where he toiled and died
To serve a tyrant's pride
For thee I weep'

From every mountain side
Upon the Ocean's tide
They call on thee
Amid thy rocks and rills
Thy woods and templed hills
I hear a voice which trills
Let all go free
Our fathers' God! to thee
Author of liberty

To thee we pray:
'Soon may our land be pure
Let freedom's light endure
And liberty secure
Beneath thy sway'

Another song that contributed to their controversy was "We Wait Beneath the Furnace Blast." Written by John Greenleaf Whittier in 1862, this song caused a condemnation from Generals Stephan Kearny and William Franklin who were both opposed to abolition. When General George McClellan heard of the song he suspended the Singing Hutchinson's pass to perform in front of Union troops. It wasn't until President Lincoln heard of the song, its performance, and the Hutchinson's suspension, that a compromise was established. President Lincoln was quoted as saying during the controversy: "It is just the character of song that I desire the soldiers to hear." I have included the entire text below.

We wait beneath the furnace blast, the pangs of transformation
Not painlessly does God recast, and mold anew the nation
Hot burns the fire, where wrongs expire
Nor spares the hand, that from the land
Uproot the ancient evil

The handbreadth cloud the sages fear'd
Its bloody rain is dropping
The poison plant the fathers spared, all else is ever topping
East, West, South, North, is curses earth
All justice dies, and fraud and lies
Live only in its shadow

What gives the wheat field blades of steel?
What points the rebel cannon?
What sets the roaring rabble's heel?
On the old star spangled pennon?
What beaks the oath, of the men of the South?
What whets the knife? For the Union's life?
Hark to the answer: SLAVERY!

Then waste no blows on lesser foes, in strife unworthy freemen
God lifts today the veil and shows, the features of the demon!
O North and South, its victims both
Can ye not cry, "Let Slavery die!"

And union find a freedom?

What though the cast and spirit tear, the nation in his going?
We who have shared the guilt must share
The pang of his overthrowing!
Whate'er the loss, whate'er the cross
Shall they complain, of present pain?
Who trust in God's hereafter?

For who that leans on His right arm, was ever yet forsaken?
What righteous cause can suffer harm, if he its part has taken?
Though wild and loud, and dark the cloud
Behind its folds, His blood upholds
The calm sky of tomorrow!

Above the maddening cry for blood
Above the wild war drumming
Let Freedom's voice be heard, with good, the evil overcoming
Give prayer and purse, to stay the Curse
Whose wrong we share, whose shame we bear
Whose end shall gladden Heaven!

In vain the bells of war shall ring, of triumphs and revenges
While still is spared the evil thing, that severs and estranges
But, blest the ear, that yet shall hear
The jubilant bell, that rings the knell
Of Slavery forever!

Then let the selfish lip be dumb, and hushed the breath of sighing
Before the joy of peace, must come, the pain of purifying
God give us grace, each in his place
To bear his lot, and murmuring not
Endure and wait and labor!

Another protest song of the Singing Hutchinsons was "The New Emancipation Song." It was a direct call for the freedom of the slaves from their wage-less labor and the liberty for all Americans. The song went so far as to criticize the Border States which stayed in the union during the war while also maintaining their system of legal slavery.

Oh! Give the slaves their freedom, you surely do not need them
And no longer clothe and feed them, in these United States

For they all sigh for freedom, they all sigh for freedom
For they all sigh for freedom in these United States

Then the slave no longer belabor, but act the part of neighbor
And hire white men to labor in these United States

Already the salvation of our slave-holding nation
Demands emancipation of slaves in the States

Then renounce your cruel knavery of keeping men in slavery
For it's getting quite unsavory e'en in the Border States

Oh, let not our free soil be degraded by the toil
Of the men whom you despoil in these United States

Release from bondage dreary each darkey and his deary
And don't send 'em to Liberi' from these United States

Esteem it but a fable that white men are not able
To take the place of sable slaves in the States

And hire maids whose pretty faces the rose and lily graces
To keep your pleasant places in these United States

If you wish to be commended let not slavery be extended
But its reign quickly ended in these United States

One of the Singing Hutchinsons' favorites was "The Liberty Ball" written by Jesse Hutchinson. It was a direct protest song against slavery. The first two verses of the song clearly identify the focus of their derision and the solution of freedom for all.

Come all ye true friends of the nation
Attend to humanity's call
Come aid in the slaves' liberation
And roll on the liberty ball (3x)
Come aid in the slaves liberation
And roll on the liberty ball

We're foes unto wrong and oppression
No matter which side of the sea
And ever intend to oppose them
Till all of God's image are free (3x)
And ever intend to oppose them
Till all of God's image are free

The issue of slavery and states' rights finally came to a head with the election of Abraham Lincoln on November 17, 1860, the first

64

person elected from a new political party dedicated to stopping the spread of slavery. Before the newly elected Republican was able to take the oath of office, however, seven states led by South Carolina had seceded from the union. In April of 1861, Ft. Sumter was attacked by the South Carolina militia and was surrendered to the newly forming confederacy. The Civil War had begun.

Once soldiers began gathering, training and fighting, a wealth of protest and topical songs were created and sung by people from all parts of the country. The singing soldier made his own unique contribution to the evolution of protest music in America. The songs of soldiers were used for many reasons: entertainment, expression of emotion, breaking up boredom, revelry, taps, marching and protest. Some songs were patriotic and used for recruitment. Others were derivatives of Minstrel tunes that started a few decades earlier. Our focus here will be those songs that can be clearly defined as protesting the conditions of the soldier in their daily drudgery, the expression of political opinions about the war, the sadness that accompanies war, the southern objection to Lincoln and the use of songs as propaganda and recruitment. Not only were the singing of songs an integral part of the soldier's life during the American Civil War, studying these singing soldiers gives us insight as to the evolution of topical singing in the United States.

It is also important to identify two writers whose work make up a large portion of the protest songs created during this era: George F. Root and Henry C. Work. Root was born in 1830 in Sheffield, Massachusetts and raised in North Reading. He studied music in New York where he eventually taught at the Abbott Institute for Young ladies and Boston's Academy of Music. Root wrote dozens of popular songs and musical numbers earning himself an honorary PhD in music from the University of Chicago. According to Ace Collins, author of Songs Sung Red White and Blue, "Lincoln might have led the government and Grant the army, but it was Root who would lead the spirits of all Americans with music." Henry Work was born in 1832 in Connecticut and trained as a printer. He used his knowledge of printing and publishing to get his first song published in 1853. Thereafter, he succeeded in publishing dozens of popular songs. The work of both of these men can be seen and heard throughout the music of the Civil War era.

One of the first songs written as a direct result of the war was "Maryland, My Maryland." Set to the tune of "Lauriger Horatius" (which is better known as the Christmas tune "O Tannenbaum"), the

65

song is from a nine-stanza poem written by James Ryder Randall. The original poem was written following the 6th Massachusetts Regiment's march through Maryland and the subsequent attack on them by confederate sympathizers. It was written in direct response to that event. The first verse clearly states the reason for the song.

> Maryland, My Maryland
> The despot's heel is on thy shore
> His torch is at thy temple door
> Avenge the patriotic gore
> That flecked the streets of Baltimore
> And be the battle queen of yore
> Maryland! My Maryland!

Northerners responded with their own version of "Maryland, My Maryland," criticizing the cleanliness of the southern soldier. The song called the southern soldier a "shock-less horde," an "unwashed reb," and a "filthy fellow." While the officers were referred to as "drunken generals on my floor," the song said that the confederate army would "dirty every stream and creek" in the nation.

There were many songs written about missing loved ones because of the war. "The Vacant Chair" by Henry S. Washburn expressed the sadness at their "noble Willie" who "strove to bear our banner" to "uphold our country's honor." "Home, Sweet Home" by John Howard Payne expressed the idea that a soldier was an "exile from home" because of war. "Somebody's Darling" by Marie Ravenal de la Coste was written from the perspective of a visitor or a nurse to a "ward of the clean white washed walls where the dead slept and the dying lay." There the person saw "somebody's darling so young and so brave weary still on his sweet pale face." Another was "The Southern Soldier Boy" written by Captain G.W. Alexander. This song was about the pride and fear parents felt after sending their sons off to war with the knowledge that they may never see them again. "Just After the Battle" written by George F. Root was from the perspective of a wounded soldier lying in a battle field waiting for the morning. The third verse describes the "field of battle strewn with dying and with dead" while "amid (his) fallen comrades (he) must wait till morning's dawn."

Songs were so important to both sides during the war, there was an incident when both armies actually joined together to sing. On the evening of December 30, 1862, as the two armies bedded down for the night not less than 700 yards from each other, a group of northerners started playing "Yankee Doodle" and "Hail, Columbia." Southern musicians responded with "Dixie" and "The Bonnie Blue Flag." Somehow one of the songs morphed into a rendition of "Home, Sweet Home" and eventually other soldiers joined in. Within minutes both armies were singing in unison. The following morning the two armies slaughtered each other in what became known as the Battle of Stones River (or the Battle of Murfreesboro). For a few minutes the previous evening, music brought the two armies some peace.

"Tenting on the Old Camp Ground" was a very popular Civil War song written in 1863 by New Hampshire draftee Walter Kittredge who would eventually join the Singing Hutchinson Family. It expressed the drudgery of a soldier's life, the sorrow of being away from loved ones and their desire that the war would end. The final verses condemn the deaths caused by the war and the tears that are shed for those who are lost.

We're tenting tonight on the old camp ground
Give us a song to cheer
Our weary hearts, a song of home
And friends we love so dear

Many are the hearts that are weary tonight
Wishing for the war to cease
Many are the hearts looking for the right
To see the dawn of peace

We've been tenting tonight on the old camp-ground
Thinking of days gone by
Of the loved ones at home that gave us the hand
And the tear that said, "Good-bye!"

We are tenting tonight on the old camp ground
The fires are flickering low
Still are the sleepers that lie around
As the sentinels come and go

Alas for those comrades of days gone by
Whose forms are missed tonight
Alas for the young and true who lie
Where the battle flag braved the fight

No more on march or field of strife
Shall they lie so tired and worn
No rouse again to hope and life

When the sound of drums beat at morn

We are tired of war on the old camp ground
Many are dead and gone
Of the brave and true who've left their homes
Others been wounded long

We've been fighting today on the old camp ground
Many are lying near
Some are dead, and some are dying
Many are in tears

Many are the hearts that are weary tonight
Wishing for the war to cease
Many are the hearts looking for the right
To see the dawn of peace
Dying tonight, dying tonight
Dying on the old camp ground

One of the most popular songs of the Civil War was "All Quiet on the Potomac." It was a haunting song adapted by John Hewitt, based on a poem written by Ethel Lynn Beers, and put to music written by W.H. Goodwin. The first verse was a direct attack on the idea that a single soldier killed is not as important as the death of an officer. This verse expressed this idea that all soldiers should be mourned, not just the officers.

All quiet along the Potomac, tonight
Except here and there a stray picket
Is shot as he walks on his beat to and fro
By a rifleman hid in the thicket
'Tis nothing: a private or two now and then
Will not count in the news of the battle
Not an officer lost: only one of the men
Moaning out, all alone, the death rattle

The "Drummer Boy of Shiloh" was about the last utterance of a young dying man who was serving as a drummer boy in the army. Written by William "Shakespeare" Hays in 1862, it expressed the sadness that accompanies war, especially when the victim is so young.

On Shiloh's dark and bloody ground
The dead and wounded lay
Among them was a drummer boy
Who beat the drum that day

A wounded soldier held him up
His drum was by his side
He clasped his hands and raised his eyes
And prayed before he died

Look down upon the battlefield
Oh Thou, Our Heavenly Friend
Have mercy on our sinful souls
The soldiers cried, "Amen."
There gathered 'round a little group
Each brave man knelt and cried
They listened to the drummer boy
Who prayed before he died

"Oh, Mother," said the dying boy
"Look down from heaven on me
Receive me to thy fond embrace
Oh, take me home to thee
I've loved my country as my God
To serve them both I've tried"
He smiled, shook hands —death seized the boy
Who prayed before he died

Each soldier wept then like a child
Stout hearts were they and brave
They wrapped him in his country's flag
And laid him in the grave
They placed by him the Bible
A rededicated guide
To those that mourn the drummer boy
Who prayed before he died

Ye angels 'round the throne of grace
Look down upon the braves
Who fought and died on Shiloh's plain
Now slumbering in their graves
How many homes made desolate
How many hearts have sighed
How many like that drummer boy
Who prayed before he died

Another song written from the perspective of a young man was penned by the very successful songwriter, Henry C. Work. "Just Before The Battle Mother," written in 1862, was a protest against the war that kept families apart. It was also a song of longing and loneness that is suffered by all soldiers. The second verse directly expressed these sentiments.

> Oh, I long to see you, mother
> And the loving ones at home
> But I'll never leave our banner
> Till in honor I can come
> Tell the traitors all around you
> That their cruel words we know
> In every battle kill our soldiers
> By the help they give the foe

George Cooper wrote a song with the same theme. "For the Dear Old Flag I Die" expressed the sentiment of a dying drummer boy. In his last breath, the dying boy tells his mother "For the honor of our land, and the dear old flag I die."

As the war dragged on President Lincoln saw no recourse other than to institute a draft. In March of 1863 the Conscription Act was signed into law and "all able body" men were now eligible for the draft. There was an exception, however, for anyone who could come up with three hundred dollars. The draft and its accompanied exemption incited riots in New York and inspired Henry C. Work to write "Grafted into the Army."

> Our Jimmy has gone for to live in a tent
> They have grafted him into the army
> He finally pucker'd up courage and went
> When they grafted him into the army
> I told them the child was too young, alas!
> At the captain's fore quarters, they said he would pass
> They'd train him up well in the infantry class
> So they grafted him into the army
>
> Oh, Jimmy farewell! Your brothers fell
> Way down in Alabarmy
> I thought they would spare a lone widder's heir
> But they grafted him into the army
>
> Dressed up in his unicorn--dear little chap
> They have grafted him into the army
> It seems but a day since he sot in my lap
> But they grafted him into the army
> And these are the trousers he used to wear
> Them very same buttons--the patch and the tear

But Uncle Sam gave him a brand new pair
When they grafted him into the army

Now in my provisions I see him revealed
They have grafted him into the army
A picket beside the contented field
They have grafted him into the army
He looks kinder sickish--begins to cry
A big volunteer standing right in his eye!
Oh! what if the ducky should up and die
Now they've grafted him into the army

Songwriter Tony Pastor took the popular patriotic song "We Are Coming Father Abraham" and turned it into a protest against the three hundred dollar exemption. The idea behind this song could be heard again in the 1969 Creedence Clearwater Revival hit "Fortunate Son."

We are coming, Father Abraham
Three hundred dollars more
We're rich enough to stay at home
Let them go out that's poor
But Uncle Abe, were not afraid
To stay behind in clover
We'll nobly fight, defend the right
When this cruel war is over

"John Brown's Body," written in 1861, was used specifically as a marching song by the Massachusetts 12th Regiment. Their first public performance of the song was July 18 on State Street in Boston, Massachusetts. They sang it so many times in public the 12th Regiment became known as the "Hallelujah Regiment." Ironically, as the song became popular and spread to other military units, an accident occurred drowning Sgt. John Brown of the 12th regiment in the Shenandoah River. This depressed the regiment preventing them from ever singing the song again.

The song's melody came from a religious hymn that originated in the early 19th century called "Say, Brothers, Will You Meet Us." As the war dragged on, "John Brown's Body" spread throughout the nation and became one of the most popular marching songs of the era.

John Brown's body lies a- mouldering in the grave
John Brown's body lies a-mouldering in the grave
But his soul goes marching on

Glory, glory, hallelujah (x2)
His soul goes marching on

He's gone to be a soldier in the Army of the Lord…
John Brown's knapsack is strapped upon his back…
John Brown died that the slaves might be free…
The stars above in Heaven now are looking kindly down…

There were many versions of this song written in honor of John Brown's dedication to the abolition of slavery. One of those versions was called "The John Brown Song," and has been attributed to William W. Patton.

Old John Brown's body lies moldering in the grave
While weep the sons of bondage whom he ventured all to save
But tho he lost his life while struggling for the slave
His soul is marching on

John Brown was a hero, undaunted, true and brave
And Kansas knows his valor when he fought her rights to save
Now, tho the grass grows green above his grave
His soul is marching on

He captured Harper's Ferry, with his nineteen men so few
And frightened "Old Virginny" till she trembled thru and thru
They hung him for a traitor, themselves the traitor crew
But his soul is marching on

John Brown was John the Baptist of the Christ we are to see
Christ who of the bondmen shall the Liberator be
And soon throughout the Sunny South the slaves shall all be free
For his soul is marching on

The conflict that he heralded he looks from heaven to view
On the army of the Union with its flag red, white and blue
Heaven shall ring with anthems o'er the deed they mean to do
For his soul is marching on

Oh, soldiers of Freedom, then strike, while strike ye may
The death blow of oppression in a better time and way
For the dawn of old John Brown has brightened into day
And his soul is marching on

Julia Ward Howe heard "John Brown's Body" one night in Washington, D.C. and decided that the Union needed a more uplifting song than one about a man rotting away in the ground. That evening, unable to sleep, Julia Howe wrote new words to the melody and came up with "The Battle Hymn of the Republic." Since then, this song has been used as a patriotic song of recruitment and loyalty to equality and justice. Its creation, however, was a direct protest against the gruesome "John Brown's Body."

Mine eyes have seen the glory
Of the coming of the Lord
He is trampling out the vintage
Where the grapes of wrath are stored
He has loosed the fateful lightening
Of His terrible swift sword
His truth is marching on

I have seen Him in the watch-fires
of a hundred circling camps
They have builded Him an altar
in the evening dews and damps
I can read His righteous sentence
by the dim and flaring lamps
His day is marching on

I have read a fiery gospel
Writ in burnished rows of steel
"As ye deal with my condemners
So with you my grace shall deal"
Let the Hero, born of woman
Crush the serpent with his heel
Since God is marching on

He has sounded forth the trumpet
That shall never call retreat
He is sifting out the hearts of men
Before His judgment-seat
Oh, be swift, my soul, to answer Him!
Be jubilant, my feet!
Our God is marching on

In the beauty of the lilies
Christ was born across the sea
With a glory in His bosom
That transfigures you and me
As He died to make men holy

73

Let us die to make men free
While God is marching on

Most versions of "John Brown's Body" kept the "Glory, Glory Hallelujah" chorus but added their own words. Two of them included "The President's Proclamation" written by Edna Dean Proctor and the "Marching Song of the First Arkansas (Negro) Regiment" attributed to Captain Lindley Miller, which I have included here in its entirety.

Oh, we're the bully soldiers
Of the "First of Arkansas"
We are fighting for the Union
We are fighting for the law
We can hit a Rebel further
Than a white man ever saw
As we go marching on

Glory, glory hallelujah (x3)
As we go marching on

See, there above the center
Where the flag is waving bright
We are going out of slavery
We are bound for freedom's light
We mean to show Jeff Davis
How the Africans can fight
As we go marching on!

We've done with hoeing cotton
We've done with hoeing corn
We are colored Yankee soldiers, now
As sure as you are born
When the masters hear us yelling
They'll think it's Gabriel's horn
As we go marching on

They will have to pay us wages
The wages of their sin
They will have to bow their foreheads
To their colored kith and kin
They will have to give us house-room
Or the roof shall tumble in
As we go marching on

We heard the Proclamation

Master hush it as he will
The bird he sing it to us
Hoppin' on the cotton hill
And the possum up the gum tree
He couldn't keep it still
As he went climbing on

They said, "Now colored brethren
You shall be forever free
From the first of January
Eighteen hundred sixty-three"
We heard it in the river going
Rushing to the sea
As it went sounding on

Father Abraham has spoken
And the message has been sent
The prison doors he opened
And out the pris'ners went
To join the sable army
Of "African descent"
As we go marching on

Then fall in, colored brethren,
You'd better do it soon,
Don't you hear the drum a-beating
The Yankee Doodle tune
We are with you now this morning
We'll be far away at noon
As we go marching on

Some protest songs were written as abolitionist minstrel tunes and then became popular among black soldiers. One was George F. Root's "De Day ob Liberty's Comin'." It was written in slave dialect because it was intended to be used in a minstrel show.

Darkies don't you see de light
De day ob liberty's comin', comin'
Almost gone de gloomy night
De day ob liberty's comin
High! ho! de darkies sing
Loud! loud! dar voices ring
Good news de Lord he bring
"Now let My people go"

Just you look and see dat light
De day ob liberty's comin', comin'
Almost gone de gloomy night
De day ob liberty's comin'

De Union folks dey wait so long
We tink dey neber was comin', comin'
And Secesh he get so strong
We tint dey neber was comin'
Now Uncle Abe he say
Come massa while you may
And for de slabe we'll pay
For we must let him go

White folks let us help ye trou
De day ob liberty's comin', comin'
We can fight and die for you
De day ob liberty's comin'
Yes! yes! we'll shout and sing
Loud! loud! our voices ring
Soon! soon! de mighty King
Will let His people go

O de Lord will bring it right
De day ob liberty's comin', comin'
From dis drefful bloody fight
De day ob libery's comin'
Shout, darkeys, shout and sing
Loud let your voices ring
Soon! soon! de mighty King
Will let His people go

Similar to the theme found in Root's song was "Kingdom Coming (Year of Jericho)." It was written by Henry C. Work in 1862 depicting what would happen to plantation owners as the union army marched through the south. Once again, it was written in slave dialect because it was intended to be performed by a minstrel group. The song was popular in the north among whites and blacks and was heard being sung by black soldiers marching into Richmond in the final days of the war.

Say, darkies, hab you seen de massa
wid de muffstash on his face
Go long de road some time dis mornin'
like he gwine to leab de place?

He seen a smoke way up de ribber
whar de Linkum gunboats lay
He took his hat, and lef' berry sudden
and I spec' he's run away!

De massa run, ha, ha!
De darkey stay, ho, ho!
It mus' be now de kingdom coming
an' de year ob Jubilo!

He six foot one way, two foot tudder
and he weigh tree hundred pound
His coat so big, he couldn't pay the tailor
an' it won't go halfway round
He drill so much dey call him Cap'n
an' he got so drefful tanned
I spec' he try an' fool dem Yankees
for to tink he's contraband

De darkeys feel so lonesome
libbing in de loghouse on de lawn
Dey move dar tings into massa's parlor
for to keep it while he's gone
Dar's wine an' cider in de kitchen
an' de darkeys dey'll have some
I s'pose dey'll all be cornfiscated
when de Linkum sojers come

De obserseer he make us trouble
an' he dribe us round a spell
We lock him up in de smokchouse cellar
wid de key trown in de well
De whip is lost, de han'cuff broken
but de massa'll hab his pay
He's ole enough, big enough
ought to known better dan
to went an' run away

Henry C. Work wrote a follow-up to the previous song called "Babylon is Fallen." He used the same dialect that was popular in the minstrel tunes of the day to express the sentiments of the slave. Like the previous song, these works were popular among abolitionists and the more radical elements of northern intellectuals.

Don't you see de black clouds Risin' ober yonder
Whar de Massa's ole plantation am?
Nebber you be frightened Dem is only darkeys
Come to jine an' fight for Uncle Sam

Look out dar, now! We's a gwine to shoot
Look out dar - don't you understand?
Babylon is fallen! Babylon is fallen
And we's a gwine to occupy de land

Don't you see de lightnin' Flashin' in de canebrake
Like as if we gwine to hab a storm?
No! you is mistaken 'Tis de darkey's bay'nets
An' de buttons on dar uniform

Way up in de cornfield, Whar you hear de tunder
Dat is our ole forty-pounder gun
When de shells are missin', Den we load wid punkins
All de same to make de cowards run

Massa was de Kernel, in de rebel army
Ebber sence we went an' run away
But his lubley darkeys, Dey has been a watchin'
An' dey take him pris'ner tudder day

We will be de massa, He will be de servant
Try him how he like it for a spell
So we crack de Butt'nutts. So we take de Kernel
So de cannon carry back de shell

The following song is a clear recruitment number using the protest against slavery as the root rallying cry. Written by R.H. Stoddard, "To the Men of the North and West" explains the main reason for the war: to fight against slavery.

Men of the North and West
Wake up your might
Prepare, as the rebels have done
For the fight!
You cannot shrink from the test
Rise! Men of the North and West!

They have torn down your banner of stars
They have trampled the laws
They have stifled the freedom they hate

78

For no cause!
Do you love it or slavery best?
Speak! Men of the North and West!

They strike at the life of the state
Shall the murder be done?
They cry, "we are two!" and you?
"We are one!"
You must meet them, then, breast to breast
On! Men of the North and West!

Not with words; they laugh them to scorn
And tears they despise
But with swords in your hands
and death in your eyes
Strike home! Leave to God all the rest
Strike! Men of the North and West!

"Tramp, Tramp, Tramp" was another song written by George F. Root. It protested the conditions of prisoners in the war. The first and last verses expressed the desire of the prisoners to go home.

In the prison cell I sit
Thinking mother, dear, of you
And our bright and happy home so far away
And the tears they fill my eyes
In spite of all that I can do
Though I try to cheer my comrades and be gay…

So within the prison cell
We are waiting for the day
That you'll come to open wide the iron door
And the hollow eye grow bright
And the poor heart almost gay
When we think of seeing home and friends once more

Southerners wrote their own version of "Tramp, Tramp, Tramp" using the same melody as the George F. Root version. The fourth verse expressed a theme of protest.

In the cruel stockade-pen
Dying slowly day by day
For weary months we've waited all in vain
But if god will speed the way

Of our gallant boys in gray
I shall see your face, dear mother, yet again

Another prison song was written from the perspective of a northern soldier serving time in a Charleston, South Carolina prison. Called "Down in Charleston Jail," it was written by Sergeant Johnson of the 54th Massachusetts infantry, with the melody from "When this Cruel War is Over." It protested the condition of the prison and mentions the fact that he was captured at the Battle of Fort Wagner. The first verse sets up the song.

When I enlisted in the army
Then I thought it was grand
Marching through the streets of Boston
Behind a regimental band
When at Wagner I was captured
Then my courage failed
Now I'm dirty, hungry, naked
Here is Charleston jail

Black soldiers had a wealth of marching songs that were considered protest songs. One such example was "Give Us a Flag." The lyrics have been attributed to a private in the 54th Massachusetts Regiment, the first group of black soldiers in the Civil War. It is clear from the song that only the black soldier will save the Union.

Fremont told them when the war it first begun
How to save the Union
And the way it should be done
But Kentucky swore so hard
And old Abe he had his fears
Till every hope was lost
But the colored volunteers

O, give us a flag
All free without a slave
We'll fight to defend it
As our Fathers did so brave
The gallant Comp'ny A
Will make the rebels dance
And we'll stand by the Union
If we only have a chance

McClellan went to Richmond

With two hundred thousand brave
He said "keep back the niggers"
And the Union he would save
Little Mac he had his way
Still the Union is in tears
Now they call for the help
Of the colored volunteers

Old Jeff says he'll hang us
If we dare to meet him armed
A very big thing
But we are not at all alarmed
For he first has got to catch us
before the way is clear
And "that's what's the matter"
With the colored volunteer

So rally, boys, rally
Let us never mind the past
We had a hard road to travel
But our day is coming fast
For God is for the right
And we have no need to fear
The Union must be saved
By the colored volunteer

The South also had songs of their own that exhibited the traits of protest. One song, "Rebels," collected by retired US Air Force Colonel Walbrook D. Swank, had a different version of the same war. It was the north that was violating the rights of the states to govern their own affairs. The song used the name rebel to remind the listener that the founding fathers, notably Washington, Adams, Jefferson, Hamilton, Hancock and Madison, were also considered rebels.

Rebels! 'tis a holy name!
The name our fathers bore
When battling in the cause of Right
Against the tyrant in his might
In the dark days of yore…

Rebels! 'tis our dying name!
For, although life is dear
Yet, freemen born and freemen bred

81

We'd rather live as freemen dead
Than live in slavish fear

Then call us rebels, if you will
We glory in the name
For bending under unjust cause
And swearing faith to unjust laws
We count a greater shame

Here is the third and fourth verse from a number called the "Confederates Song." This song clearly points out Lincoln as the invader and violator of the southerner's right to self-government. It calls on all sons of the Confederacy to fight "both day and night."

Traitorous Lincoln's bloody band
Now invades the freeman's land
Arm'd with sward and firebrand
'Gainst the brave and free

Arm ye, then, for the fray and fight
March ye forth both day and night
Stop not till the foe's in sight
Songs of chivalry…

Here is the second verse from another song called "A Cry to Arms." It was a call to southerners to give up their old tools from the farm for the war effort.

The despots rove your fairest lands
And, till he flies or fears
Your fields must grow but armed hands
Your sheaves be sheaves of spears
Give up your mildew and to rust
The useless tools of gain
And feed your country's sacred dust
With floods of crimson rain…

"Goober Peas" was another song that was popular in the south but was not written down until its publication in 1866. It was known to be sung by many southern confederates as they realized their dire situation and skimpy rations. The goober peas in the song were the peanuts that many confederate soldiers subsisted on in the waning days of the war. The author of the lyric is listed as A. Pindar while the music was written by P. Nutt. Somebody certainly had a sense of humor!

Sitting by the roadside on a summer's day
Chatting with my mess-mates, passing time away
Lying in the shadows underneath the trees
Goodness, how delicious, eating goober peas

Peas, peas, peas, peas
Eating goober peas
Goodness, how delicious
Eating goober peas

When a horse-man passes
The soldiers have a rule
To cry out their loudest
"Mister, here's your mule!"
But another custom
Enchanting-er than these
Is wearing out your grinders
Eating goober peas

Just before the battle
The General hears a row
He says "The Yanks are coming
I hear their rifles now"
He turns around in wonder
And what d'ya think he sees?
The Georgia Militia
Eating goober peas

I think my song has lasted almost long enough
The subject's interesting
But the rhymes are mighty tough
I wish the war was over
So free from rags and fleas
We'd kiss our wives and sweethearts
And gobble goober peas

"Bonnie Blue Flag" was one of the more popular patriotic songs the south used for recruitment and motivation. Written by Harry McCarthy in 1861, the song sends the message that southerners were fighting for the freedom of their land against the tyranny of the northern oppressive government trying to take away sovereign southern rights. Referencing confederate President Jefferson Davis and Vice President Alexander Stephens by name, the song had political and patriotic messages.

We are a band of brothers
And native to the soil
Fighting for the property
We gained by honest toil
And when our rights were threatened
The cry rose near and far
"Hurrah for the Bonnie Blue Flag
That bears a single star!"

Hurrah! Hurrah!
For Southern rights hurrah!
Hurrah for the Bonnie Blue Flag
That bears a single star

As long as the Union
Was faithful to her trust
Like friends and like brothers
Both kind were we and just
But now, when Northern treachery
Attempts our rights to mar
We hoist on high the Bonnie Blue Flag
That bears a single star

First gallant South Carolina
Nobly made the stand
Then came Alabama
Who took her by the hand
Next quickly Mississippi
Georgia and Florida
All raised on high the Bonnie Blue Flag
That bears a single star

Ye men of valor, gather round
The banner of the right
Texas and fair Louisiana
Join us in the fight
Davis, our loved president
And Stephens statesman are
Now rally round the Bonnie Blue Flag
That bears a single star

And here's to old Virginia
The Old Dominion State
Who with the young Confederacy

At length has linked her fate
Impelled by her example
Now other states prepare
To hoist on high the Bonnie Blue Flag
That bears a single star

Then cheer, boys, cheer
Raise the joyous shout
For Arkansas and North Carolina
Now have both gone out
And let another rousing cheer
For Tennessee be given
The single star of the Bonnie Blue Flag
Has grown to be eleven

Then here's to our Confederacy
Strong are we and brave
Like patriots of old we'll fight
Our heritage to save
And rather than submit to shame
To die we would prefer
So cheer for the Bonnie Blue Flag
That bears a single star

One of the more unique protest songs that came out of the Civil War was used by both the north and south. "Battle Cry of Freedom," written by George F. Root, became a rallying cry for both armies fighting to their deaths. Both camps saw themselves a fighting for freedom and rights, while they saw their enemy as doing the exact opposite. In the original, the author clearly established that the cause of the war was the conflict between freedom and slavery.

Oh, we'll rally round the flag, boys, we'll rally once again
Shouting the battle cry of freedom
We will rally from the hillside, we'll gather from the plain
Shouting the battle cry of freedom!

The Union forever! Hurrah, boys, hurrah!
Down with the traitor, up with the star
While we rally round the flag, boys, rally once again
Shouting the battle cry of freedom!

We are springing to the call with a million freemen more...
And we'll fill our vacant ranks of our brothers gone before...

We will welcome to our numbers the loyal, true and brave…
And although he may be poor, he shall never be a slave…

So we're springing to the call from the East and from the West…
And we'll hurl the rebel crew from the land we love best…

The song was so popular that a southerner used the same melody and rhythm to create a new song for the southern cause. This time it's the Confederacy that was fighting against tyranny and oppression.

Our flag is proudly floating on the land and on the main
Shout, shout the battle cry of Freedom!
Beneath it oft we've conquered, and we'll conquer oft again
Shout, shout the battle cry of Freedom!
Our Dixie forever! She's never at a loss!
Down with the eagle and up with the cross!
We'll rally 'round the bonny flag, we'll rally once again
Shout, shout the battle cry of Freedom!

Our gallant boys have marched to the rolling of the drums…
And the leaders in charge cry out, "Come, boys, come!"…
They have laid down their lives on the bloody battle field…
Their motto is resistance "To tyrants we'll not yield!"…
While our boys have responded and to the fields have gone…
Our noble women also have aided them at home...

Arguably the most popular song that came out of the Civil War was "Dixie." The irony of this number is that the original version was written by a northerner from Ohio, Daniel Decatur Emmett and eventually became the most popular song for the confederacy. Emmett wrote it for the minstrel troupe he was working in called the Bryant Minstrels. Originally titled "I Wish I Was In Dixie Land," the song was first performed by the Bryant Minstrels on April 4th 1859 in New York and was listed in the program as a "Plantation Song." It contained the dialect that was heard in many of the minstrel songs of the day written by whites, which were supposed to depict the culture of the slaves. I have used the version that includes the dialect. There are many other versions in print that have been translated into modern English.

I wish I was in de land ob cotton
Old times dar am not forgotten
Look Away! Look Away!
Look Away! Dixie Land

In Dixie land whar I was born in
Early on one frosty mornin'
Look Away! Look Away!
Look Away! Dixie Land

I wish I was in Dixie
Hooray! Hooray!
In Dixie land I'll take my stand
To live and die in Dixie

After a version of the song was performed at the Jefferson Davis inauguration on February 18, 1861, it was picked up by others and it spread throughout the south. By the end of the war, there were dozens of versions being sung in the south and north. For an excellent description of the origin and expansion of this song see: <u>Singing The New Nation</u> by E. Lawrence Abel.

Near the end of the war, songs coming out of the south were less patriotic and idealistic and more based on the reality that the war was not going well for the confederacy. "Hard Times in Dixie" clearly expressed this protest against the difficulties that engulfed the entire south, especially those communities in the path of the armies of Generals U.S. Grant and Benjamin Butler. The irony of this song is its perspective. As you read the song you may realize that the author is actually pleased about the "Hard Times in Dixie."

Hear the mournful music swell
It's hard times in Dixie!
Hear the rebellion's funeral knell
Hard times in Dixie!
Everything is going wrong
Rations short and faces long
And the burden of their song

Is hard up in Dixie
Rations high and funds so low
Foemen come and niggers go
Worst of all the Yankees know
We're hard up in Dixie

Grant is close up on their track
Its hard times in Dixie
Southern fire won't turn him back
Hard times in Dixie

With his heroes tested well
What cares he for shot or shell
Southern brag or Southern swell
They're hard up in Dixie

Uncle Abe don't flinch a bit
For hard times in Dixie
Tough as any rail he's split
Hard up in Dixie
Holding out his honest hands
Welcoming all loyal bands
Abraham well understands
They're hard up in Dixie

Butler with his soldiers true
Makes hard times in Dixie
When he came the rebels knew
Hard times in Dixie
Johnny Rebs don't see the fun
Want begins and credit's done
White man works and darkey runs
They're hard up in Dixie

Beat the drum and toll the bell
For hard times in Dixie
Chant rebellion's funeral knell
Hard times in Dixie
And while over land and sea
Floats the banner of the free
Traitors shall forever be
As hard up in Dixie

After the war's conclusion, the south was controlled by northern soldiers and bankers. "Down on Penn's Farm" was a song that protested the treatment of citizens of southern states who were only trying to make a living. In this song we see the exploitation of the southern plantation owner by carpetbaggers and bankers following Lee's surrender at Appomattox.

Come you ladies and gentlemen, and listen to my song
I'll sing it to you right, but you might think it's wrong
May make you mad, but I mean no harm
It's just about the renters on Penny's farm

It's hard times in the country
Out on Penny's farm

Now you move out on Penny's farm
Plant a little crop of 'bacco and a little crop of corn
He'll come around to plan and plot
'Til you get himself a mortgage on everything you got

You go to the fields and you work all day
Till way after dark, but you get no pay
Promise you meat or a little lard
It's hard to be a renter on Penny's farm

Now here's George Penny come into town
With a wagon load of peaches, not a one of them sound;
He's got to have his money or somebody's check;
Pay him for a bushel and you don't get a peck.

George Penny's renters they'll come into town
With their hands in their pockets and their head hanging down.
Go in the store and the merchant will say,
"Your mortgage is due and I'm looking for my pay."

Down in his pocket with a trembling hand,
"Can't pay you all, but I'll pay you what I can."
Then to the telephone, the merchant makes a call,
He'll put you on the chain gang, (if) you don't pay it all.

The final song we will examine in this chapter is "Oh, I'm a Good
Old Rebel." Probably the most direct protest song in this collection, it
comes from the southern perspective after the fall of the confederacy.
Attributed to Major Innes Randolph of the Confederate army, "I'm A
Good Old Rebel" expresses the "hate" the southerner had for the
"constitution" and "the Yankee Nation and everything they do."

Oh, I'm a good old Rebel soldier, now that's just what I am
For this "Fair Land of Freedom" I do not give a damn
I'm glad I fit against it, I only wish we'd won
And I don't want no pardon for anything I done

I hates the Constitution, this "Great Republic," too
I hates the Freedman's Bureau and uniforms of blue
I hates the nasty eagle with all its brags and fuss
And the lying, thieving Yankees, I hates 'em wuss and wuss
I hates the Yankee nation and everything they do

I hates the Declaration of Independence, too
I hates the "Glorious Union" -- 'tis dripping with our blood
And I hates their striped banner, and I fit it all I could

I followed old Marse Robert for four years, near about
Got wounded in three places, and starved at Point Lookout
I cotched the "roomatism" a'campin' in the snow
But I killed a chance o' Yankees, and I'd like to kill some mo'

Three hundred thousand Yankees is stiff in Southern dust
We got three hundred thousand before they conquered us
They died of Southern fever and Southern steel and shot
But I wish we'd got three million instead of what we got

I can't take up my musket and fight 'em now no more
But I ain't a'gonna love 'em, now that's for sartain sure
I do not want no pardon for what I was and am
And I won't be reconstructed, and I do not care a damn

Of the hundreds of songs created as a direct result of the conditions on the battlefield and the home front, only a small selection has been chosen for this examination. While protest was only one element of a singing soldier, it played a major part in their survival. When the soldiers returned home, whether it was from the battlefield or the prison, these Americans had a wealth of new songs to sing.

In the years following the Civil War, the freedom won for the slaves by the Yankee armies allowed black Americans to express their emotions and opinions in many forms of music. Ballads of sadness and strength were written by blues artists and music expressing freedom and improvisation were created by the jazz performers. Other Americans sang protest songs to express their feelings and political opinions. Coal miners wrote song-stories, migrant workers wrote ballads of suffering, and cowboys sang about loneliness and misery. Many of these musical genres (except for many coal mining song-stories which can be traced to Europe) are rooted directly in the music of the settler, revolutionary, slave, abolitionist or soldier. It was not until the expansion of the Industrial Revolution that the art of singing protest songs became an organizing tool for unionization and the demand of working people to make a living wage in the United States.

Chapter Four:
The Industrial Revolution: Singing Their Way to Unionism

If there ever comes a time
When I have more than a dime
They will have to put me under lock and key
For they've had me broke all along
I can only sing this song
Of the workers and their misery

From the traditional song:
"Beans, Bacon, and Gravy"

The Industrial Revolution produced a wealth of protest songs that borrowed from traditions already established and created new traditions all their own. In this chapter we will focus on protest songs primarily written following the Civil War to the birth of the IWW that deal with the Industrial Revolution and its effects on people. The Industrial Revolution was a change in the way people work and the location of their labors. With the creation of the first flour mill in 1787 by Oliver Evans and the invention of the Cotton Gin in 1793 by Eli Whitney, America was industrializing with machines taking the role of human endurance. Even with these new technological developments, in 1800 97% of Americans still lived on farms in rural areas. But that would quickly change. There were many artisans and craftsmen in the early republic, but they worked their craft by themselves (or maybe with an apprentice) at their own workbench and in their own home or shop. With the development of water power, and the ability to distribute energy throughout a building, people now had the ability to run an entire factory. At first it was the descendants of English and Dutch settlers that built and worked the early factories along with some Irish and other western European immigrants. Over time the increased competition and changing market forces, required the factories to cut their costs. Their need for cheap labor was met by other European immigrants looking for a better life. Eventually women and children joined the ranks of the factory workers. These workers labored long hours, in poor working environments and for meager wages. By the end of the Civil War the effects of the Industrial Revolution were felt in many corners of the now re-united America. Those effects were heard in the songs of troubadours and troublemakers in the ranks of railroad workers, coal miners, convict laborers and industrial unionists.

93

One of the earliest protest songs that dealt with the Industrial Revolution was created in the 1830s and called "The Lowell Factory Girl." The factory system established in Lowell Massachusetts along the banks of the Merrimack River was supposed to be starkly different than the dingy factories of England. At first the conditions were reasonable, but as time wore on circumstances changed. Competition grew with other factories, hours were increased, wages were cut, and workers quotas were raised. In order to compete, textile mills, like the ones in Lowell, hired girls from the farms of New England and daughters of English immigrants. For many of these young women it was a maturing experience with educational and romantic opportunities, but for others is was miserable. They worked 12-14 hours a day, six days a week; they worked in factories that were flammable, polluted and filled with loud and dangerous textile looms; and they had to deal with sexual harassment, low wages and limited privacy. Eventually these girls and women left the factory to be replaced by eastern and southern European immigrants.

I have selected seven verses of the eighteen verse "The Lowell Factory Girl" to include here. This song was found by John Greenway in the Harris Collection at Brown University and printed in <u>American Folksongs of Protest</u>.

When I set out for Lowell
Some factory for to find
I left my native country
And all my friends behind

But now I am in Lowell
And summon'd by the bell
I think less of the factory
Than of my native dell

The factory bell begins to ring
And we must all obey
And to our old employment go
Or else be turned away

Come all ye weary factory girls
I'll have you understand
I'm going to leave the factory
And return to my native land...

No more I'll get my overseer

To come and fix my loom
No more I'll say to my overseer
Can't I stay out till noon...?

Then since they've cut my wages down
To nine shillings per week
If I cannot better wages make
Some other place I'll seek

I do not like my overseer
I do not mean to stay
I mean to hire a Depot-boy
To carry me away...

Charles D. Halker compiled and examined what he called song-poems from 1865 to 1895. He called his study For Democracy, Workers, and God, and found that "between 1865 and 1895 some forty three English language publications printed nearly 2,600 original song-poems." He also concluded that:

> A wide range of subjects and topics also occupied the song-poets attention. Writers issued, for example, strike song-poems, that reported on and encouraged support for striking workers. Workers who crossed picket lines could be subjected to severe opprobrium: song-poems described scabs and blacklegs as loathsome creatures.... Elsewhere song-poets directed criticism toward economic exploitation forcing women into prosecution. Others examined the impact of marginal wages on families, particularly those children who worked to ensure family survival. Still others considered problems of the workplace – the degradation of labor, unspeakable working conditions, unemployment, substandard wages, company stores, discrimination based on age, and the hardships of minors, to name a few.

One of the most popular and longest lasting songs protesting the growing Industrial Revolution in America was about "John Henry." This song is about the competition between man and machine. It is the battle between the brute strength and determination of the human species and the new tools created in the Industrial Revolution. At the end of the battle, John Henry managed to win the competition and

95

drilled deeper than the machine. According to Edith Fowke and Joe Glazer in Songs of Work and Protest:

> Many people claimed to have known John Henry, but their accounts cannot be made to agree. Some say he was black, some say white. Some say he was of average size, others that he was a giant. They insist that he outdrove a steam-drill with his hammer and steel and died from the effort, although the real-life John Henry appears to have died in a cave-in.

Archie Green examined the significance of John Henry in American folklore in Wobblies, Pile Butts, and Other Heroes and wrote:

> John Henry in ballad, rhythmic chant, children's story, and pictorial form comes closer than any other folk hero to personifying our work experience…. Skill, strength, and endurance, although virtues, lead to a pyrrhic victory. Ultimately he signifies an individual defeated by industrial might....

There are dozens of songs dedicated to the feat of John Henry. In each version, John Henry always dies in the face of industrial advancement. He may have won the short term battle (and proving the worth of human labor) but by dying in the effort, he loses to the advancing Industrial Revolution. Throughout American history, John Henry is always the hero in the conflict between man and machine. This theme of human endurance crosses centuries in American popular culture. Below is the concluding verse from a version collected by John and Alan Lomax in American Ballads and Folk Songs:

> Dey took John Henry to de graveyard
> An' dey buried him in de san'
> An' every locomotive come roarin' by
> Says, "Dere lays a steel-drivin' man
> Lawd, Lawd, dere lays a steel-drivin' man

Railroad work was as difficult as any labor in the early 19th century America. Immigrants, especially the Irish who had been escaping the potato famine since the 1830s were prime labor resources for the companies dedicated to connecting the United States with rail. "Pat Works on the Railway" was a song that was frequently sung by the Irish who labored constructing the railroads. One verse expresses the danger of the job:

> In Eighteen hundred and forty five
> I found myself more dead than alive
> I found myself more dead than alive
> From working on the railway

"Drill, Ye Tarriers, Drill" was a song that protested the dangerous working conditions that railroad builders labored under and the cheap bosses they worked for. Published in 1888, it was written by Thomas F. Casey, a New Yorker in the "entertainment" business who had previously worked on a "blasting gang." The final two verses exhibit elements of protest.

> Now the new foreman was Jean McCann
> By god, he was a blamed mean man
> Last week a premature blast went off
> And a mile in the air wend big Jim Geoff

> The next time pay day come around
> Jim Geoff a dollar short was found
> When asked what for, came his reply
> "You were docked for the time you were up in the sky"

As early as 1863 there was a protest song written for Boston printers. These workers went on strike in opposition to a printer's pay scale they felt was exploitation of their skills.

> Rouse, Workingmen, will ye crouch down
> Beneath employers' threatening frown?
> Are ye not men?
> We ye submissive bow the neck
> To yoke oppressive at their beck
> Like goaded beasts?

> Have ye not rights as well as they?
> Are they to rule and ye obey
> Like abject slaves
> No! Justice, honor, manhood, all
> That man ennobles, sternly call
> For union firm

> Yield but the right they now contest
> Ye to the winds may fling the nest

97

Nor hope to rise
But lower, deeper, baser sink
Till robber of e'en the right to think
As well as act

H.C. Dodge wrote a parody of the song "My Country 'Tis of Thee" which he called "The Future America." Published in <u>Bakers Journal</u> in 1889, this song protested the inequity of wealth and income distribution in America primarily because of bribery and political corruption. Parodies of this melody are heard throughout the history of American music.

My country, 'tis of thee
Land of lost liberty
Of thee we sing
Land which the millionaires
Who govern our affairs
Own for themselves and heirs
Hail to thy king

Land once of noble braves
But now of wretched slaves
Alas! Too late
We saw sweet freedom die
From letting bribers nigh
Our unprized suffrage buy
And mourn thy fate

Land where the wealthy few
Can make the many do
Their royal will
And tax for selfish greed
The toilers till they bleed
And those not yet weak-kneed
Crash down and kill

Land where the rogue is raised
On high and loudly praised
For worst of crimes
Of which the end, must be
A hell of cruelty
As proved by history
Of ancient times

My country, 'tis of thee
Betrayed by bribery
Of thee we sing
We might have saved thee long
Had we, when proud and strong
Put down the cursed wrong
That makes a king

Another parody was written in 1890 by Ralph Hoyt. Here is one verse:

Our country, 'tis of thee
Sweet land of knavery
Of thee we sing
Sweet land of Jobs and Rings
And various crooked things
Our social system brings
Full many a sting

One of the earliest union songs of this era was "Step by Step" taken from the preamble of the American Mineworkers Association constitution. It expressed the idea that only through unity will the lives of industrial workers be improved. Through unity comes solidarity and through solidarity comes strength.

Step by step the longest march can be won, can be won
Many stones can form an arch, singly none, singly none
And by union what we will can be accomplished still
Drops of water turn a mill, singly none, singly none

Another pro-union number, "Song of Labor" was written by "a German piano and furniture polisher" named Karl Reuber. You can hear the Christian influence and the Abolitionist fervor in this number.

Now that want and distress doth labor oppress
What shall we sing for Labor's song?
What shall we plead against Mammon's greed
Base selfishness and grievous wrong?
"Close the rank – close the rank, still closer ever
Let Union be our high endeavor!"

For the coal and the ore earth's depths you explore
Your strong arm and courage make fruitful the soil
Yes, heroes all when King Labor doth call
And what reward have you for all your toil?

Mammon all freemen slave would make
Then unite – unite, for Freedom sake!

In vain, church's preaching, in vain Christian teaching
If manhood be nothing, and gold be all
And humanity's claim is naught but a name
If while heaping up wealth we our brother enthrall
O brothers! O sisters! Let speed the good cause
And inscribe on our flag – "better life, better laws!"

Labor's heroes, O ne'er in life's battle despair
For your cares and your toil behold Victory nigh
Together unite – and be steadfast in right
Be ready to live – and be ready to die
Be ready and steady to battle life's wrong
And "Union forever!" be Labors song!

Coal mining was a major life-blood of the Industrial Revolution. The demand and increased production of coal during this period of history was staggering. Between 1850 and 1900 the U.S. output of coal went from 8.4 million tons per year to 270 million tons per year. By 1918 American had reached its peak of production with 680 million tons of coal each year. For almost four years, while America was helping fuel the Great War in Europe over 700,000 people were working in the coalfields of America. These coal mines were dirty and dangerous. The air quality was extremely poor and the possibility of cave-ins were a daily reality.

One song that miners used to protest their conditions was "Only a Miner." It was borrowed from earlier folk-singing traditions that used the beginning phrase "Only a…" then completing it with whatever difficult occupation the singer had. (It could be "Only a Cowboy" or "Only a Tramp" etc.) "Only a Miner" was sung in the 1880s and eventually recorded in the 1920s and then again in the 1960s. It clearly protests the difficult working conditions of those in the coal mines. With lack of daylight, no clean air and the daily danger of cave-ins the life of the coal miner was difficult and treacherous.

The hard-working miners, their dangers are great
Many while mining have met their sad fate
While doing their duties as miners all do
Shut out from the daylight and their darling ones, too

He's only a miner been killed in the ground

100

Only a miner, and one more is found
Killed by an accident, no one can tell
His mining's all over, poor miner, farewell

He leaves his dear wide, and little ones, too
To earn them a living as miners all do
While he was working for those whom he loved
He met a sad fate from a boulder above

With a heart full of sorrow we bid him farewell
How soon we may follow, there's no one can tell
God pity the miners, protect them as well
And shield them from danger while down in the ground

The death of a miner was part of the life of the community.
Whenever there was an accident, families waited in fear for news of
who was in the mine at the time of the collapse. Aunt Molly Jackson
wrote and sang a song about this very subject. Called "Poor Miner's
Farewell," Jackson was able to convey the profound sadness that a
miner's death causes to entire families in mining communities.

Poor hard working miners, their troubles are great
So often while mining they meet their sad fate
Killed by some accident, there's no one can tell
Their mining's all over, poor miner's farewell!

Only a miner, killed under the ground
Only a miner, but one more is gone
Only a miner but one more is gone
Leaving his wife and dear children alone

They leave their dear wives and little ones, too
To earn them a living as miners all do
Killed by some accident, there's no one can tell
Their mining's all over, poor miner's farewell!

Leaving his children thrown out on the street
Barefoot and ragged and nothing to eat
Mother is jobless, my father is dead
I am a poor orphan, begging for bread

When I am in Kentucky so often I meet
Poor coal miners' children out on the street
"What are you doing?" to them I have said
We are hungry, Aunt Molly, and we're begging for bread"

"Will you please help us to get something to eat?
We are ragged and hungry, thrown out on the street"
"Yes, I will help you," to them I have said
"To beg food and clothing, I will help you to get bread"

Aunt Molly Jackson talked about her personal experience with her brother's accident in a coal mine:

> My brother, Richard Garland, was mashed up in the coal
> mines – it took fifteen men to raise a piece of slate off of
> him – 'til they could get his body out – it caught him just
> in his shoulders here, and every bone in him was just
> mashed – (there was) nothing that you could tell that was
> him, only just from his face and head.

Another song about dying in the mine was called "Only a Miner Killed in the Mine." It probably comes from another variant called "Only a Miner Killed in the Breast" from the 1890s. Here is the third and fifth verse collected by Archie Green in his masterpiece analysis of coal mining songs, Only a Miner:

Unconscious of dangers the night hours fled
They heard not the crash of a rock over head
Till it fell like a bolt to the death blow of one
At the feet of his comrade he sank with a moan

Oh! Mother, Joes dead! He was killed in the mine
The telegram trembled along oe'r the line
That the fate that she feared had oe'r taken her boy
Struck down in his manhood, her pride and her joy

Some songs were written from the perspective of the children. It was a constant fear of all mining families that dad would not return home from work one day. Any accident could cause serious injury or even death. "Don't Go Down in the Mine, Dad" was one such number from the perspective of the child. The fear was real and the work was deadly.

A miner was leaving his home for his work,
When he heard his little child scream;
He went to his bedside, his little white face,
"Oh, Daddy, I've had such a dream;
I dreamt that I saw the pit all afire,
And men struggled hard for their lives;

102

The scene it then changed, and the top of the mine
Was surrounded by sweethearts and wives."

"Don't go down in the mine, Dad,
Dreams very often come true;
Daddy, you know it would break my heart
If anything happened to you;
Just go and tell my dream to your mates,
And as true as the stars that shine,
Something is going to happen today,
Dear Daddy, don't go down the mine!"

The miner, a man with a heart good and kind,
Stood by the side of his son;
He said, "It's my living, I can't stay away,
For duty, my lad, must be done."
The little one look'd up, and sadly he said,
"Oh, please stay today with me, Dad!"
But as the brave miner went forth, to his work,
He heard this appeal from his lad:
"Don't go down in the mine, Dad" (etc)

Whilst waiting his turn with the mates to descend,
He could not banish his fears,
He return'd home again to his wife and his child,
Those words seem'd to ring through his ears,
And, ere the day ended, the pit was on fire,
When a score of brave men lost their lives;
He thank'd God above for the dream his child had,
As once more the little one cries:
"Don't go down in the mine, Dad" (etc)

Another song from the perspective of the children of mining
families was "The Dream of the Miner's Child." It exhibits the fear that
all mining children had of losing their father. Woody Guthrie learned
this as a young boy in Oklahoma and taught himself to play it.
According to Woody:

The soft coal mines, the lead and zinc mines around
Henryetta, were only seventeen miles from my home
town, Okemah, and I heard their songs... I sold
newspapers, sang all of the songs I picked up. I leaned to
jig dance along the sidewalks to things called portable

phonographs and sang for my first cancered pennies the "Dream of the Miners' Child"....

The next protest song is based on an actual event. Known as the Coal Creek War (or Coal Creek Rebellion), "the struggle began in 1891 when coal mine owners in the Coal Creek watershed attempted to replace free coal miners with convicts leased out by the state government. Over a period of just over a year, the free miners continuously attacked and burned prison stockades and company buildings, hundreds of convicts were freed, and dozens of miners and militiamen were killed or wounded in small-arms skirmishes." They were protesting the fact that convict labor was being used to replace paid labor. The Buchanan in the song was the Governor John P. Buchanan, the chief executive of the state of Tennessee. I have included the song's entire text as collected by Archie Green.

My song is founded on the truth
In poverty we stand
How hard the millionaire will crush
Upon the laboring man
The miner's toiling under ground
To earn his daily bread
To clothe his wife and children
And see that they are fed

Some are from Kentucky
The place known as my birth
As true and honest-hearted man
As ever trod this earth
The Governor sent the convicts here
And works them in the back
The captain and his soldiers
Are leading by in rank

Although the mines are guarded
The miners true and fair
They mean to deal out justice
A living they declare
The corruption of Buchanan
Brought the convicts here
Just to please the rich man
And take the miner's share

The miners acted manly
When they turned the convicts loose
You see, they did not kill them
And gave them no abuse
But when they brought the convicts here
They boldly marched them forward
The miners soon were gathered
And placed them under guard

Soon the miners did agree
To let them take their place
And wait the legislature
To act upon the case
The law has made no effort
To lend a helping hand
To help the struggling miner
Or move the convict band

Buchanan acted cruelly
To put the out to toil
He says he has not room enough
For the convicts in the wall
He has no law to work them
Only in the pen
Why should they be on public work
To rob the laboring man?

I am in sympathy with the miners
As everyone should be
In other states they work free labor
And why not Tennessee?
The miners true and generous
In many works and ways
We all should treat them kindly
Their platform we should praise

The Lord in all His wisdom
Will lend a helping hand
And if we hold out faithful
God will strive with man
He gives us happy sunshine
A great and glorious light
He'll give us food and raiment
If we'll only serve Him right

The convicts themselves had songs of protest. Convicts were used in many cases as cheap labor to do dangerous jobs for local businesses. One number was "Convict Song" probably sung in the 1890s.

Guns on their shoulders
The bullets made of lead
All them guards is a-guardin' fer
Is that ole fat grease an' bread

Walk around ald Asheville
You'll think you are a sport
Fifteen minutes an' you're arrested
An' Judge Brown got yer bound over to court

They'll take yer over before ole Judge Shaw
A mighty cruel man, he'll try yer mighty well
He'll try his best ter send
Yer poor soul down to hell

Long before the 2012 Occupy Wall Street radicals were deriding the 1% in support of the 99%, there was a song written by Mrs. S.M. Smith called "Labors Ninety Nine." This song clearly protests against the rich and their efforts to keep the fruits of the earth away from the poor working class. It specifically mentions those who "dig… in the dusty mine."

They toil in the fields, the Ninety-and-nine
For the fruits of the mother earth
They dig and delve in the dusky mine
And the bring its treasures forth
But the wealth released by their sturdy blows
To the hands of the one forever flows

From the sweat of their brown the desert blooms
And the forest before them falls
Their labor has builded humble homes
And cities with lofty halls
But the one owns cities and homes and lands
While the ninety-and-nine have empty hands

It was after the Civil War that workers started advocating for the 8-hour work day. A steelworker in 1892 described the long hours workers labored in the factory:

We go to work at seven in the morning and get through at night at six. We work that way for two weeks and then we work the long turn and change to the night shift of thirteen hours. The long turn is when we go on at seven Sunday morning and work through the whole twenty-four hours up to Monday morning. That puts us onto the night turn for the next two weeks, and the other crew onto the day.

"The Eight Hour Day" was a song created to advocate for a shorter work day. The song probably originated in the 1890s when this was a major political issue. The writers of this number took a revolutionary tune and adapted it to the cause of unionization and the eight hour movement. "The Eight Hour Day" took the melody from "Free Americay" which took the melody from "The British Grenadiers." "The Eight Hour Day" called on all workers to strike for the eight hour day.

> We're brave and gallant miner lads, who work all under ground
> With courage and good nature, none finer can be found
>
> We work both late and early, and get but little pay
> To support our wives and children, in free Americay
>
> And when this strike is at an end, and we have gained the day
> We'll drink to health to our miner boys, both near and far away
>
> Eight hours we'd have for working, eight hours we'd have for play
> Eight hours we'd have for sleeping, in free Americay...
>
> If Satan took the blacklegs, I'm sure t'would bid no sin
> What peace and happiness t'would be, for us poor workin' men
>
> Eight hours we'd have for workin', eight hours we'd have for play
> Eight hours we'd have for sleeping, in free Americay

Another song dealing with this same subject was written by I.G. Blanchard and Reverend Jesse H. Jones. Called "Eight Hours" this song calls on all workers to join together for the fight for better hours and the ability to actually "feel the sunshine" during the day. Charles D. Halker, in Democracy, Workers, and God, categorized this song as the "official song of the eight hour movement." Here is the first verse.

> We mean to make things over, we are tired of toil for naught
> With but bare enough to live upon, and never an hour for thought

We want to feel the sunshine, and we want to smell the flowers
We are sure that God has will'd it, and we mean to have eight hours
We are summoning our forces from the shipyards, shop and mill
Eight hours for work, eight hours for rest, eight hours for what we will
Eight hours for work, eight hours for rest, eight hours for what we will

It is important to note that working people have been advocating for reasonable working hours since the beginning of contract labor. This next number collected by John Greenway in <u>American Folksongs of Protest,</u> was a call for a twelve hour work day. "Six to Six" was written sometime early in the 19th century and probably in the industrial northeast. Written to the tune of "Adam and Eve" this song condemns the sun-up to sun-down work hours and calls on people to join their struggle. It compares the work of black slaves to others and identifies the slaves as better off than those that work more than 12 hours a day. I have included here the first verse.

In days now gone the working man begun, sires
To work with the sun, and keep on till he was done, sires
The bosses were as bad as the overseers of blackees
Because they wished the working men to be no more than lackies
The niggers have their tasks, and when done they may spree it
But the jers they were asked to stick to work as long as they could see it
The blackees they had friends of all varieties
But the workies made themselves their own abolition societies
O dear! Oh dear! Why didn't they fix
The hours of labor from SIX to SIX

A consistent theme of protest from the post-Civil War era up until the modern era was the untrustworthiness of the politician. One song, "The Dodger" dates to 1884 when the campaign of James Blaine of Maine was being criticized as someone who was dodging all the important issues of the day, especially the concerns of westerners and farmers.

Oh, the candidate's a dodger, yes, a well-known dodger
Oh, the candidate's a dodger, yes, and I'm a dodger too
He'll meet you and treat you and ask you for your vote
But look out, boys, he's a-dodgin' for your vote

We're all a-dodgin', Dodgin', dodgin', dodgin'
Oh, we're all a-dodgin' out the way through the world

Oh, the lawyer, he's a dodger, yes, a well-known dodger
Oh, the lawyer, he's a dodger, yes, and I'm a dodger, too
He'll plead your case and claim you for a friend
But look out, boys, he's easy for to bend

Oh, the preacher, he's a dodger, yes, a well-known dodger
Oh, the preacher, he's a dodger, yes, and I'm a dodger, too
He'll preach the gospel and tell you of your crimes
But look out, boys, he's dodgin' for your dimes

Oh, the merchant, he's a dodger, yes, a well-known dodger
Oh, the merchant, he's a dodger, yes, and I'm a dodger, too
He'll sell you goods at double the price
But when you go to pay him you'll have to pay him twice

Oh, the farmer, he's a dodger, yes, a well-known dodger
Oh, the farmer, he's a dodger, yes, and I'm a dodger, too
He'll plow his cotton, he'll plow his corn
But he won't make a livin' as sure as you're born

Oh, the sheriff, he's a dodger, yes, a well-known dodger
Oh, the sheriff, he's a dodger, yes, and I'm a dodger, too
He'll act like a friend and a mighty fine man
But look out, boys, he'll put you in the can

Oh, the general, he's a dodger, yes, a well-known dodger
Oh the general, he's a dodger, yes, and I'm a dodger, too
He'll march you up and he'll march you down
But look out, boys, he'll put you underground

Oh, the lover is a dodger, yes, a well-known dodger
Oh, the lover is a dodger, yes, and I'm a dodger, too
He'll hug you and kiss you and call you his bride
But look out, girls, he's telling you a lie

Another song from the gilded age that protested the politician whose only concern is getting votes was "The Workingman's Song." Written by Irish immigrant Michael McGovern, this number complained that the politician acts like he cares about workers only during election season.

They tell me I'm a "sovereign"
That I am truly free
And yet no wealth idle men
Have e'er hobnobbed with me

109

The only time they bow to me
Is when they seek my vote
To place them where their hands may be
E'er clutching Labor's throat

The wealth I toil for goes away
To plutocrat and lord
While I but get starvation pay
Below a slaves reward
Of mansions capped with spire and dome
By Hudson, Thames, Rhine
The poorhouse is the only home
Which I may claim as mine

Politicians were not the only targets of protest singing in the gilded age. Many of the clergy were opposed to unionization and the disruption that it caused. Some of the clergy supported the corporations by calling for the workers to be peaceful and passive. Shady Maguire wrote a number that pointed out that the clergy's indifference to the plight of the worker as a form of betrayal.

'Be patient!' the preacher keeps telling
Poor souls without clothing or food
When rolling in richest of broadcloth
And aping a sanctified mood

They'll feed you on text from Scriptures
And ask why you dare to complain
While at the same time they're regaling
On porter-house steak and champagne

The birth of the People's Party in the late 19th century was based on the idea that farmers and rural people didn't have representation in the government. Although never successful in becoming a major force in national politics, they did have some local electoral success and had their own protest songs. I have included here the chorus of a song called "People's Party Song" collected by John Greenway in American Folk Songs of Protest.

Hark! See the people are advancing
In solid columns to the flight
We will let the bosses see
We're determined to be free
And for bullets we'll use ballots in the fight

Near the end of the 19th century a protest song was created about an event in the nation's capital. As the nation's unemployment rate reached around 18% and the plight of workers and their families grew worse each day because of the economic depression, a group of workers demanded assistance from their government. In April of 1894 a group of fed up Americans, estimated to be in the thousands, and led by labor leader John Coxey, marched on Washington DC. While the event ended in defeat for the workers and mass arrests, including Coxey, it also resulted in a new protest song called "On To Washington." Notice the use of the Civil War classic "John Brown's Body" for the tune and refrain.

> We're headed straight for Washington
> With leaders brave and true
> The foremost men the mighty men
> Who fight the Wall Street crew
> They lead the people's army forth
> Injustice to undo
> And truth goes marching on
>
> Glory Glory Hallelujah (x3)
> Truth goes marching on

Another number about the same event was titled "Coxey Army." The Grover mentioned in the song was President Grover Cleveland who called out the US Army to suppress the marchers.

> Bring the good old bugle, boys, we want to tell in song
> The Coxey Army's marching from town of Massillon
> Soon they'll meet old Grover, a good four million strong
> Marching in the Coxey Army
>
> Hurrah! Hurrah! We want the jubilee
> Hurrah! Hurrah! Hard working men are we
> We only want a chance to live in this land of the free
> Marching in the Coxey Army
>
> Coxey is our leader, from the state of Ohio
> When we get to Washington, he'll let the legislature know
> That we are all working men, and not tramps "on the go"
> Marching in Coxey Army

Here is one more song about Coxey's Army called "Go Join Coxey's Army" written by O. DuBois. I have included three verses and the chorus.

I suppose you've heard of Coxey, and his army on the tramp
'Tis composed of various elements, from the worker to the scamp
They are marching on to Washington, our Congressmen to see
They propose to change existing laws, to suit us all to a T

Then go join Coxey's army, if you want to see the earth
In a Pullman car you'll ride, with the doors hung on the side
If you go join Coxey's army…

And when, upon their uppers
They will reach the White House door
And Cleveland reaches for his gun
They'll travel on some more
They'll make them work for all they get
And, where will Coxey be then-He'll be in the stew, and so will you
If you follow up Coxey's band…

Then he'd better go and join Coxey's army, be an officer in the line
He can work his game of bluff, all the farmers' kids can cuff
Which he can't do with Uncle Sam's army
To battle or to die

"Hold the Fort" was a Civil War song that made a transition to a protest song supporting unionism. According to Edith Fowke and Joe Glazer in their <u>Songs of Work and Protest,</u> "the title comes from a famous incident… (in) October 1864, when Union troops were trapped in a fort at Allatoona Pass, near Atlanta, (and) General Sherman sent a message which was signaled by flags from mountain to mountain…. Despite heavy attacks, the men held the fort until Sherman's army rescued them." You can see from the lyrics below, that if looked at in a different context, the song could also be about working people fighting for unionism.

We meet today in freedom's cause
And raise our voices high
We'll join our hands in union strong
To battle or to die

Hold the fort for we are coming
Union men be strong
Side by side keep pressing onward

112

                        Victory will come

                 Look my comrades see the union
                       Banner waving high
                 Reinforcements now appearing
                        Victory is nigh

                 See our numbers still increasing
                       Hear the bugles blow
                 By our union we shall triumph
                        Over every foe

                 Fierce and long, the battle rages
                       But we do not fear
                 Help will come whenever it's needed
                       Cheer my comrades cheer

The Nights of Labor picked up the theme of the song and converted it to "Storm the Fort."

                   Toiling millions now are waking
                       See them marching on
                   All the tyrants now are shaking
                       Ere their power is gone

                 Storm the fort, ye Knights of Labor,
                       Battle for your cause;
                 Equal rights for every neighbor,
                       Down with tyrant laws

                 Lazy drones steal all the honey
                     From hard labor's hives
                 Bankers control the nation's money
                       And destroy your lives

                 Do not load the workman's shoulder
                       With an unjust debt
                 Do not let the rich bondholder
                       Live by blood and sweat

              Why not should those who fought for freedom
                     Wear old slavery's chains
                 Workingmen will quickly break them
                       When they use their brains

                               113

The Knights of Labor were a union of working men fighting for reasonable hours and fair wages. They also understood the value of singing to build membership, unity and express the spirit of the workers. According to Robert E. Weir in his study of the Knights called <u>Beyond Labor's Veil: The Culture of the Knights of Labor,</u>

> The KOL understood that music, religion, and organizing went hand in hand. The KOL singing tradition was part of nineteenth-century working-class culture, and a link in the unbroken chain of social protest singing that connected life and the workplace. The Order inherited a rich social protest tradition from groups such as the Philadelphia carpenters, New England textile operatives, the Ten Hour Movement, the Greenback Labor Party, and the Grand Eight Hour League. Much of KOL song was simply built on existing form and convention: broadsides, folksong structure and parodies of familiar tunes…. Further, KOL journals printed scores of lyrics with testimonials of how popular particular songs were in given locals, and few socials failed to include music on their programs.

According to Terence V. Powderly leader of the Knights of Labor, singing was an important part of the organization. The quality of singing had nothing to do with the effort. It was all about unity and solidarity.

> Understand, no one member was selected to sing alone; all joined in; someone led, of course, but we all tried to sing and if all didn't do it right the volume of sound enabled us to escape detection and, being a forgiving lot of mortals, no effort was ever made to ferret out and punish the offenders of harmony.

Identified by Robert Weir as "one of the more popular labor songs of the day," the song "The March of Labor" proclaimed that change was coming and it was unified labor that was winning the battle for a living wage.

> Hurrah! The dawn is breaking
> Ye toiling hearts arise
> The despots now are quaking

Hear not their frantic cries
Too long they're on us trampled
White slaves oppressed we were
The galling chain
We'll rend in twain
And gain our victory
March, march, march
From sea to rolling sea
Ten million strong we'll march along
To labor's victory

Written by Thomas Selby and published in the <u>Journal of United Labor</u> in 1885, "Nights of Labor" expressed protest against those who are trying to break them up and calling for unity in their struggle.

Nights of Labor stand for action
Never let an outside faction
In our ranks to cause distraction
Listen to the call

Shoulder stand to shoulder
Then we'll march the bolder
The air is free and we must be
No longer bond, but freemen

'Tis our noblest aspiration
To improve our generation
Raise the standard of our nation
And defend our cause

Men from every land and nation
Join our ranks and take your station
If you're toilers of creation
Join our noble band.

This next number was printed in the <u>Journal of Labor</u> in 1887 and has the same theme as the previous number and also adds a little stab at spineless politicians. (A nabob is a conspicuously wealthy man.)

Ye valiant Knights of Labor, rise
Unfurl your banner to the skies
And go to work and organize
Until the world is won

See the lordly nabobs quake

See the politicians shake
Labor now is awake
Justice will be done

Another Nights of Labor song was written by Thomas Leahy and called "Come Join the Nights of Labor Boys." It points out that all the wealth of the nation is created by the masses of working people but controlled by the select few. The song calls for the fruits of labor to be controlled by those who created it.

We build gilded carriages, fine mansions and halls
But not for the brave sons of labor
And we go to work when the bell or whistle calls
But where are the fruits of our labor

While the law has the banker and broker for pets
Who fatten on the fruits of labor
The brawny wealth producer, a thought never gets
Though working day and night at labor

The bite of the usurer, the landlord and rent
And the trader who lives on labor
Swallow up between them, the wealth by nature sent
To cheer the hearts and homes of labor

Labor forever, hurrah! Boys, hurrah
'Tis the life of the nation, the prop of the law
And we'll raise it to that station, where no man can draw
Millions from our labor, hurrah? Boys, hurrah

"If We Will, We Can Be Free" was written for the Knights of Labor and became a favorite of its members. According to John Greenway in American Folksongs of Protest, this song was sung "at the close of each session" of the organization. Here is the first verse.

Base oppressors, cease your slumbers
Listen to the people's cry
Hark! Uncounted, countless numbers
Swell the peal of agony
Lo from Labor's sons and daughters
In the depths of misery
Like the rush of many waters
Comes the cry "We will be free"
Comes the cry "We will be free"

Here is a verse from a song that was common in the Kansas Chapter of the Knights of Labor.

Hear the pleadings of the workers
As they toil from day to day
Let it be our aim and object
To drive the hungry wolf away
Extending to our toiling brothers
Everywhere a helping hand
Give protection to the workers
Needy ones all o'er the land

The protest songs of the gilded age from railroad workers, miners and members of the Knights of Labor set the stage for the next wave of protest singing. Robert Weir put it well when he wrote:

The link between Ralph Chaplin, the IWW, and the KOL may strike some readers as tenuous, even contrived. But if one considerers the many dimensions in which legacies are formed and operate, it assuredly is not.... While a few specific songs remain from the KOL era, the bulk of the Order's legacy lies in its role in keeping alive the tradition of social protest singing, and in inspiring future labor singers and songwriters to continue that tradition.

The protest songs of working people reflected the hard conditions that they labored and lived under. Whether it was railroad workers, convict laborers, coal miners or industrial unionists; people sang about what ailed them and what would cure those problems. They called out to others to join their fight for a better life and against injustice. When the Nights of Labor came onto the scene in the late 1800s they understood how a song can be used to recruit and build unity among people who are hurt and need a shot of uplifting energy. The Knights of Labor were able to collect and organize songs as well as inspire the writing of new songs to meet new conditions. It was not until the birth of the Industrial Workers of the World, however, that protest singing become more militant and even revolutionary. It was the protest songs of the railroad workers, coal miners, convict workers, and industrial unionists (especially the members of the Knights of Labor), that set the stage for the next generation of troubadours and troublemakers.

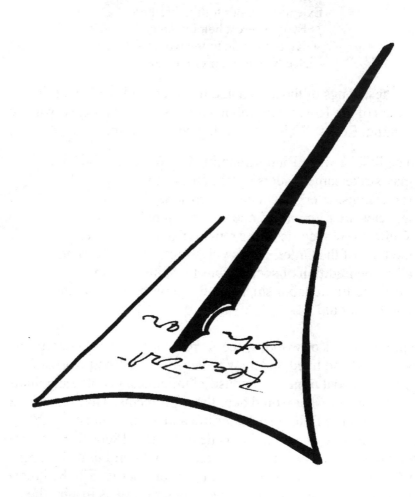

Chapter Five:
Labor & Radical Politics:
The Music of Ralph Chaplin, Joe Hill & the IWW

"Don't waste any time mourning - Organize!"

Joe Hill

The first example of organized revolutionary protest singing in the twentieth century was directed against industrial capitalism and the hardships that result from unchecked corporate power. The Industrial Workers of the World (IWW), or Wobblies, built an organization that was rooted in the idea that songs can move people to revolutionary action, even between people of different languages. The IWW was dedicated to overthrowing the capitalist system and creating a new socialist utopia in its place. The use of songs in this struggle was instrumental to the IWW. They believed that songs should be used as a weapon against those with economic or political power. Ralph Chaplin and Joe Hill were two such troubadours and troublemakers of the IWW who used lyrical talent to write dozens of songs for the radical labor organization. Many of their songs became standards not only in the IWW organization, but other labor organizations throughout America. The IWW and the martyred Joe Hill re-invigorated the use of protest songs and advocated violent rebellion and communist revolution.

The IWW was founded in Chicago in 1905 as a national union for all working people. The Wobblies recognized the historical and emotional potency of music and disseminated protest songs to build membership and arouse opposition to capitalism. It was the first radical organization in America to fully utilize the power and symbolism of songs to advance a political position. Wobblies solidified mainstream America's connection between protest songs and American labor that continued for the next 100 years.

They sang "The Internationale" at the first IWW convention in 1905. It was originally written in 1871 by Eugene Pottier as a poem and in 1888 it was set to music by Pierre Degeyter. Below is the translation made in 1900 by Charles H. Kerr for his collection called <u>Socialist Songs</u>.

Arise, ye prisoners of starvation
Arise, ye wretched of the earth
For justice thunders condemnation

119

A better world's in birth
No more tradition's chains shall bind us
Arise, ye slaves! No more in thrall
The earth shall stand on new foundations
We have been naught - We Shall Be All

'Tis the final conflict, let each stand in his place
The Industrial Union, shall be the Human Race

We want no condescending saviors
To rule us from their judgment hall
We workers ask not for their favors
Let us consult for all.
To make the thief disgorge his booty
To free the spirit from its cell
We must ourselves decide our duty
We must decide and do it well

The law oppresses us and tricks us,
The wage slave system drains our blood
The rich are free from obligation
The laws the poor delude
Too long we've languished in subjection
Equality has other laws
"No rights", says she "without their duties
No claims on equals without cause"

Behold them seated in their glory
The kings of mine and rail and soil
What have you read in all their story
But how they plundered toil?
Fruits of the workers' toil are buried
In strongholds of the idle few
In working for their restitution
The men will only claim their due

We toilers from all fields united
Join hand in hand with all who work
The earth belongs to us, the workers
No room here for the shirk
How many on our flesh have fattened!
But if the noisome birds of prey
Shall vanish from the sky some morning
The blessed sunlight then will stay

The IWW used songs as a weapon to disrupt harmony between the classes. Their philosophy of non-cooperation placed the IWW ideologically closer to the vision of European theorists like Karl Marx, rather than American visionaries like Edward Bellamy. Bellamy was convinced that industrial socialism was the inevitable outcome of capitalism. He also believed that economic and political revolution would come slowly and peacefully. Bellamy speculated that capitalists would realize that their status in society was a temporary "link... in the evolution of the true industrial system." Wobblies, on the other hand, could not wait for power; they joined Karl Marx's call for immediate revolution. The IWW Manifesto, agreed to in January 1905, outlines this economic philosophy:

> This worn out and corrupt system offers no promise of improvement and adaptation.... This system offers only a perpetual struggle for slight relief within wage slavery. It is blind to the possibility of establishing an industrial democracy, wherein there shall be no wage slavery, but where the workers will own the tools which they operate, and the product of which they alone will enjoy.... Separation of craft from craft renders industrial and financial solidarity impossible. Union men scab on union men; hatred of worker for worker is endangered, and the workers are delivered helpless and disintegrated into the hands of the capitalists. All power should rest in a collective membership.... without affiliation with any political party.

The IWW's first major act of disruption was also the first documented "sit down strike in American History." It occurred on December 10, 1906, when three thousand Wobbly workers waged a strike against a General Electric plant in Schenectady, New York. These activities were the founding blocks of future generations of protest radicals. The actions of the IWW made them a prominent force in American labor and a radical political influence on the development of future songs of American protest. Richard Brazier, talented member of the IWW, expressed the importance of songs to their revolutionary labor movement: "We want our songs to stir the workers to action, to awaken them from our apathy and complacency that has made them accept their servitude as though it had been divinely ordained."

The IWW recruited the worst victims of capitalist exploitation: unskilled laborers, outcast immigrants, and non-white Americans. The IWW saw the potential strength in mobilizing the divergent populations in America and crossed all racial, ethnic, and religious barriers. Wobblies accepted African Americans, Native Americans, Asian and European immigrants, as well as Jews and Catholics. These workers believed that while they were competing for the same jobs, businesses were taking advantage of the economic situation by exploiting worker competition and lowering wages. These abused peoples spoke the same language of exploitation that the IWW professed.

America's growing population provided the IWW with many disgruntled workers to recruit. In 1860 the population of the nation had reached thirty million. By the turn of the century, it more than doubled, reaching over seventy five million. Immigration was a major factor in this growth. Between 1890 and 1917 over seventeen million people came to the United States from Europe and Asia.

The Wobblies collected and printed songs as part of their recruitment and organizing efforts. The first of these lyric and poem collections were called "song-cards." When these cards became too small to accommodate the emerging new Wobbly talent, a committee was created to organize and construct a larger collection. J. H. Walsh, one of its chief promoters, helped to convince the committee that songs from the nearby communities should make up most of the first issue. He was confident that as the popularity of the songbook grew, writers from across the nation would begin contributing. The first issue was published in Spokane, Washington in 1909, under the title: Songs of the Industrial Workers of the World (eventually becoming known as the Little Red Song Book). The songbook contained the same material as the song-cards plus short stories and cartoons. It was about thirty pages in length and sold over ten thousand copies within the first month of being printed. Workers sold them at meetings, brought them to factories, and passed them out at strikes and labor rallies.

The songbook was very popular with the workers because of its convenient size, populist message, and cheap cost. The song collection was deliberately organized and constructed to address the problems of individual workers. Even the shape of the songbook was designed so it could be carried in the overalls of industrial workers. The IWW wanted to make it easy for the masses to identify with the organization and relate their own personal struggles with those of other Wobblies.

Workers recognized this link between the songs and their own lives and accepted the book as "the Wobbly bible."

The songbook's success in recruiting and mobilizing workers contradicted those who believed that scientific indoctrination was the only way to win support from workers. Dialectical radicals believed that the communication of industrial unionism could only be accomplished through technical and philosophical language. The failure of this approach was due to the complexity of the language, which was usually very difficult for the average laborer to understand. The Wobblies, however, proved that an organization could spread politics through songs and verse rather than literature and academic publications. The songbook defied ideological wisdom and became the most popular and largest selling IWW publication.

The cover of the songbook was red with two IWW slogans; "An Injury to One Is An Injury To All" and "Labor Is Entitled To All It Produces." Above the slogans were the title and the organization's logo. On the inside cover was the IWW preamble:

> The working class and the employing class have nothing in common. There can be no peace so long as hunger and want are found among millions of working people and the few, who make up the employing class, have all the good things of life.

> Between these two classes a struggle must go on until the workers of the world organize as a class, take possession of the earth and the machinery of production, and abolish the wage system....

> It is the historic mission of the working class to do away with capitalism. The army of production must be organized, not only for the everyday struggle with capitalists, but also to carry on production when capitalism shall have been overthrown. By organizing industrially we are forming the structure of the new society within the shell of the old.

The IWW's use of songs as part of their strategy was influenced by the singing practices of the Salvation Army. The Salvation Army was very successful at attracting attention, recruiting volunteers, and soliciting contributions with the performance of patriotic and spiritual songs. When recruitment competition intensified between the Salvation Army and the IWW, Wobblies adopted Salvation Army tactics in their strategy. The incident marking this transition was the Spokane Washington free speech fight of 1909. The trouble started when the local government issued a ruling that restricted free speech on the city streets. The wording of the decree gave the Salvation Army the right to speak on the city streets while denying labor unions, such as the IWW, the same privilege. This was a deliberate blow to IWW recruitment efforts in the city. One day the Salvation Army confronted the IWW recruiting on the city streets and began their brass band in an attempt to drown out the Wobbly speaker. Wobblies sang along with the Salvation Army but changed the lyrics to suit their message of economic protest.

The Wobblies also borrowed from the songs of American Protestantism. They adapted not only certain songs but also their style of singing. The IWW attempted to capture the spirit of Protestant "revivalism" by linking the importance of worker solidarity to the tradition of singing and praying in church. Fred Thompson, a Wobbly historian, believes there are similarities between the activities of a church and the IWW. He pointed out that members of both organizations gather to build unity, improve personal strength, and defend certain beliefs. Wobbly songwriters strengthened this association by politicizing many religious hymns. They sang to promote economic justice instead of the glory of God and His gift of heaven.

A major aspect of IWW's image was the perception that the labor organization promoted violence. The first act of violence by a Wobbly was on Saturday, December 30, 1905, when Harry Orchard used an explosive device to assassinate former Idaho Governor Frank Stevenberg. Although the motive for the murder is still unclear, the trial that followed the event created an image of Wobblies as anarchists and violent revolutionaries. Mainstream America labeled Wobblies as destructive radicals and rejected IWW politics.

Wobblies argued that workers were the victims of violence and not the perpetrators of it. The IWW defined capitalism itself as a form of violence: "the very conditions of capitalist production, private property, and the wage system is an industrialized act of violence." They maintained that workers, not the owners and bosses, were the victims of violence. The Wobblies insisted that they endorsed nonviolent tactics to initiate public attention to the exploitation of the workers. The official IWW position was that it was not trying to promote violence or "sabotage," but only attempting to "explain it" to the worker.

The Wobblies took the term "sabotage" from a European tradition of the first French industrial workers. The wooden shoes of these French workers were called "sabots." The story goes that the French laborers took off their "sabots," put them in the machines, and halted production; thus the term "sabotage."

The IWW concluded that industrial sabotage was a form of direct action against the perpetrators of violence. According to Wobbly Frank Bohen, "direct action is... any action taken by workers directly at the point of production with a view to bettering (working) conditions." The IWW believed that any sabotage aimed at an industry that exploits its workers, was a necessary part of the evolutionary process towards proletarian revolution. Wobblies viewed all private property as a primary component of worker exploitation. They considered it destructive to the human spirit and saw its elimination as a necessary step in liberating the worker.

One of the misconceptions regarding sabotage is the belief that its goal is to terrorize or even murder members of the bourgeoisie. According to IWW propagandist Walker C. Smith, who wrote the pamphlet, Sabotage: It's History Philosophy & Function (published in 1913) "sabotage does not seek nor desire to take human life." He continued:

> Sabotage is the destruction of profits to gain a definite revolutionary economic end. It has many forms. It may mean damaging of raw materials destined for a scab factory or shop. It may mean the spoiling of a finished product. It may mean the displacement of parts of machinery or the disarrangement of a whole machine where that machine is the same one upon which the other machines are dependent for material. It may mean working slow. It may mean poor work.... In fact, it has as many variations as there are different lines of work.

The Wobblies considered songs a part of promoting this direct action and educating their members about the concept. Ralph Chaplin was one of the greatest writers of protest songs for the labor organization. He wrote promoting sabotage entitled "That Sabo-Tabby Kitten." It created an image of a cat who was hiding and ready to pounce on an industrial factory. The cat criticized society's elite occupations and called on workers to sabotage the tools of the exploiters.

> If you are down and the boss is gloating
> Trust in me instead of voting...
>
> On every wheel that turns I'm riding
> No one knows, though, where I'm hiding...
>
> The fight is tough and you can't see through it
> Shut your traps and a cat will do it...
>
> Lawyers have no bunk to fill me
> Cops and soldiers cannot kill me...
>
> Step on things that the bone-heads bow to
> Come with me and I'll show you how to...
>
> This world should have but free men in it
> Let me show you how to win it
> Hurry now! Wonder how? *MEOW - SABOTAGE*

"Up From Your Knees" was also penned by Chaplin to a Civil War tune called "Song of a Thousand Years." It was originally printed in the Joe Hill Memorial Edition of the <u>Little Red Song Book</u> (ninth edition) in 1916. The song certainly shows the poetic skill of the author and his passion for the Wobbly cause.

> Up from your knees, ye cringing serfmen!
> What have ye gained by whines and tears?
> Rise! they can never break our spirits
> Though they should try a thousand years.
>
> A thousand years, then speed the victory
> Nothing can stop us nor dismay
> After the winter comes the springtime
> After the darkness comes the day
>
> Break ye your chains; strike off your fetters
> Beat them to sword--the foe appears
> Slaves of the world, arise and crush him
> Crush him or serve a thousand years
>
> Join in the fight --the Final Battle
> Welcome the fray with ringing cheers
> These are the times all freemen dreamed of

Fought to attain a thousand years

Be ye prepared; be not unworthy
Greater the task when triumph nears
Master the earth, O Men of Labor
Long have ye learned-a thousand years

Over the hills the sun is rising
Out of the gloom the light appears
See! at your feet the world is waiting
Bought with your blood a thousand years

Another song credited to Ralph Chaplin was "Paint 'er Red." Chaplin gives credit for the song's creation to West Virginian Elmer Rumbaugh. Ironically this song was being sung only a few years before the Russian Revolution of 1917 when landless hungry peasants were crying out for "Peace, Land and Bread!" In this number Chaplin (or Rumbaugh) was calling for revolution in the factory and the government in order to create "One Big Industrial Union."

Come with us you workingmen and join the rebel band
Come you discontented ones and lend a helping hand
We march against the parasite to drive him from the land
With One Big Industrial Union

CHORUS: Hurrah! hurrah! we're gonna paint 'er red!
Hurrah! hurrah! The way is clear ahead!
We're gaining shop democracy and liberty and bread
With One Big Industrial Union.

In factory and field and mine we gather in our might
We're on the job and know the way to win our hardest fight
For the beacon that shall guide us out of darkness into light
Is One Big Industrial Union.

Come on you fellows, get in line, we'll fill the boss with fears
Red's the colour of our flag, it's stained with blood and tears,
We'll flout it in his ugly mug and raise our loudest cheers
For One Big Industrial Union.

"Slaves", they call us, "working plugs", inferior by birth
But when we hit their pocketbooks, we'll spoil their smiles of mirth
We'll stop their dirty dividends and drive them from the earth
With One Big Industrial Union.

> We hate their rotten system more than any mortals do
> Our aim is not to patch it up but build it all anew
> And what we'll have for government when finally we're through
> Is One Big Industrial Union.

Ralph Chaplin was the author of many protest songs printed in the Little Red Song Book. Some of those included "The IWW Prison Song" (written in honor of Wobblies in prison for striking and organizing), "The Commonwealth of Toil" (about starving factory workers dreaming for the day they will claim the earth), "May Day Song" (in honor to the international holiday for all working people), "All Hell Can't Stop Us" (written while in the Leavenworth Penitentiary in Kansas about the emancipation of the industrial worker), "Mourn Not the Dead" (calling for workers to mourn those not active in the struggle), "To My Little Son" (a letter to his son from jail put to music), "The Red Feast" and "Someday a Silent Guard" (about surviving the Paint Creek Miner battlefield in Kanawha, West Virginia between armed capitalist thugs and industrial workers armed with a flag), "The Song of the Rail" (about life traveling on the boxcars as a hobo or migrant worker), and "November" (written to honor those striking workers who died for the cause of industrial unionism).

Ralph Chaplin's most famous song, however, was "Solidarity Forever." It has become the unofficial anthem for the American labor movement and in the words of Chaplin himself: the song was "full of revolutionary fervor." It is also an easy song to teach and learn. Over the years, I have been able to successfully lead many high school history classes in singing this song, and it always ends with students smiling and laughing. Written to the Civil War tune "John Brown's Body" (with the Glory Glory Hallelujah refrain) the melody is easily recognizable by young and old alike.

> When the union's inspiration through the workers blood shall run
> There can be no power greater anywhere beneath the sun
> Yet what force on Earth is weaker than the feeble force of one but
> The union makes us strong
>
> Solidarity Forever, Solidarity Forever, Solidarity Forever
> For the union makes us strong
>
> Is there aught we hold in common with the greedy parasite
> Who would lash us into serfdom and would crush us with his might
> Is there anything left to us but to organize and fight?

For the union makes us strong

It is we who plowed the prairies, build the cities where they trade
Dug the mines and build the workshops, endless miles of RR laid
Now we stand outcast and starving 'mid the wonders we have made but
The union makes us strong

They have taken untold millions that they never toiled to earn
But without our brain and muscle not a single wheel can turn
We can break their haughty power, gain our freedom when we learn that
The union makes us strong

In our hands is placed a power greater than their hoarded gold
Greater than the might of armies magnified a thousand-fold
We can bring to birth a new world from the ashes of the old for
But the union makes us strong

"Solidarity Forever" (and the IWW itself) was immortalized in American literature by James Jones' <u>From Here to Eternity</u>.

> You don't remember the Wobblies. You were too young.
> Or else you weren't born yet. What they really were was a
> religion. They were welded together with a vision we
> don't possess. It was their vision that made them great.
> And it was their belief that made them powerful. And
> sing! You never heard anyone sing the ways those guys
> sang unless it was for a religion. Bunches of them, ten or
> twenty at a time, out in the harvest fields or in one of
> their free speech fights, sitting in the barred windows of
> the second floor of the jail singing the songs that Joe Hill
> had written for them or Ralph Chaplin's "Solidarity
> Forever," a singing that swelled through the town until
> nobody could escape it.

Ralph Chaplin wrote about the creation of his masterpiece, "Solidarity Forever," in a 1961 essay titled "Why I Wrote 'Solidarity Forever.'" I have excerpted portions below.

> When I wrote "Solidarity Forever", I had no way of
> knowing that less than half a century later it would be
> keynoting the none-too-reassuring news that an unborn
> generation would learn about on tomorrow's
> newscasts.... It was originally designed to meet the

needs of a nonconformist, nonpolitical labor organization that was critical of the crudely divided craft unions of the times and practiced voluntary libertarian teamwork at the point of production to obtain its objectives through the "One Big Industrial Union"…. I wrote "Solidarity Forever" at a time when there was a life-or-death struggle between fiercely competitive ideological groups to see which of them would shape the future the then embryonic left-wing labor movement. It was a knockdown-drag-out fight with no holds barred, and every available weapon from gentle persuasion to brass knuckles was used to gain a fair or unfair advantage…. "Solidarity Forever" was written on the assumption that we knew where we were going and knew how to get there…. I didn't write "Solidarity Forever" for ambitious politicians or for job-hungry labor fakirs seeking a ride on the gravy train. I wrote it, or thought I was writing it, for a bunch of "timber beasts", "gandy dancers" and "harvest stiffs" who wouldn't have had a full belly or a place to flop if they hadn't learned to become "the stick-together guys that organize." These were my people, and they looked to me to write this kind of song for them….

Another prolific songwriter for the IWW was Richard Brazier. He served as an editorial board member of the Little Red Songbook and had many of his songs printed there. While his songs did not enjoy the popularity of other writers like Ralph Chaplin or Joe Hill, his contributions cannot be overstated. His lyrical contributions include the following songs:

"A Dream"
"Come and Get Wise"
"Come Join the One Big Union, Do"
"Farewell, Joe"
"Gone Are the Days"
"Good-Bye Dollars; I Must Leave You"
"Hey, Polly!"
"If You Workers Would Only Unite"
"I'll Remember You"
"It Is the Union"

"Making the Camps Like Home"
"Meet Me in the Jungles, Louie"
"That Old Red Button"
"The Child Slaves"
"The Eight-Hour Song"
"The Long, Long Fight"
"The Master Class Are Feeling Fine"
"The Suckers Sadly Gather"
"The Workers of the World Are Now Awaking"
"The Workers, So They Say"
"They Are All Fighters"
"We Will Unite"
"When You Wear that Button"
"Working Folk, Do You Hear?"
"Working Folk, You Are Called Upon"
      (aka: "Working Men, You Are Called Upon")
"You Can't Stop the March of the Toilers"

One of the most descriptive songs of worker hardships in the IWW catalog was "Workingmen, Unite!" Written by E.S. Nelson, the song made a direct assault on capitalism and called for its abolition:

Conditions are bad, and some of you are sad
You cannot see your enemy, the class that lives in luxury
You workingmen are poor, will be forevermore
As long as you permit the few, to guide your destiny

Shall we still be slaves, and work for wages?
It is outrageous, has been for ages
This earth by right, belongs to toilers
And not to spoilers of liberty

The master class is small, but they have lots of 'gall'
When we unite to gain our right, if they resist we'll use our might
There is no middle ground, this fight must be one round
To victory, for liberty, our class is marching on...

Workingmen Unite, we must put up a fight
To make us free from slavery, and capitalistic tyranny
This fight is not in vain, we've got a world to gain
Will you be a fool, a capitalist fool, and serve your enemy?

There were other songwriters that made major contributions to the IWW song catalog. While there are many songs that were anonymous,

131

the following is comprehensive list of known contributors to the <u>Little</u> <u>Red Songbook</u>: George G. Allen, Charles Ashleigh, Thomas Borland, Frank Brechler, John Brill, Ralph Cheney, Raymond Corder, Ethel Comer, Laura Payne Emerson, James Ferriter, Joe Foley, Harrison George, T.E. Hawkins, John Healy, Charles James, Ed Jorda, Harold R. Johnson, John F Kendrick, George Lambert, A. Layton, Dan Liston, Gerald Lively, James Morris, William Morris, Vera Moller, John E Nordquist, Charles M. Robinson, Philips Russell, Joachim Raucher, Loren Roberts, T-bone Slim, H.S. Salt, J.E. Sinclair, Herbert Tulin, William Whalen, and Bertram Lester Weber.

One of the most prolific and popular of the Wobbly songwriters was Joe Hill. He was the most significant contributor to the tradition of protest singing in the United States and the most prominent songwriter in American labor. Almost a quarter of all the eighty-six known Wobbly songs were written by Hill, making him the most successful contributor of any IWW songwriter. He understood the people he wrote for and captured their attention by evoking an emotional response with satirical references to important economic issues in the plain language that workers understood. He borrowed different lyrics and concepts from other genres and created what has been called the "Wobbly idiom." Ralph Chaplin praised Hill's songs as "simple, forceful, and subliminal... full of lilting laughter and keen edged satire... full of fine rage and finer tenderness." Fred Fisher wrote, "Wherever Joe Hill was, he somehow felt like the workers and he wrote for them a song."

Hill understood the significance of music in communicating messages of discontent. He wrote:

> A pamphlet, no matter how good, is never read more than once, but a song is learned by heart and repeated over and over... (and) will succeed in reaching a great number of workers who are too unintelligent or too indifferent to read a pamphlet or an editorial on economic science.

Hill was born Joel Emanuel Hagglund on October 7, 1879, in Gaule, Sweden. He came to America in 1902 and joined the IWW in 1908. Much of what we know about him is based on speculation and hearsay evidence, but there is good reason to believe he participated in many labor strikes against different industries. One of the best books written about the mysterious life of Joe Hill was by Gibbs Smith called

Joe Hill. What is certain about the legacy left by Hill is that workers viewed him as a committed radical and the wealthy saw him as a threat to their economic power.

The protest songs written by Joe Hill illustrate why corporate leaders saw him as a threat to the stability of the national economy. One song that openly criticized the capitalist system was "Workers of the World, Awaken!" It called on all workers to escape from their current economic situation and join the "fight for... emancipation." The song called on workers to "crush the greedy shirkers" who "take the wealth that... belongs to you by right." The song's language plainly set out a radical course of action for workers to disrupt American capitalism.

Workers of the world, awaken
Break your chains, demand your rights
All the wealth you make is taken
By exploiting parasites

Shall you kneel in deep submission?
From your cradles to your graves
Is the height of your ambition?
To be good and willing slaves
Arise, ye prisoners of starvation
Fight for your own emancipation
Arise, ye slaves of every nation
In one Union Grand

Our little ones for bread are crying
And millions are from hunger dying
The means the end is justifying
'Tis the final stand...

In "Where the Frazer River Flows" Hill expressed feelings of exploitation, and worker victory:

Fellow workers pay attention
To what I'm going to mention
For it is the clear contention
Of the workers of the world
That we should all be ready
True-hearted, brave and steady
To rally 'round the standard
When the Red Flag is unfurled
Where the Frazer River flows

Each fellow worker knows
They have bullied and oppressed us
But our union grows
And we're going to find a way boys
For shorter hours and better pay, boys
And we're going to win the day boys
Where the Frazer River Flows...

"There is Power in a Union" was another of Joe Hill's many songs that emphasized worker struggle and international solidarity. Hill criticized those who cooperated with managers and bosses and called upon "workers from every land" to join the "Industrial band" and get all "the earth can supply." It gave the overworked and underpaid a reason to believe that solidarity would lead them away from despair and into prosperity. The Wobblies made a conscious effort to convert "gospel hymn" songs into numbers that protested working conditions and recruited workers into the IWW.

Would you have freedom from wage slavery?
Then join in the grand Industrial band
Would you from mis'ry and hunger be free?
Then come! Do your share, like a man

There is pow'r, there is pow'r
In a band of workingmen
When they stand hand in hand
That's a pow'r, that's a pow'r
That must rule in every land
One Industrial Union grand...

Another important song of Joe Hill's advocated sabotage. Titled "Ta-ra-ra Boom De-ay," it was about the satisfaction of farm workers after using sabotage to halt food production. The act of agricultural violence was a way of getting back at the owner for deplorable working conditions.

I had a job once threshing wheat
Worked sixteen hours with hands and feet
And when the moon was shining bright
They kept me working all night
One moon-light night I hate to tell
I 'accidentally' slipped and fell
My pitch-fork went right in between some cog wheels
Of that thresh machine

134

Ta-ra-ra boom de-ay!
It made a noise that way
And wheels and bolts and hay
Went flying ev'ry way
That Stingy rube said,
'Well! A thousand gone to hell'
But I did sleep that night
I needed it all right...

Two of Hill's most famous songs were "The Preacher and the Slave" and "Casey Jones, the Union Scab." The first song, printed in the third edition of the IWW Songbook, was not only a criticism of the Salvation Army's promise of a "pie in the sky when you die," but also a call to workers to "fight hard for children and wife" and "fight for freedom" until "the world and its wealth" is won by all workers. The second song, printed in the fourth edition of the IWW Songbook, was an attack on "union scabs" who worked for a company even though strikes were engaged. In "Casey Jones" the main character was killed in a train accident and then sent to heaven. After arriving, he "went scabbing on the angels just like he did to workers on the S.P. line." These songs exhibit Hill's satirical wit and humor while protesting working conditions and calling for worker solidarity against oppressive capitalists.

"Coffee An'" was a song that was originally credited to another writer when it was first published in the Little Red Song Book in 1912. In 1922 the song was finally credited to the martyred Wobbly. One of the cheapest foods available to an out of work and broke worker was a doughnut. Hill used humor and wit (with a little bit of racism prevalent at the time) to convey the struggle of an out of work American just looking for food.

An employment shark the other day I went to see
And he said come in and buy a job from me
Just a couple of dollars, for the office fee
The job is steady and the fare is free

Count your pennies, count them, count them one by one
Then you plainly see how you are done
Count your pennies, take them in your hand
Sneak into a Jap's and get your coffee an'

I shipped out and worked and slept in lousy bunks
And the grub it stunk as bad as forty-'leven skunks
When I slaved a week the boss he said one day
You're too tired, you are fired, go and get your pay

When the clerk commenced to count, Oh holy gee!
Road, school and poll tax and hospital fee
Then I fainted, and I nearly lost my sense
When the clerk he said: "You owe me fifty cents"

When I got back to town with blisters on my feet
There I heard a fellow speaking on the street
And he said: "It is the workers' own mistake
If they stick together they get all they make"

And he said: "Come in and join our union grand
Who will be a member of this fighting band?"
"Write me out a card," says I, "By Gee!
The Industrial worker is the dope for me"

Count your workers, count them, count them one by one
Join our union and we'll show you how it's done
Stand together, workers, hand in hand
Then you will never have to live on coffee an'

"Mr. Block" was a Hill song inspired by a cartoon created by and drawn by Ernest Riebe that ran regularly in the <u>Industrial Worker</u>. The cartoon was about a worker that rejected the teachings of the IWW and stayed with the tired and worn out capitalist system. I can't help but think of the term "blockhead" made famous by the Peanuts cartoon created by Charles Shultz where Lucy is always calling Charlie Brown a "blockhead." Joe Hill's song (and the <u>Industrial Worker</u> cartoon) had the same connotation as Lucy insulting Charlie Brown. Mr. Block was so ignorant that he believed the lies of the American government when it came to social mobility, electoral integrity, and even the Spanish American War. At the end of the song Mr. Block was looking for the famous robber barons (Vanderbilt and Rockefeller) when told to look "down below" in hell.

Please give me your attention, I'll introduce to you
A man that is a credit to "Our Red White and Blue"
His head is made of lumber, and solid as a rock
He is a common worker and his name is Mr. Block
And Block he thinks he may

Be President someday

Oh Mr. Block, you were born by mistake
You take the cake, you make me ache
Tie a rock on your block and then jump in the lake
Kindly do that for Liberty's sake

Yes, Mr. Block is lucky; he found a job, by gee!
The sharks got seven dollars, for job and fare and fee
They shipped him to a desert and dumped him with his truck
But when he tried to find his job, he sure was out of luck
He shouted, "That's too raw
I'll fix them with the law"

Block hiked back to the city, but wasn't doing well
He said "I'll join the union -- the great A. F. of L."
He got a job next morning, got fired in the night
He said, "I'll see Sam Gompers and he'll fix that foreman right"
Sam Gompers said, "You see
You've got our sympathy"

Election day he shouted, "A Socialist for Mayor!"
The "comrade" got elected, he happy was for fair
But after the election he got an awful shock
A great big socialistic Bull did rap him on the block
And Comrade Block did sob
"I helped him to his job"

The money kings in Cuba blew up the gunboat Maine
But Block got awful angry and blamed it all on Spain
He went right in the battle and there he lost his leg
And now he's peddling shoestrings and is walking on a peg
He shouts, "Remember Maine
Hurrah! To hell with Spain!"

Poor Block he died one evening, I'm very glad to state
He climbed the golden ladder up to the pearly gate
He said, "Oh Mister Peter, one word I'd like to tell
I'd like to meet the Astorbilts and John D Rockefell"
Old Pete said, "Is that so?
You'll meet them down below"

"Scissor Bill" is a song penned by Joe Hill that had the same attitude as "Mr. Block." It was about people who didn't believe in the organizing efforts of the IWW and preferred to get along with the status quo. "Scissor Bill" also criticized nativists who complained about immigrants and foreigners in America and believed everything their government told them. The song ends with a familiar reference to the promise of "pie in the sky when you die" and the punishment the ignorant will receive in death.

You may ramble 'round the country anywhere you will
You'll always run across that same old Scissor Bill
He's found upon the desert, he is on the hill
He's found in every mining camp and lumber mill

He looks just like a human, he can eat and walk
But you will find he isn't, when he starts to talk
He'll say, "This is my country," with an honest face
While all the cops they chase him out of every place

Scissor Bill, he's a little dippy
Scissor Bill, he has a funny face
Scissor Bill, should drown in Mississippi
He is the missing link that Darwin tried to trace

And Scissor Bill he couldn't live without the booze
He sits around all day and spits tobacco juice
He takes a deck of cards and tries to beat the Chink
Yes, Bill would be a smart guy if he only could think

And Scissor Bill he says: "This country must be freed
From Niggers, Japs and Dutchmen and the gol durn Swede"
He says that every cop would be a native son
If it wasn't for the Irishman, the sonna fur gun

Scissor Bill, the "foreigners" is cussin'
Scissor Bill, he says: "I hate a Coon"
Scissor Bill, is down on everybody
The Hottentots, the Bushmen and the man in the moon

Don't try to talk your union dope to Scissor Bill
He says he never organized and never will
He always will be satisfied until he's dead
With coffee and a doughnut and a lousy old bed

And Bill, he says he gets rewarded thousand fold
When he gets up to Heaven on the streets of gold
But I don't care who knows it, and right here I'll tell
If Scissor Bill is goin' to Heaven, I'll go to Hell

Scissor Bill, he wouldn't join the union
Scissor Bill, he says, "Not me, by Heck!"
Scissor Bill, gets his reward in Heaven
Oh! Sure. He'll get it, but he'll get it in the neck

Joe Hill wrote "The Tramp" to the well-known Civil War tune "Tramp Tramp Tramp" we reviewed in chapter three. Using the tune from George F. Root, Hill was able to utilize a very familiar melody to convey the frustration that a homeless person seeking work had to deal with. Wherever he went, nobody wanted him. Even when he went to Hell looking for a place to stay, the devil kicked him out because he's a hobo.

If you all will shut your trap
I will tell you 'bout a chap
That was broke and up against it, too, for fair
He was not the kind that shirk
He was looking hard for work
But he heard the same old story everywhere

Tramp, tramp, tramp, keep on a-tramping
Nothing doing here for you
If I catch you 'round again
You will wear the ball and chain
Keep on tramping, that's the best thing you can do

He walked up and down the street
'Till the shoes fell off his feet
In a house he spied a lady cooking stew
And he said, "How do you do
May I chop some wood for you?"
What the lady told him made him feel so blue

'Cross the street a sign he read
"Work for Jesus," so it said
And he said, "Here is my chance, I'll surely try"
And he kneeled upon the floor
'Till his knees got rather sore
But at eating-time he heard the preacher cry

Down the street he met a cop
And the Copper made him stop
And he asked him, "When did you blow into town?
Come with me up to the judge"
But the judge he said, "Oh, fudge

139

Bums that have no money needn't come around"

Finally came that happy day
When his life did pass away
He was sure he'd go to heaven when he died
When he reached the pearly gate
Santa Peter, mean old skate
Slammed the gate right in his face and loudly cried

In despair he went to Hell
With the Devil for to dwell
For the reason he'd no other place to go
And he said, "I'm full of sin
So for Christ's sake, let me in!"
But the Devil said, "Oh, beat it! You're a 'bo!"

Joe Hill wrote a song for what has been considered one of the greatest triumphs of the IWW: *The Lawrence Textile Strike of 1912* better known as the *Bread and Roses Strike*. "John Golden and The Lawrence Strike" (aka "A Little Talk With Golden") was written to the tune of "A Little Talk With Jesus." In six verses, Joe Hill was able to capture the attitude of workers toward the leader of the American Federation of Labor Textile Workers Union, John Golden.

In Lawrence, when the starving masses struck for more to eat
And wooden-headed Wood he tried the strikers to defeat
To Sammy Gompers wrote and asked him what he thought
And this is just the answer that the mailman brought

A little talk with Golden, makes it right, all right
He'll settle any strike, if there's coin in sight
Just take him up to dine, and everything is fine
A little talk with Golden, makes it right, all right

The preachers, cops and money-kings were working hand in hand
The boy in blue, with stars and stripes were sent by Uncle Sam
Still things were looking blue, 'cause every striker knew
That weaving cloth with bayonets is hard to do

John Golden had with Mr. Wood a private interview
He told him how to bust up the "I double double U"
He came out in a while and wore the Golden smile
He said: "I've got all labor leaders skinned a mile"

140

John Golden pulled a bogus strike with all his "pinks and stools"
He thought the rest would follow like a bunch of crazy fools
But to his great surprise the "foreigners" were wise
In one big solid union they were organized

That's one time Golden did not, make it right, all right
In spite of all his schemes, the strikers won the fight
When all the workers stand, united hand in hand
The world with all its wealth, will be at their command

The strike began when the mills in Lawrence complied with a 1911 Massachusetts law prohibiting women and children from working more than 54 hours a week. In order to make accounting easer and the scheduling of work bells more efficient, most of the mills cut the hours of all workers to 54 hours a week. That also meant that each worker's pay would be cut an average of 2 hours pay a week.

The strike was known as a singing strike. According to a journalist who reported from Lawrence, Ray Stannard Baker, "It was the first strike I ever saw which sang. I shall not soon forget the curious life, the strange, sudden fire of the mingled nationalities at the strike meetings when they broke into song." Journalist Mary Heaton Vorse attended one of the many meetings in Lawrence and wrote "Then at the end of the meeting, they sang. It was as though a spurt of flame had gone through the audience." Vorse continued: "this was a new kind of strike…. It was the spirit of the strikers that seemed dangerous. They were confident… they sang. They were always marching and singing." In fact there were many reports in local newspapers describing parades of workers singing IWW songs while waving the American flag.

The strike even got its own song. It was a poem written by James Oppenheim who had experienced the turmoil in Lawrence first hand. The song is called "Bread and Roses."

As we come marching, marching in the beauty of the day
A million darkened kitchens, a thousand mill lofts gray
Are touched with all the radiance that a sudden sun discloses
For the people hear us singing: "Bread and roses! Bread and roses!"
As we come marching, marching, we battle too for men
For they are women's children, and we mother them again
Our lives shall not be sweated from birth until life closes
Hearts starve as well as bodies; give us bread, but give us roses!

As we come marching, marching, unnumbered women dead
Go crying through our singing their ancient cry for bread
Small art and love and beauty their drudging spirits knew
Yes, it is bread we fight for -- but we fight for roses, too!

As we come marching, marching, we bring the greater days
The rising of the women means the rising of the race
No more the drudge and idler -- ten that toil where one reposes
But a sharing of life's glories: Bread and roses! Bread and roses!

As the strike wore on John Golden, the President of the American Federation of Labor Textile Workers Union, seemed to be working against the striking Wobblies, especially when he testified against the IWW in congressional hearings regarding the Lawrence strike. According to Bruce Watson, author of Bread and Roses a comprehensive look at the Lawrence Textile Strike of 1912, John Golden attempted to undermine the efforts of the IWW in Lawrence by pitting skilled workers against the striking unskilled workers. Watson wrote:

> Golden and leaders of Lawrence's Central Labor Union
> invited weavers, spinners, and other skilled workers to
> formulate a separate set of demands. Once these had
> been determined craft by craft, they would be presented
> to mill owners. If craftsmen got a slight wage increase,
> their return might cause a rush back to the mills. Then
> the IWW could be run out of town.

Considering all the songs we reviewed above, Joe Hill was definitively one of the greatest contributors to the IWW Little Red Songbook. Many of his songs are still being recorded today by folkies and rockers alike. Below is a complete alphabetical list of the songs penned by the martyred Wobbly.

"Casey Jones - The Union Scab"
"Coffee An'"
"Don't Take My Papa Away From Me"
"Down In The Old Dark Mills"
"Everybody's Joining It"
"The Girl Question"
"It's A Long Way Down To The Soup line"
"Joe Hills's Last Will"
"John Golden and The Lawrence Strike"

142

"Mr. Block"
"Nearer My Job To Thee"
"The Old Toiler's Message"
"The Preacher And The Slave"
"The Rebel Girl"
"Scissor Bill"
"Should I Ever Be A Soldier"
"Stung Right"
"Ta-ra-ra Boom De-ay"
"There Is Power In A Union"
"The Tramp"
"We Will Sing One Song"
"What We Want"
"Where The Fraser River Flows"
"The White Slave"
"Workers Of The World, Awaken"

One of the main components of Joe Hill's immortality as a protest minstrel was his martyrdom at the hands of the state of Utah. If he had lived and faded into the fabric of American industrial culture, his legacy may not have been so profound. However, his execution became a symbol of working class oppression by capitalists and the US government. Before the court-ordered death sentence was carried out, Hill wrote words that were powerful enough to be used by a generation of political activists fifty years later. The circumstances surrounding Hill's death, his attitude during and after the trial, and people's reaction to it, guaranteed a place for him as a martyr for radicalism in America. In Wayne Hampton's Guerrilla Minstrels, Hill was described as a man "whose voice was stilled but whose songs live on... in the struggle for social justice in America."

The trial leading to Hill's execution did not confirm the events of the evening of January 10, 1913 when John G Morrison (a grocer and ex-policeman) and his son Arling were murdered. One hundred years later, however, William Adler did extensive research on Joe Hill for his book The Man Who Never Died and found evidence that the killer of John Morrison was probably Frank Z Wilson who was a known criminal with many convictions and at least sixteen aliases. Adler also found that the probable shooter of Joe Hill was Otto Appelquist, motivated by jealousy over Hill's relationship with Hilda Erickson. Adler also concluded that the anti-IWW attitude in Utah among the state's political and economic leadership made it almost impossible for Hill to have a fair trial.

Joe Hill was arrested at 11:30 pm, January 13, 1913 and accused of shooting and killing John G. Morrison and his son Arling. Hill refused to speak in his own defense and did not cooperate with defense attorneys. After only eleven days of trial, Hill was found guilty of first degree murder on June 28, 1913. His lack of cooperation with the defense attorneys, the fact that Hill's own gunshot wound was unexplained and the radical reputation of Wobblies in Utah, probably contributed a great deal to his conviction. The Supreme Court of Utah refused to hear an appeal of the guilty verdict even after hearing Hill's multiple requests for a "new trial - a fair trial...." Hill continued his jail cell plea to whoever would listen: "If I cannot have a new trial, I am willing to give my blood as a martyr that others may be afforded fair trials."

Many people came to Hill's defense in calling for a new trial. IWW President Bill Hayward, Minister from Sweden Wilhelm Ekengren, AFL President Samuel Gompers and President Woodrow Wilson are only some of the famous people advocating for Hill. Even Helen Keller sent a letter to President Wilson explaining:

> I believe Joseph Hillstrom has not had a fair trial and the
> sentence passed upon him is unjust. I appeal to you as
> official father of all the people to use your great power
> and influence to save one of the nation's helpless sons.

Wobbly bard Ralph Chaplin wrote a number in Joe Hill's honor while he was on death row. Put to the tune of "The Red Flag," Chaplin reminded the listener of the songs Hill wrote and his dedication to the Wobbly cause. Chaplin wrote that by defending the rights of Joe Hill, the workers were defending the cause of the IWW.

A rebel we have known for long
Who's thrilled us often with his song
Has fallen on an evil day
They seek to take his life away

No harm to him can we allow
He needs our help and needs it now
He's in their dungeon, dark and grim
He fought for us; we'll stand by him

They'd fill his warrior heart with lead
And gloat to see him safely dead
His voice forever hushed and still
Our singing fighting brave Joe Hill

His spirit gloried in the fight
In labors sure resistless might
And ONE BIG UNION, staunch and strong
This was the burden of his song

His heart was hot with burning hate
Against the bosses, small and great
He told what haughty Sub-cats do
And all about the wooden shoe

The "long-haired preachers" feared his name
He fills apologists with shame
While "Mr. Block" so bland and Meek
With Scissor-bill did take a sneak

Now boys we've known this rebel long
In every land we've sung his song
Let's get him free and the he may see
The day of our great victory

He made them hate him high and low
They feared his tuneful message so
He'd fight for us while he had breath
We'll save him from the jaws of death

It may not have been recognized at the time, but the conviction and execution of Hill became a symbol of capitalist oppression and an example of future state sponsored repression of radical Americans. The national government eventually used its power not only to destroy the IWW, but also any organization or individual perceived as subversive and threatening to national security or the status quo. Hill's execution was only the beginning of the US government's efforts to suppress singers of American protest songs. This persecution lasted well into the 1950s with the American government's persecution of Pete Seeger in the House of Un-American Activities and the 1970s with the deportation efforts of the Nixon Administration against John Lennon.

One of Joe Hill's most profound sayings was written in a letter to a friend from jail. Hill wrote: "I die like a true blue rebel. *Don't waste any time mourning - organize!"* He even wrote his "Last Will and Testament" in the form of a song.

My will is easy to decide
For there is nothing to divide
My kin don't need to fuss and moan
'Moss does not cling to rolling stone'
My body?-Oh!-If I could choose
I would to ashes it reduce
And let the merry breezes blow
My dust to where some flowers grow
Perhaps some fading flower then
Would come to life and bloom again
This is my last and final will
Good luck to all of you
Joe Hill

In the midst of the controversy surrounding the arrest and indictment of Hill (and one year before his murder trial), the IWW held what became known as the "first great counter-culture festival and media event of the century." As an effort to enlighten workers in New York City about a strike in Paterson, New Jersey, a festival was held on June 7, 1913, in New York City's Madison Square Garden. The Wobblies wanted to expose the hardships of Paterson's striking workers to New York laborers. The historic importance of this event was its successful combination of drama, music, and politics to protest worker exploitation and the inhuman working conditions that American capitalism perpetuated.

The organizer of the event was Harvard graduate John Reed. He participated in the Paterson strike and was arrested during that activity. After his release, Reed spent time at the home of Mabel Dodge and other radicals from Greenwich Village. He allegedly overheard a conversation about the lack of publicity the strike was receiving and interrupted someone who suggested a festival to spread the worker's message. He volunteered his services and said, "My name is Reed... we'll make a pageant of the strike! The first in the world." He immediately began organizing the festival to spread the strikers' message. His goal was to present a realistic but symbolic dramatization of the strike in Paterson.

The "Pageant of Paterson" was an economic, political, and social statement financially backed by Mabel Dodge and endorsed by the

IWW. Over fifteen thousand people attended the festival, and most of them had a copy of the Wobbly songbook. These people sang the IWW songs and created a moving experience for everyone present. The festival included all the significant events from the strike. It began with the walkout of workers and the murdering of innocent spectators. It included strong speeches on labor issues and ended by creating an image of a labor utopia. Mabel Dodge said of the event:

> For a few electric moments there was a terrible unity
> between all these people. They were one: the workers
> who had come to show their comrades what was
> happening across the river and the workers who had
> come to see it. I have never felt such a high pulsing
> vibration in any gathering before or since.

The Paterson Pageant was a symbolic success but a financial failure. They charged a low fee for non-IWW members and gave free admission to IWW members. Although the Paterson strikers were promised the profits from the festival, the workers only received an explanation from Elizabeth Gurley Flynn. She said, "Nothing could have been made with one performance on such a gigantic scale...." Not accepting this justification, the strikers felt cheated by the people whom they believed were trying to help.

The pageant represented the last extensive effort of the Wobblies to influence economic conditions in America. This endeavor, however, set the precedent of combining music, art, culture and politics for the purpose of protest. The festival called for worker solidarity, requested sympathy from other workers, and demanded a worker revolution. The pageant was also the first event to successfully illustrate how symbolic politics can be used as a powerful weapon in spreading a message. This Wobbly experiment prepared the way for future American radicals who used festivals of art and music to express social and political discontent; the most famous of these was the Woodstock Music and Arts Festival in the summer of 1969 in Bethel, New York.

By the end of the World War I, the IWW ceased to exist as a powerful force in labor unionism and protest singing. This decline of influence was caused by their own political positions on important issues. It gave their opposition fuel for their criticism. Ole Hanson, former Mayor of Seattle wrote that "The IWW publish and sing songs filled with sacrilege and hatred, songs reeking of the mire, glorifying crime, encouraging revolt, debauching the hearer, and ridiculing God and good, and all that it is sweet and dear to true men and women everywhere."

The IWW denounced war and called on workers in all American industries to start a massive strike. The IWW also endorsed the Russian Revolution of October 1917 and launched specific strikes against industries that were significant to the American war effort in Europe. These actions led to national hysteria called the Red Scare and a government sponsored effort to eliminate the IWW. This suppression became the model used by the US to eliminate future movements of social and political change.

Between June 1917, and March 1918, the IWW initiated strikes against the lumber and copper industries for better working conditions and an eight hour day. The Wilson Administration recognized how important these raw materials were to the war effort and appointed a Mediation Commission to help resolve the disputes and end the strikes. The Commission on Lumber concluded that "the introduction of the basic eight hour day in the pacific northwest lumber industry is indispensable as a measure of national need." The Commission on Copper found that "neither sinister influences nor the IWW can account for these strikes. The explanation is to be found in un-remedied and remediable industrial disorders."

Even after the commission reported that the labor unrest was not a result of foreign infiltration, the Wilson Administration still concluded that the IWW was trying to disrupt the ability of the United States to engage in war. Industrial representatives agreed with President Wilson and attempted to influence public opinion to stop the strikes and eliminate the Wobblies. They manipulated America's fear of foreign infiltration and accused Wobblies of disloyalty to the United States. The American congress reacted to these accusations with the passage of the Espionage Act on June 15, 1917, and the Sedition Act on May 16, 1918. Between 1917 and 1919 over three hundred IWW members were arrested by agents of the federal government. The American people reacted to the charges of un-Americanism by physically harming individual Wobblies in vigilante actions. The Espionage and Sedition laws legitimized government suppression and provided super-patriots with a justification for Wobbly bashing. While the Wilson Administration eliminated all IWW strongholds, there were reports of Wobblies being "hanged… horsewhipped... tortured, mutilated, and scalded" by vigilantes.

The combined actions of the government and the American citizenry practically eliminated the IWW as an influential organization in American politics and labor unionism. The demise of the IWW did not end protest singing in the United States, but only temporarily subdued its strength as a political weapon. The activities, philosophy, and songs of the IWW were instrumental in the American public's connection between radical union politics and protest singing. The Wobblies made a lasting connection between exploited workers and protest singing which contributed significantly to the use of music by future oppressed people and exploited workers. By the 1930s, American labor adopted the radical traditions carried on by the singing Wobblies to further their cause. They sang about injustice, exploitation, oppression, and continued to associate topical songs with oppressed peoples by addressing mostly the economic concerns of those people. The legacy and traditions created by early twentieth century American troubadours and troublemakers like Ralph Chaplin and Joe Hill, can be heard throughout the next 100 years of American protest music. In the next chapter we examine the protest songs and minstrels of the 1930s and 40s, especially Woody Guthrie and Pete Seeger.

Chapter Six:
Woody Guthrie, Pete Seeger & the Songs of Patriotic Radicalism

A singing army is a winning army, and a singing
Labor Movement cannot be defeated. When
hundreds of men and women in a labor union
sing together, their individual longing for dignity
and freedom are bound into an irrepressible
force.

John L. Lewis, President C.I.O.

The enormity of the Great Depression made a significant impact on the expansion of protest music in American culture and created a number of musical troubadours and troublemakers. The calamity of the depression exhibited the weakness of capitalism and turned many Americans to radical politics. Some people viewed the depression as uncontrollable and compared it to the great biblical tragedies of human history. The depression took away the homes and jobs of Americans, and threatened to take away the idealistic dreams of financial security millions had worked for. These catastrophic economic conditions re-invigorated the tradition of protest singing in the US and exposed topical music to many Americans in different regions of the country. The protest songs of the thirties and forties opposed capitalism's lack of economic fairness towards working people and helped expose the traditional music of common, ordinary American folk to mainstream and urban society.

Woody Guthrie was probably one of the most notable protest singers of the depression era. Because of his unique style and diverse repertoire, Woody was described as "a proletarian revolutionary from the pages of a Steinbeck novel." Guthrie's topical material and distinct persona made him a symbol of protest in American folklore. His messages of optimism and strength were combined with the desire to change the economic system and class structure of the nation. He wanted to use his music to help bring about change in people's lives and their working conditions. Woody wrote to Alan Lomax, a folklorist and assistant director of the Folk Song Archive in the Library of Congress, about the power and meaning of songs.

A folk song is what's wrong and how to fix it, or it could
be who's hungry and where their mouth is, or who's
carrying a gun, and where the peace is - that's folklore
and folks made it up because they seen that the
politicians couldn't find nothing to fix or nobody to feed
or give a job of work [to].

Born in Okemah Oklahoma, on Sunday, July 14, 1912, Woodrow
Wilson Guthrie was named as a tribute to the Democrats most recent
presidential nominee. He didn't initially envision a career in music until
he realized that performing came naturally and people enjoyed
watching him. He also found that he could earn money from an
audience by playing harmonica and dancing. Woody first attempted a
stringed instrument after noticing an old guitar in Shorty Harris' local
store and persuaded the owner to give it to him. He then asked his
Uncle Jeff to teach him some chords, and practiced almost every day
trying to remember the songs his mother sang to him when he was a
baby.

A major influence on Woody's development as a singer of protest
songs was his experience of the Great Dust Bowl of Oklahoma in the
mid-1930s. A lack of rainfall and torrential winds dried out cornfields
and grass pastures. The wind and sand removed nutrient-rich top soil,
killed crops, and made planting much more difficult the following
season. The agricultural catastrophe resulted in massive unemployment
and the bankruptcies of family farms. John Steinbeck's description of
this horror in the novel, <u>The Grapes of Wrath</u>, influenced Guthrie's
view of people who survived these conditions. After Guthrie saw the
movie made from the novel, he began a project of his own as a musical
reflection of what he saw, called <u>Dust Bowl Ballads</u>.

Released five years after the worst of the dust storms subsided, this
album was not immediately popular with the general public. Over time,
however, <u>Dust Bowl Ballads</u> became recognized by a new generation
coming of age in American cities that discovered these songs as a new
form of political protest. One of the songs, "The Great Dust Storm,"
paralleled Steinbeck's ability to summarize the environmental and
economic tragedy. The song dealt with more than just the storm; it was
a testament to the many problems that farmers faced in the 1930s. It
captured the feeling of an old broadside ballad from the colonial days
by starting the song with a date and continuing with a description of one
of the worst dust storms to hit the Midwest.

In "Dust Can't Kill Me," Woody sang about how some people lost their farms. He alluded to how farmers were encouraged to go into debt by promises of increased production and warnings about the gamble of competing with large plantations. In the environmental depravation of the Great Dust Bowl, many farmers had poor harvests and could not pay their debts. This put some family farms in financial trouble and even bankruptcy. Guthrie believed that Americans were losing their livelihood to banks and mortgage institutions in the name of industrial progress, greed, and uncontrolled capitalism. Woody sang that even though farmers are losing everything they still have their honor and pride.

Another relevant protest song on the album was "Blowing Down this Road." In this number Guthrie sang about travelers who were looking for a job in order to feed their children and families. After each verse that detailed people's struggle in the depression and dust bowl. Woody sang that he wasn't going to tolerate being treated like the scum of the earth. The song protested the way people were treated because of their class or income level. The song also protested the conditions working people were forced to live and work under.

Guthrie continued the theme of discrimination against the poor with "Do Re Mi." In this song Woody sang about people who attempted to make things better by migrating to California. He sang about how people needed money, which he called "Do Re Mi," to prevent being stopped and sent away at the state border. At strategic points around Los Angeles, sentries were ordered to turn people away suspected of looking for work. Guthrie sang that even though people were doing their best to find a job anywhere they could, the people and the border would turn them away.

In "I Ain't Got No Home In This World Anymore," Guthrie tried to solicit sympathy for the working people who suffered the effects of the nation's bad economic and environmental conditions. He sang about the troubadours who traveled looking for any kind of work they could find. He sang about police harassment and the struggles of families without a home.

Another song Guthrie wrote during this same period was in response to a Tin Pan Alley number by Irving Berlin called, "God Bless America." While traveling, Guthrie heard the song on the radio a number of times and grew angry because it "told people not to worry... God was in the driver's seat." Guthrie believed that working people had to make a good life for themselves in this world because nobody else would do it for them. He reacted to "God Bless America" by writing a song titled "God Blessed America For Me." He tried to convey a message that America belongs to hard-working people, not the affluent or those with political power. The song eventually became "This Land is Your Land," a very popular song in American culture.

The version that is well known in America is not the same as Woody's original. A verse that pointed out the song's message of capitalist protest has been removed from many traditional songbooks and public performances. The main point of the song is that the American land is for all the people and not just a select few. The most important verse is an attack on the concept of private property. Guthrie made sure that his son Arlo knew the verse condemning private property so that America would never forget.

Over the years between 1936 and 1942, Woody was a rambling traveler. He experienced more pain and suffering than many American's would ever witness in a lifetime. Sometimes with no destination in mind and usually without any money, Guthrie looked for a free ride. The large numbers of people searching the countryside for employment made free transportation difficult to find and Guthrie, like many others, ended up traveling by box car. These freight trains were full of men from different parts of the country who passed the time by telling stories and singing songs. This form of transportation gave Guthrie the opportunity to live with the really down trodden, the most desperate, and the most helpless Americans. He saw "starving children with distended bellies... running sores, dysentery, lice and worms..." and realized it was not unusual to see starving people in dirty migrant communities close to farms with plenty of food. It was at this stage in his life that Guthrie developed his opinion about America's class system. He was convinced that the nation was divided by an economic class structure: the rich and the poor. Woody considered himself poor like the people he traveled with and incorporated this suffering into his music. According to Cisco Houston, Woody's one-time musical partner, the singing Okie "spent a third of his life starving, a third working and a third creating...."

Guthrie's exposure to the different conditions under which Americans lived was very important to his evolution as an influential protest singer. By traveling the country in box cars, singing protest songs, and learning the ideology of labor radicals; Woody absorbed many aspects of these roaming strangers and developed songs that addressed their ruined lives and the economic system that allowed it to happen. He learned songs, stories, and mannerisms from all parts of the country and incorporated them into his repertoire. According to Richard A. Ruess:

> Guthrie's importance to the folklorist lies not in his negligible contributions to oral tradition but in his role as spokesman for various groups.... In other words, Guthrie was a unique distillation of the cultural experiences of several groups possessing folk elements, at once a mirror in which they saw themselves and their most articulate and able chronicler.

One song that Woody performed while on the road was "Going Down the Road Feeling Bad." Sometimes referred to as "Lonesome Road Blues," Guthrie called this song "the Okie anthem." He attempted to depict the desperate feelings of people who never seemed to get a break. Over the years this song has been covered by rock bands like the Grateful Dead and even used is a South Park episode that was a parody of the film *Grapes of Wrath.*

Guthrie first became interested in radical leftist politics in the mid-thirties when his experiences on the road with starving children and striking miners made him ready to challenge the establishment. He sang for communists because at this time in American history it seemed that capitalism was to blame for all the ills in the country. Communists were active in helping poor, hardworking Americans who were exploited by the system. Leftist audiences identified with Guthrie's songs about the despair of life on the unemployed road and especially loved the way he sang the word "politician." He had a way of expressing more protest with that one word than any leftist document or literature of economic or political opposition. Guthrie commented about his performing for communists: "Left-wing, right-wing, chicken-wing - it's all the same thing to me. I sing my songs whenever I can sing 'em."

Guthrie developed opinions about American society that were similar to those of American communists. His political and economic philosophy did not come from a book on Marxist theory of dialectical materialism, but from the realities of the Great Depression, Oklahoma's dust bowl years, and the songs, stories and people he met in his travels. Guthrie's lyrical wit expressed people's dissatisfaction with capitalism and supported working Americans everywhere. Defining Woody's ideological positions is not a simple task. Wayne Hampton described

Guthrie as being "at one with the tradition of the Wobblies," while Joe Klein describes him as having "a philosophy, but no opinions." However he is viewed, Guthrie certainly dedicated his life to worker solidarity in making "One Big Union."

Guthrie's songs were different from those of Joe Hill and the Wobblies in two ways. One was the form of music the message of protest was attached to. While the songs of the IWW were based on religious hymns and urban based popular songs, Woody's style was a smorgasbord of material from different areas of the vast American nation. The second difference was the people he identified with and sang about. Wobbly protest music was primarily aimed at workers in the lumber and coal industries; whereas Woody prided himself in representing the Okies from the farms in the mid-west. Woody did not sing about men thrown out of steel mills; he identified with the struggle of the dust bowl refugee. Guthrie's vision of a worker paradise was not the handing over of the nation to the industrial workers, but liberating Okie farmers who were forced on the road in search of work. Woody tried to represent them by capturing a home-grown feel in his songs. According to John Steinbeck:

> Woody... sings the songs of a people and I suspect that
> he is, in a way, that people. Harsh voiced and nasal...
> there is nothing sweet about Woody, and there is nothing
> sweet about the songs he sings. But there is something
> more important for those who will listen. There is the
> will of a people to endure and fight against oppression. I
> think we call this the American spirit.

To Guthrie, the closer the performer or writer is to the audience, the more significant and relevant the music will be. He said, "The best stuff you can sing about is what you see and if you look hard enough you can see plenty to sing about." His songs were identified by their representation of people's struggles and viewpoints. He even once mentioned that he wrote "songs that said what everybody in (the) country was thinking." Sometimes, Guthrie went a little far and claimed that in order to write a song about something one had to be part of the event or situation. He also believed that if a performer loses his connection with the audience, "there is just one way to save yourself, and that's to get together and work and fight for everybody."

156

During his shortened career, Guthrie wrote over a thousand songs, poems, short stories, two autobiographical books: <u>Bound for Glory</u> and <u>Seeds of Man</u>, a work of fiction: <u>House of Earth: A Novel</u>, political and economic commentaries, as well as cartoons in the socialist-worker newspaper: *Peoples World.* His distinct style and diverse repertoire were reflected by the usage of different words and phrases when writing songs, stories and articles. When performing, he would often forget a verse and make up a new one that related to the audience or a particular issue. He combined the idea of storytelling with politics and distinguished himself from other singers of his time. His life, songs, beliefs, and personal philosophy as well as the intensity with which others imitated him, attributed to his mythologization. Woody explained how he viewed some of his best work on a radio (WNEV) program on December 31, 1944:

> I am out to sing songs that will prove to you that this is your world and that if it has hit you pretty hard and knocked you for a dozen loops, no matter how hard it run you down nor rolled over you, no matter what color, what size you are, how you are built, I am out to sing the songs that make you take pride in yourself and your work. And the songs that I sing are made up for the most part by all sorts of folks just about like you.

Another important development in the thirties was the American Communist Party's adoption of American folk music to further its cause. American communists originally used Russian and European classical songs to propagate their position and entertain workers, but by the mid 1930's, the party adopted the strategy of the IWW and accepted songs from American writers for propaganda purposes. Communists recognized that music can be used as a weapon in the class struggle and that every songwriter is a valuable part of that endeavor. They wanted a songwriter to prop up like the Wobblies promoted Joe Hill. They initiated the American Music League to help promote traditional and topical American songs as the music of the working class. They believed that using folk singers as a propaganda tactic was an ideal way to battle the established culture of the bourgeoisie.

Some of the people the League promoted were the radical singers already known among certain groups such as Aunt Molly Jackson, Woody Guthrie, and Huddie Ledbetter (Leadbelly). Leadbelly's anticapitalist attitude was an ideal expression for communists to exploit. Born in the midst of poverty and racism in 1879, Leadbelly developed his distinctive singing and guitar style while imprisoned at work farms and prison camps. According to Pete Seeger, "this modern age will not produce again such a combination of genuine folk artist and virtuoso." His most famous protest song, which attacked both racism and capitalism, was written after he moved to the nation's capital. By using the term bourgeois, Leadbelly made himself the darling of American communists. He called it "Bourgeois Blues."

Part of this communist endorsement of American folk music was the "popular front." The communists promoted cooperation between all the Left's factions and endorsed the temporary tolerance of capitalism. This plan was initiated for two primary reasons. The first was to recruit new members for the Communist Party among the American masses. The second reason was to combat the rise of international fascism. This philosophy of cooperation promoted the idea that "Communism is Twentieth Century Americanism." The Popular Front emphasized anti-fascism and democracy, rather than communist ideology, economic theory, and the evils of capitalism. At first, Americans considered the Communist Party immaterial to the labor struggle in the United States, but by the early thirties, Americans looked to communism as a possible solution to their economic problems. The appearance of Soviet economic success in Europe and communist support for the workers in American labor disputes convinced many Americans that the Communist Party was the only political organization in the US dedicated to the improvement of working conditions. The most significant aspect of the Popular Front, however, was its exposure of radical singers like Guthrie and Leadbelly to new audiences in urban America.

A leftist group that was specifically formed in the mid-thirties to use songs to oppose capitalism was the Composers Collective. It was a branch of New York's Pierre Degeyter Club and a division of the communist Workers' Music League. It used songs to promote communist ideology and printed the first Workers Songbook in 1934. The songbook became a voice for exploited workers and reiterated the Wobbly conviction that "music is a weapon in the class struggle."

The forward to the songbook clearly stated their position.

> Music Penetrates Everywhere
> It Carries Words With It

It Fixes Them in the Mind
It Graves Them in the Heart
Music is a Weapon in the Class Struggle.

This organization attempted to combine communist culture with the culture of American folk music. It had two basic goals: to exploit the association between art and politics and expose political songs to a large number of people. The collective was successful in bridging gaps between propaganda songs of the radical left and the music of ordinary working people. Even though the organization only lasted two years and rejected the songs of the IWW, it did manage to expose many performers and writers to new audiences.

Another major contributor to the expansion of protest music in American culture was Pete Seeger. By committing himself to advancing the idea that folk music represents ordinary people, Seeger became a major catalyst in the development of protest music eventually representing the grievances of American youth. This transition was not what Seeger intended, but became his most significant contribution to the musical genre.

Pete Seeger was born on May 3, 1919, in Paterson, New York, into a musical family. Pete's father, Charles Seeger, had a tremendous influence on him. Charles was devoted to collecting traditional American music. In 1936 he brought Pete to the 9th Annual Folk Song and Dance Festival. Pete was so impressed by what seemed like a wondrous spectacle from the Middle Ages, he fell in love with this music and the common people it represented. Although he came from an upper middle class background, Pete Seeger spent his entire life in support of working people everywhere.

Seeger's decision to commit his life spreading the music of ordinary people was reinforced by an experience in college. He was from a financially secure family and given the opportunity to study at Harvard University. It was an encounter with sociology Professor Sorokin that convinced Seeger that Harvard was not where he wanted to be. When he asked the Professor why he used such big words, Seeger received the following response: "You have to impress people you know." At that point Seeger remembers thinking: "If this is the sort that's teaching here, I'm not going to bother studying anymore." Seeger then decided to pursue an education about the real world by learning from people who live in it and playing the music that represented these people.

By 1939 Seeger toured with the Vagabond Puppeteers and developed his musical talent and radical political philosophy. Eventually, Seeger concluded that he wanted to be part of building a singing labor union. In the summer of 1940 Seeger traveled with Woody Guthrie and learned much from the Okie spokesman. He absorbed all the stories, jokes, talking blues, songs and traditional ballads Woody could offer. He expanded his own knowledge of music folklore and developed a commitment to singing union protest songs for American laborers. According to Robbie Lieberman, Seeger believed it was possible to "make a singing labor movement, take up where Joe Hill left off, and carry the tradition on."

Seeger formed the Almanac Singers to help build what he envisioned as a singing labor movement. In December of 1940, Pete performed with Lee Hays at the Jade Mountain Restaurant in Greenwich Village, New York. After a few performances, Lee's roommate, Millard Lampell, started playing with them. By February of 1941 they were officially recognized as the Almanac Singers when Pete, Lee, and Millard were invited to perform at a National Youth Congress in Washington D.C. They took their name from the Farmer's Almanac, which Seeger said was a guide to the earth. He wanted the Almanac Singers to become a guide for those fighting for a better life for everyone. Some of the Almanacs' material also ended up in the AFL-CIO Songbook, which was used by union members.

The Almanacs were a significant part of the evolution of protest songs for two primary reasons. One was that they were the first singing group of traditional and labor songs to promote working class culture in an urban environment as an attempt to give it a wider public appeal. The second was their position as the holders of the Wobbly tradition. Their position as an heir was realized when Elizabeth Gurley Flynn gave them most of Joe Hill's personal annals. This "official passing of the torch" from one generation of singing radicals to another became the symbol of the evolving radical America from the "Lyrical Left" to what has become known as the "Old Left."

The creation of the Almanac Singers was a major step in the dissemination of radical politics in urban America. A big part of this was when Woody Guthrie joined the group in June of 1941, and exposed some of his protest material about the economic conditions of unemployed migrant farmers to new audiences. In 1940 some leftist radicals discovered Guthrie's music and followed his career into the Almanac Singers. These urban leftists saw Guthrie as the protest singer from the Dust Bowl and associated the Almanac Singers in this same context. Many urban radicals viewed the Almanacs, with Seeger and Guthrie as strong influences, as the embodiment of a new form of political expression. With the Almanacs as a guiding force, topical songs became a staple form of political opposition in urban communities. The Almanacs also influenced many other writers and singers to perform traditional ballads and original protest songs.

One failure of the Almanac Singers was their appearance of being controlled by the security interests of the Soviet Union and the politics of American communists. This was obvious when the group made decisions about what songs to sing based on the politics of the situation. The most dramatic political illustration of this was Woody's position on the Second World War. Woody defended the communists when the Soviets took advantage of the Hitler-Stalin Pact of August 23, 1939, and invaded Poland. He explained his support by pointing out "that communists still were the only people organizing the migrants in the San Joaquin Valley to fight the cotton growers...." Woody wrote a song supporting the actions of the Soviet Union in Poland called "More War News."

Woody wrote another song which criticized President Roosevelt's position on the European war. When the President announced his policy of providing aid to Finland in a speech to an American Youth Congress meeting in New York City in 1940, the reaction of the Left stifled the popular front. Woody supported the American Left's rejection of Roosevelt's slow attempt to ally the US with Great Britain and wrote "Why Do You Stand There in the Rain." The last verse of the song clearly pointed out Guthrie's ability to make fun of the US government and oppose the President's policy.

Along with Guthrie, the Almanac Singers wrote songs expressing their opposition of the widening war in Europe. On October 16, 1940, when the US government registered sixteen and a half million men for the military draft, the Almanac Singers opposed the action with the song called "The Ballad of October 16." It clearly criticized the hypocrisy of politicians who say one thing and then do another. In this case the Almanac Singers castigated FDR for saying he would keep us out of the war while clearly planning eventually to enter it.

As soon as Nazi Germany invaded the Soviet Union, Guthrie and the Almanac singers changed their tune and started writing songs in favor of US involvement in the war. The release of their first pro-war song, "Reuben James," made them appear to be stooges of the Soviet

Union. The American public was quickly convinced that the Almanacs were "slavishly" dedicated to the security of Soviet communism. While some questioned the intentions of the Almanac Singers, they were still praised as the first folk singers in New York City to write propaganda songs for the United States. With the saying "This Machine Kills Fascists" written across his guitar, Guthrie's place as an American patriot was secured among the American masses.

The Almanac Singers' biggest influence on urban America was Talking Union, a collection of traditional mining and industrial union songs. This record was the ultimate expression of folk music used as a weapon in the class struggle. Recorded in late spring of 1941, Talking Union turned out to be their most influential and longest lasting musical contribution to the ongoing struggle of American labor. Some were written by the Almanacs while others were adapted from traditional pieces. In the introduction to the album's liner notes, Seeger wrote:

> Like hymns and patriotic songs, union songs are songs with a message.... A few of these songs, however, prove worthwhile enough in melody and lyrics to warrant being passed on by one generation of workers to the next. It is our hope that these belong in that category.

The original 1941 release was a collection of six songs: "Get Thee Behind Me," "The Union Maid," "All I Want," "Talking Union," "The Union Train," and "Which Side Are You On?" (It was re-released in 1955 with seven additional labor songs from Seeger's union song bag.) "Get Thee Behind Me" attacked politicians as well as company men who tried to convince people to reject union organizing. The song conveyed a message of solidarity and told workers that they need to tell a politician: "send him back to hell." "The Union Maid" praised wives of union workers and called on others to support their efforts by following their lead, while "Talking Union" was a talking blues that told workers that the only way to receive "higher wages" was to organize workers into a union. The end of the song condemned the tactics that industries and governments use to break up unions. "The Union Train" was a simple song that told workers that the union was the only way to true liberation.

The most significant protest song on the album was "All I Want." It was written in the early 1930's by Jim Garland, a young blacklisted mine worker from Harlan County, Kentucky. The chorus rejected the flashy affluence of the rich and asked for something very simple: a job. The second verse described the feeling of many workers when they saw all the profits from their labor going to someone who never earned the rewards. The last verse was an obvious protest against the two party system that apparently did not address the issues important to workers. If the government is supposed to represent the people and their needs, then the political parties should be the voice and vehicle for these issues to be heard. Workers felt abandoned by the system and called for the victory of a new political party.

Talking Union reflected decades of union protest songs and became the most influential of all the Almanacs' music. These songs took the words and feelings of exploited workers and adapted them to a musical form that was recognized by ordinary laborers and people in urban communities. Unfortunately, as the songs on the album became somewhat popular, it was not the labor movement that identified with them. The songs became symbolic protest statements of political radicals and bohemians from America's urban communities. They used these songs to oppose contemporary urban American society.

Other significant songs of the Almanacs were material from the days of the IWW. "Casey Jones" was a Joe Hill song about scabs who work during a strike. In this song, the Almanac Singers captured both the wit and seriousness of the original, while protesting a continuous problem for unions: strike-breakers. "Solidarity Forever," a song written by Ralph Chaplin when the Wobblies were strong and vital, was basically a call to all working men to join the union. It was also an explanation to workers as to why they deserved power in America's economic and political system. The Almanac Singers spread "Solidarity Forever" among the labor unions and made it a regular at rallies and labor strikes.

By the summer of 1942 the Almanac Singers failed to stay together as a functioning group. According to music historian Serge Denisoff, there were four main reasons for the dissolution of the group: the material they performed was either outdated or created opposition, the press regularly attacked the group, the American military recruited Almanac members for the war effort, and/or there was a general lack of interest in their type of music. Although short, their life as a group helped expand the tradition of singing protest songs. By exposing the art of singing in protest to urban communities, the Almanacs provided training for the next generation of topical performers. It was the effort of the Almanacs in the forties that helped convince radicals that songs can be used as a weapon in political struggles.

The founding of People's Songs Inc. (PSI) by Pete Seeger in 1946 was another major step in the expansion of protest songs outside the realm of labor. Similar to the goals of the Almanacs, PSI wanted to popularize traditional labor songs and establish a "singing labor movement." The organization was formed on December 31, in the basement of Seeger's Greenwich Village apartment. Seeger was joined by Woody Guthrie, Lee Hays, Josh White, Bess Hawes, Millard Lampell and Earl Robinson. The organization sent performers to different union rallies and labor strikes to perform, usually for little or no pay. According to Fred Hellerman, "the stated purpose (of the group) was to change the world.... Another purpose, a good purpose, was becoming a central point for people with like interests and goals to establish contact." He added that, "songs can heighten awareness and show people they're not alone in dealing with problems." Seeger brought PSI into a historical context when he said: "In a way we thought we could pull together the experiences of the Wobblies and Joe Hill, the experiences of black churches and white churches, (and) the experiences of folk musicians...."

PSI utilized the continuing tradition of printing songs of protest (traditionally called Broadsides) by publishing a periodical called: People's Songs Bulletin. The collection emphasized the use of songs to initiate worker political participation. The Preamble to the People's Songs International Constitution confirmed their belief in the concept of a utopian nation in which everyone contributes to the good of the community. It stated: "songs of any people truly express their lives, their struggles and their highest aspirations.... (PSI will) fight for peace, for a better life for all, and for the brotherhood of man." Felix Landau, one time Executive Secretary of PSI, said that the organization would use "every musical means available to bring the democratic message to the American people."

The organization's political leanings and song content were very suitable to America's leftist groups such as the American Labor Party, the Socialist Party and the American Communist Party. Even though most of their audiences were from these groups, People's Songs were significantly more independent from communists than the Almanac Singers. The communists were only interested in People's Songs for entertainment. In fact, the American Communist Party never made any financial contributions to the organization. Communists also viewed protest songs differently than PSI. While the communists disregarded the significance of songs to liberate oppressed workers, PSI believed that folk music with messages of change would have a stronger impact on people than political speeches or pamphlets about scientific economics. Even though there was no direct connection between communists and PSI, the organization's leftist positions and sympathy for communists connected the two together in the minds of many ordinary Americans.

Some mainstream American listeners and broadcasters were intrigued by the work and dedication of PSI. In 1946, the November issue of *Fortune* pointed out the important influence songs had on people. The article said that a "song helps strikers over tense hours, and if the tune is catchy it may do more to persuade the public than an armful of press releases." A 1947 issue of the <u>Christian Science Monitor</u> pointed out PSI's importance to the American tradition of protest singing. They said PSI would help "circulate the still all-too-neglected folk heritage of poetry and song...." By the summer of 1946 young people were learning to play the many traditional songs PSI promoted in their songbooks and performances. Even the <u>Manual of Techniques</u> of the Congress of Industrial Organizations had a section entitled Music for Political Action. It informed members that "parodies of favorite old songs are the easiest to write and the most effective political songs. By taking a familiar folk song and writing new 'socially significant' words for it... you can create a potent weapon."

The American public's attraction to People's Songs began to wane by the end of the decade primarily because of rising anti-Communist sentiments. The end of the Second World War left two former allies with opposite political and economic ideologies poised with powerful military forces. President Truman reacted to Russia's huge Red Army and its offensive posture by proposing to involve America everywhere in the world to promote capitalist democracy. With the Soviet Union occupying Eastern Europe and the Truman Doctrine being put into action, red-baiting returned to America at a level the nation had not seen since the twenties.

PSI's relationship with labor organizations also worsened because of domestic tensions. Due to the intensifying Cold War, labor unions eliminated radicals from their membership. Members of the CIO were reported to fear that communists would take over the United States and repeat the aggressive and oppressive actions of Stalin in Eastern Europe. The CIO officially stated: "We the delegates... resent and reject efforts of the communist party, or other political parties and their adherents to interference in the affairs of the CIO." As workers and unions moved to distance themselves from communists and PSI, Seeger and his organization became associated more with Stalin's aggressive international posture, than the struggles of American workers. Because PSI was willing to sing for communists while Stalin was becoming unpopular among CIO workers, the organization drifted away from their main audience of industrial workers. Consequently, as PSI was rejected by American labor, subscriptions to their bulletin also increased by over a thousand. These new subscribers were urban radicals and not the intended audience of industrial workers.

PSI was kept barely alive by their participation in the presidential campaign of Progressive Party candidate, Henry Wallace. The campaign's use of topical songs made the most significant connection between folk music and presidential politics in the history of American elections. "The Wallace-Taylor campaign inspired countless scores of songs, but only thirty or so appeared in 'Peoples Songs.' Most are lost to posterity, but some survived on fragile home-cut acetates or soundtrack recordings." Some of the songs performed and recorded by members of the PSI were "Battle Hymn of 48," "The Same Old Merry Go-Round," "I've Got a Ballot," "Great Day," "Wallace Button/Goodbye Harry," "Henry Wallace," "We Can Win with Wallace," "The Century of the Common Man," "Wallace Is The Man For Me," and "Yankee Doodle, Tell the Boss."

The Progressive Party saved PSI from dissolution by using their songs as a central focus of the campaign and by donating four thousand dollars to the singing organization. The Wallace campaign also reinforced a PSI concept that was unwelcome in America's anti-Communist environment; the belief that everyone is valuable and has the right to independent ideas. Even though both PSI and the Progressive Party were completely independent from the American Communist Party and the Soviet Union, they both were accused of being puppets of the Soviet Union and labeled as un-American.

The defeat of Henry Wallace and the dissolution of PSI had much to do with the public's association of both with communists, and the dramatic increase in red baiting. Even though the songs used in Wallace's presidential campaign probably did not gain any votes, PSI certainly readied Americans for a new style of political and social expression that protested not only policies of the US government but also the social structure of American society.

Although PSI folded in 1949, it made a lasting impact on urban communities and Americans with radical beliefs. In addition to their music, PSI conducted seminars on using songs in politics and created a committee to advocate radical songwriters to use songs to express their own politics. PSI succeeded in combining the music of common people with the politics of important social and economic issues. Another one of their major contributions was reinforcing the IWW's conviction that songs can and should be used as weapons in political struggles. PSI also exposed traditional and topical music to an urban audience, and strengthened the talents, philosophy, and dedication of Pete Seeger. Not until the formation of the Weavers in the fifties, did this traditional style of music become immensely popular within mainstream America culture.

The music, politics and songwriters of the thirties and forties prepared American culture for a revolution in popular music. The radicalism, talent, and enthusiasm of the people of this era, especially Woody Guthrie and Pete Seeger, made a tremendous impact on labor radicals, leftist intellectuals, and fans of traditional music. The melding of different styles of music in the thirties and forties prepared middle-class American youth of the fifties and sixties for a popular boom in folk songs. The songs and style of Woody Guthrie and Pete Seeger became the images, sounds, and influences of the children growing up in the Cold War era. The dedication of these troubadours and troublemakers to the topical songs of oppressed Americans laid the groundwork for the evolution of protest songs to the next stage of its development; massive popularity within the culture of mainstream middle-class America.

Chapter Seven:
Pete Seeger: The Johnny Appleseed of Protest Music

> If we ask who is to blame for such troublesome
> children, there can be only one answer: It is the
> parents who have equipped them with an anemic
> superego. The current generation of students is
> the beneficiary of the particularly permissive
> child rearing habits that have been a feature of
> our postwar society.
>
> Theodore Rosak

Protest music went through a period of transition in the fifties. Changes in the economic, political, and social environment in the United States had a tremendous impact on the maturation of American youth, their politics, and their music. In the early fifties, American protest music was repressed by anti-Communist hysteria, rejected by mainstream American labor fearful of being labeled as communist sympathizers, and forgotten by the general public because of growing middle-class incomes and educational opportunities for the white middle-class. Although few in number, protest songs in the early fifties still primarily expressed economic discontent. By the late fifties, however, protest songs started addressing the symptoms of anti-communism, American preparation for nuclear holocaust, and the civil rights movement. The new environment that welcomed American protest music was the college campus, the new vehicle for the protest message was the sound of rural folk music and the new subjects were issues involving social injustice, nuclear war and individuality. These new troubadours and troublemakers of the fifties were led by the Johnny Appleseed of American folk music: Pete Seeger.

The songs of the Weavers were very important to the developing musical tastes of the postwar generation. With the end of the 1948 Progressive Presidential campaign, the dissolution of People's Songs, and labor's rejection of leftist politics; topical singers were forced to find other ways to make a living. According to Pete Seeger, "The very banishment of singers such as my-self from labor-union work forced us to make a living in commercial ways, such as nightclub appearances, or giving concerts for schools and colleges." In late 1949 Seeger joined with Lee Hayes, Fred Hellerman, and Ronnie Gilbert to make another attempt at spreading traditional, topical, and labor songs throughout the United States. The difference between this new group and previous musical entities was the enormous success that the Weavers achieved. They popularized traditional music among mainstream record buyers, brought a new sound to top-forty radio, and exposed traditional songs to urban and suburban communities.

By the summer of 1950 the Weavers were a very successful singing group. Both sides of their "Tzena, Tzena"/"Goodnight Irene" record was being played on radios and jukeboxes. The single held the number one spot on the Billboard charts for thirteen straight weeks. By September, the single "Goodnight Irene" was still the number one song while "Tzena, Tzena" was at number four.

Some of the Weavers' other material was made marketable by eliminating the harsh lyrics from the songs of the Almanac Singers and People's Songs. They made traditional music a sellable product by eliminating the obvious elements of protest. The group even made a conscious effort at self-censorship in order to avoid controversy. As Fred Hellerman pointed out, "It's one thing to sing Aunt Molly Jackson at a Hootenanny, and another to sing it at the Vanguard. We were essentially a musical group." They recognized that their public responded mostly to their traditional style of music not the messages of protest.

Although the Weavers had achieved popular success and were spreading traditional songs among the masses, Seeger was not satisfied. He felt that he had "lost control over his music," and wondered if sacrificing political messages was a "sell out" to his past associations and political commitments. Seeger was angered by the producers who changed aesthetic elements and removed controversial lyrics from his songs. While the other Weavers accepted these changes, Seeger reacted by growing more uncomfortable as the group became more and more popular. He always wanted to spread traditional music among the masses, but when confronted with the realities of corporate control, Seeger realized that sacrifices needed to be made in order to become popular.

The Weavers concentrated almost entirely on non-protest material, but some topical songs from radical labor circles were recorded and performed. Not only did these few songs expose the economic hardship of American labor to American middle-class youth, they continued the IWW tradition of protesting economic radicalism with songs in the face of government repression.

One protest song the Weavers performed was written by Merle Travis, the son of a coal miner. Called "Sixteen Tons," it protested the hard conditions and low pay workers were forced to accept. The song pointed out how owners and managers charged miners high prices at company stores, while paying them very little for their labor. Some mining companies actually forced workers to go into debt to buy food, clothes, and other necessities.

Another Weavers' number of protest was "Brother Can You Spare a Dime." This song came from the days of the depression when millions were out of work and misery was commonplace. Workers felt neglected after being an important part in America's industrial expansion and a source of soldiers for national defense, only to be rejected when jobs became scarce. This song exposed the human abandonment that is part of the capitalist economic cycle.

As the popularity of the Weavers continued throughout 1950, anti-Communist fever started taking its toll on the group. According to Fred Hellerman, "The rise of the repressive action against the Left, coincid(ed) with the commercial birth of the Weavers." At first, the Weavers were able to avoid being associated with communists because their popularity on the radio was at a time when the broadcasting industry was more interested in selling records than anti-communist hysteria. But as more people were infected by the fear of communism, the radio and record industries were targeted by anti-communists. Radio was considered dangerous to American security because it was able to reach a large audience with limited effort. As popular radio entertainers, the Weavers became a focus of investigators looking for either subversive activity or publicity. The Weavers' popularity, personal history, and topical material made them easy targets of anti-communist hunters.

The strength of anti-communism in the United States was directly related to political events and rising international tensions. The end of the Second World War brought about a change in the international balance of power. The Soviet Union took an offensive posture with its military and tried to increase communist influence around the world. President Truman responded to both Soviet hegemonism and domestic demands for staunch anti-communism by committing the US to the security of countries with free market economic systems. In 1949, the same year the Soviets detonated an atomic bomb; Chinese communists gained control over the mainland and pushed Chiang Kai-shek's nationalist forces onto the island of Formosa. While Americans feared the Soviet nuclear arsenal and struggled to learn who "lost China" to communism, they also became involved in the bloody Korean Civil War. To compound these events, the illusion of national security was completely shattered on March 29, 1951, when Julius and Ethel Rosenberg were convicted of atomic espionage and sentenced to death (They were executed on June 11, 1953). By the time of the Rosenberg trial, American citizens and government officials were convinced that the United States was the target of a communist conspiracy promoted by either the Kremlin or Red China.

Following WWII, the red-baiting of Americans with radical or leftist ideas (similar to the repression of the IWW earlier in the century) officially began on March 21, 1946, when President Truman signed Executive Order 9835. This action created a government policy to insure the loyalty of federal employees. It set the stage for Senator Joseph McCarthy's accusation that over two hundred State Department employees were members of the Communist Party. The nation's fear of communism inspired the US Congress to investigate Americans for possible subversive activity. The music industry became only one of the many industries that the House Un-American Activities Committee (HUAC) looked into.

The Weavers became direct targets of anti-Communists on June 16, 1950, when Harvey Matuson hinted to the Federal Bureau of Investigation that, "the FBI should keep an eye on them." Then on June 22, 1950, an organization called Counterattack published a report called Red Channels: Communist Influence on Radio and Television. This report accused 151 entertainers of subversive activity against the United States. By implicating Pete Seeger, Red Channels blacklisted the Weavers from record companies, concert promoters, and radio stations. The hysteria against anyone with left-of-center politics frightened many people away from expressing protest in song, and thus prevented any significant protest songs from being recorded in the country during this period.

Matters became worse for the Weavers on August 9, 1951, when the head of the FBI, J. Edgar Hoover, released "confidential" information regarding the Weavers' past political associations to Ohio Governor Frank Lausche. The Governor wanted to avoid a public backlash at hiring leftist radicals and canceled the Weavers' scheduled appearance at the Ohio State Fair. The publicity of this action was followed by writing campaigns that attacked the Weavers for being associated with communists and guilty of corrupting American youth and therefore a threat to national security. Lee Hays, angered by these allegations, wrote a letter to their Decca record label.

> We would like to tell you that we have never in our lives knowingly participated in, nor contributed to, any action or cause disloyal to this country; that we are not engaged as individuals or as a group in any activity of any kind, whether professional, artistic, organizational or personal, that is unrelated to our main business of singing.

By February of 1952, the careers of the Weavers were temporarily shattered by Harvey Matuson when he testified before the House Un-American Activities Committee that some of the Weavers were members of the American Communist Party. Even though their involvement with communists was in the past, once this information became public knowledge, it was very difficult for them to get performance bookings. When they did get work, it paid very little. Even though the group did nothing illegal, the blacklisting hurt their careers. By the spring of 1953, the Weavers had no choice but to discontinue their partnership and temporarily go their own ways.

In August 1955, the same year the Weavers got back together for a reunion concert at Carnegie Hall, Seeger was called to appear at a committee hearing to answer questions about his political past and radical associates. Seeger considered different options on how to properly respond to HUAC's inquiries. Many who testified earlier used the Fifth Amendment to the US Constitution as protection to avoid self-incrimination. Pete did not want to use the Fifth Amendment because he believed that he had not broken any laws or participated in subversive activity.

When the day of his hearing finally arrived, Seeger made his position very clear, he would not "take the fifth" for protection. In fact, he didn't even recognize the authority of HUAC to ask questions regarding his personal beliefs. On August 17, 1955, Seeger defied the committee by refusing to answer their questions.

> I am not going to answer any questions as to my association, my philosophical or religious beliefs or my political beliefs, of how I voted in any election or any of these private affairs. I think these are very improper questions for any American to be asked, especially under such compulsion as this....

When challenged with suggestions that the nature and scope of his work was to promote defiance and rebellion against American society, Seeger strongly defended his right as a United States citizen to perform his music wherever he wanted to and for whom ever wished to listen.

> I love my country very dearly, and I greatly resent this implication that some of the places that I have sung and some of the people that I have known, and some of my opinions, whether they are religious or philosophical... make me any less of an American.

Seeger also defied the committee's assertion that having different beliefs than the United States government makes someone un-American.

> I feel that in my whole life I have never done anything of any conspiratorial nature and I resent very much and very deeply the implication of being called before this committee that in some way because my opinions may be different than yours... that I am any less of an American than anybody else. I love my country very deeply, sir.

On June 20, 1956, the House of Representatives voted to cite Seeger with contempt of Congress and scheduled a trial. After four years of waiting for his day in court, Seeger was found guilty on March 27, 1961, and sentenced on April 3, 1961, to one year in jail. Before being sentenced, Pete stood up for his rights as a citizen and reiterated his love for America, its basic principles, and the people that inherit it. He condemned those that suggested his songs were un-American.

> Some of my ancestors were religious dissenters who came to America over three hundred years ago. Others were abolitionists in New England in the eighteen forties and fifties. I believe that in choosing my present course I do no dishonor to them, or to those who may come after me....

Seeger's case was eventually dismissed by the Court of Appeals on May 18, 1962. The court stated that "HUAC's authority hadn't been clearly explained" to Seeger and therefore all charges would be dropped. Pete felt that the court's decision was a deliberate evasion of the basic reason for his defiance. Seeger believed the court avoided the responsibility of deciding whether the US Constitution should allow a government committee to question a citizen's political beliefs. Years after the whole episode was over, Seeger reflected on HUAC's effect on his career:

> I am far more lucky that most. The HUAC ruined the careers of many people. But my income comes from so many sources that they were not able to cut it off. From time to time, the hate groups do campaign to keep me out of an auditorium - sometimes successfully. But I have learned that many an American town has other citizens... who will indignantly insist on their right to think for themselves - to hear this music in person before judging how dangerous it might be.

From 1955 on, Seeger defied the US government's assertion that someone with leftist politics was a criminal. This battle with the self-appointed moral arm of the American people became a significant trait of his image. In the words of Doris Willens: Seeger was "the musical embodiment of bravery under fire." Seeger's radical background interested people as much as his music. Americans focused more on his growing reputation as a citizen fighting for free speech than his music. Seeger even had an inscription on his guitar similar to Woody Guthrie's "This Machine Kills Fascists." Pete's banjo read: "This machine surrounds hate and forces it to surrender." By refusing to succumb to public pressure and government investigation, Seeger became a minstrel of protest who opposed the evils of McCarthyism.

By investigating Seeger, HUAC inadvertently maneuvered him into a new environment to play his music. Seeger was unable to record or perform in the commercial market still controlled by the money and power of corporate America. Needing an audience for his music, Seeger "went underground" and performed at colleges and universities that didn't object to his presence. He exposed the music of Leadbelly, Aunt Molly Jackson, Woody Guthrie, and other contemporary writers to a new generation of Americans.

Leadbelly was a conduit for African American ballad traditions to spread into the white community. According to Pete Seeger, "this modern age will not produce again such a combination of genuine folk artist and virtuoso." Born in the midst of poverty and racism in 1879,

Leadbelly developed his distinctive singing and guitar style while imprisoned at work farms and prison camps. After being released from prison in Texas and Louisiana, Leadbelly became the favorite project of John and Alan Lomax who wanted to expose Leadbelly music to the world. Michael Simmons wrote in <u>Acoustic Guitar</u> magazine that "Leadbelly seemed to be able to remember almost every song, field holler, and dance tune he ever heard, and he was a powerful and charismatic performer." Having died in 1949 with Lou Gehrig's disease, is was for Pete Seeger to take up the mantel of spreading his music.

Leadbelly's most famous protest song was "Bourgeois Blues" which attacked both racism and capitalism. It was written after he moved to the nation's capital and had a difficult time finding a place to live. "We rode all around in the rain," Leadbelly remembered. "No colored people would take me in because I was with a white man." By using the term bourgeois, Leadbelly made himself the darling of American communists, socialists and progressives.

Aunt Molly Jackson spend the bulk of her life living in coal mining towns of rural Kentucky. Some of her better known songs are: "Dreadful Memories," "Poor Miners Farewell," "The Death of Harry Simms," "I Am A Union Women," "Disgusted Blues," and "Ragged Hungry Blues."

> Since I was a little girl I have composed songs and sung them to pass my sorrows away. Some people think my stories are too sad to be true and other folks say they are not interested in the songs I write because they are so sorrowful they cannot be true. But I have never written one word that has not been the truth, and I believe I have more troubles than any other poor woman who has ever been born.

Another important protest singer of the 1950s supported by Pete Seeger was Joe Glazer. Seeger remembers Glazer as one who has done "an extraordinary job in his life, not letting people forget the great union songs." From 1949 to the early 1980s Joe Glazer dedicated himself to the spreading of union and protest songs for working people across America. A discography of <u>Songs of American Labor Industrialization and the Urban Work Experience</u> compiled by Richard Reuss in 1983, listed twenty four albums of protest union songs recorded by Joe Glazer. In his own autobiography discography, Glazer listed more than forty seven recorded albums of union and topical songs. Archie Green wrote that Glazer "left a legacy of lasting value to the labor movement through his own songs and his recordings of union classics." Although Joe Glazer died of non-Hodgkin's lymphoma in 2006, his legacy of singing, writing and recording songs for working people will continue throughout the twenty first century.

Joe Glazer's most famous song, "The Mills Was Made of Marble" was written in 1947. It was performed and recorded by so many people that the *New York Times* reported it as an "old folk song." Joe was so pleased to see his song referred to as an "old folk song" he felt compelled to write a letter to the paper of record:

> In the normal course of events a song is not considered a folk song until the composer has been long gone from this earth and the song, as the professional scholars say, enters tradition. This is the ultimate gift a people can give a creative artist. So I thank you for characterizing my song as an "old folk song." It is a nice Labor Day present.

Pete Seeger performed protest songs throughout the 1950s wherever and whenever he could. According to singer Don McLean, Seeger "definitely pioneered what we know today as the college circuit..." and developed what became known as "cultural guerrilla tactics." By performing at leftist summer camps, radical political organizations, and colleges across the American nation, Seeger planted the roots of protest music like a "Johnny Appleseed" of folk music. According to Seeger:

> I could not hold down a job at the average college or University, but I could appear to sing some songs, and then be on my way. I kept as home base this one sector of our society which refused to knuckle under to the witch-hunters: college students.

He cultivated the spirit of individual participation in music and politics by teaching young college students that there was more to music than fun. He showed them that songs with meaning could explain history and protest unacceptable social and political conditions. Seeger used his experiences with labor unions and political organizations to teach young people to fight against injustice and maintain the right of free speech. In time, American colleges became a bastion of young people singing traditional ballads and original protest songs about their own concerns.

According to Pete Seeger the campuses were changing in the fifties.

> ...increasing numbers of young people who loved music
> found that no music school was teaching what they
> wanted, and so they had to teach themselves.
> Dissatisfied with the commercial way... many of these
> young folks found a trail used by our great-grandparents.
> It was still quite usable. In homemade music, well
> performed, they were able to simply *be themselves*.

By the late fifties, colleges were filling up with the children of Americans who experienced the Great Depression, the World War II, and the prosperity of the fifties. These parents viewed the fifties as a period in history when everything they had suffered for in the past twenty years came to fruition. The children, however, never experienced the hardships of their parents and therefore never realized the suffering their parents remembered. If the children had seen some of this hardship, they might have better understood their parents' conservative values and consumer oriented lifestyle. Instead, these young people from middle-class and working-class families questioned contradictions they saw in society. They were taught that all men were created equal, but witnessed on television the repression of southern blacks fighting for their civil rights. They were taught to go to school, get a job, get married, and have children, but watched the country prepare for nuclear war. They were told that rock'n'roll was either communist subversion or black culture, but they knew it was only music.

The US government was so zealously anti-communist, politicians actually promoted a government policy to teach history, economics, and sociology with an anti-communist theme. This effort was to educate young people with information that the United States and capitalism were good while the USSR, China, and communism were bad. According to Ronald Oakley, author of God's Children, American youth were educated with a "bland, patriotic, false interpretation of the past" and led to believe that America was a nation in which all people could live in peace as equals regardless of ethnic, racial, or religious heritage. What young people realized on their own was that the United

States had enslaved the blacks, then denied them equality and professed to other nations about freedom, while repressing diversity and free speech at home.

Although most American youth still subscribed to the fundamental conservatism of their parents, some groups of young people completely rejected the expectations of their elders and opted for a new lifestyle. One group that completely deviated from the status quo were the "Beatniks" (also called the "beat generation"). Mostly located in small communities in San Francisco, Los Angeles, and Greenwich Village; these social radicals were "descendants of the Lost Generation of the twenties and the 'bohemians' of the thirties and forties...." They rejected everything that mainstream society stood for and promoted, such as "dedication to hard work, success, materialism, patriotism, suburbanism, consumerism, conformity, and organized religion." Their lifestyle was represented by the books of Jack Kerouac and the poetry of Allen Ginsberg. They withdrew from American society and attempted to create a whole new set of mores. Although small in number, the Beats became an issue of media attention and became attractive to impressionable teenagers. This American fascination with the Beat counter-culture influenced future society dropouts, known as hippies, who emulated aspects of the Beat communal lifestyle and anti-establishment attitude.

Other young Americans opposed Cold War American society by stressing non-conformity. They rejected jobs set up by their parents and opted for social rebellion through a different lifestyle, a new language, and alternative career plans. Many of these young people became aware of a society that ignored racial injustice, accepted the threat of nuclear annihilation, and disregarded HUAC's restriction on free speech. They began to join anti-nuclear organizations and civil rights organizations trying to change American society. These young people eventually became the backbone of white America's participation in the civil rights struggles and anti-war protests of the 1960's.

In the thirties and forties college campuses were filled with jazz enthusiasts, but by 1960s musical tastes dramatically changed. By the time the young and vibrant John F. Kennedy was elected US President, it seemed that the potency of McCarthyism was fading from public attention, the call for civil rights was increasing and socially conscious protest music performed in traditional musical style was heard everywhere on college campuses. The people listening to this protest material were socially and politically aware young people who were inflamed by the need for a civil rights struggle, concerned with restrictions on their right to free speech, and afraid of global nuclear war. A major difference between this group and Seeger's traditional audience was that they did not relate to the traditional material that Seeger usually promoted. Seeger's audience identified more with new songs that described concerns about contemporary American society and international nuclear disarmament, instead of traditional songs about industrial laborers and poor working conditions.

A common trait of many in this generation was non-conformity. A song dealing with non-conformity was popular on college campuses and neighborhood coffee houses. It criticized America's acculturation process by which young people are brainwashed through schooling, to perform family responsibilities and corporate duties. Written by Melvina Reynolds, the "Ticky Tacky" song satirized parents' expectations that young people accept contemporary society. Reynolds was reportedly driving through an LA suburb when she noticed all the houses looked alike. At that moment she started to write a song about conformity and suburban living. She protested America's social plan to educate young people to fit into society's desired social structure.

People comfortable with the status quo were critical of movies, books, and ideas that threatened the stability of mainstream society. Traditional songs with topical messages and new songs dealing with contemporary issues were considered subversive. Critics made wild accusations that this music was being used by external forces to incite American youth into rebellion. What these critics failed to understand was that American youth was not being subverted by music; they were using music to express discontentment with forced conformity, a self-destructive military society, and the neglect of racial minorities.

Pete Seeger endorsed new singers who wrote protest songs about important issues of the day; and the most significant political and social issue facing the nation at that time was the existence of the nuclear bomb. In mid-1954, Seeger wrote in the pages of Sing Out!, "Where once it was agreed that the pen was mightier than the sword, perhaps now the guitar could be mightier than the bomb."

One such individual endorsed by Seeger as "a prolific new songwriter" was Ernie Marrs. Seeger described Marrs as someone who had "a great future as a writer of people's songs, in the tradition of Woody Guthrie, Joe Hill, Jimmie Rodgers, and Robert Burnes." His songs were not popular among the masses, but were heard performed by Seeger and Marrs on the college circuit, in the coffee houses of

Boston, San Francisco, and New York, and read in the pages of Sing Out!, "Plop Goes the Missile" was sung to the tune of "Pop Goes the Weasel" and criticized the millions spent for military hardware and missile technology for the Cold War spurred space-race. "Smoggy Old Smog" was another Marrs composition that used the "Dusty Old Dust" melody and pointed out the worsening problem of pollution in Los Angeles. "They'll Be Paid for Bye and Bye" questioned America's Cold War economy, the politicians leading the crusade, and the nation's preparation for global nuclear annihilation. The song made fun of McCarthyism and the restrictions on free speech while it warned the nation of the pain and suffering that accompanies nuclear war. By using the "bye and bye" phrase, Marrs also evoked memories of the singing Wobblies who were destroyed by government repression similar to McCarthyism.

While playing traditional folk music, and songs written by others, Pete would also perform some of his own compositions and adaptations. "Hold the Line" was the story of a concert in Peekskill, New York that was marred by violent racist thugs opposed to any interracial gathering. The song was originally recorded in 1949 as a six minute musical documentary that even includes a short clip of Paul Robison singing "Old Man River." Through-out the 1950s Pete sang this song to students, progressives, and unionists keeping the story of Peekskill alive.

Another one of Seeger's originals was "To My Old Brown Earth." Written in the late fifties and performed on the college circuit, Seeger was singing the seeds of the developing environmental movement. He was also telling his fans that we are all in this world together, and only together can we make this a better planet.

Probably the most popular of Pete's songs was "Turn, Turn, Turn." It was a song Pete often performed in a-cappella style. Pete took phrases from the Book of Ecclesiastes and turned a part of the Bible into a protest song. (In ten years' time, the Byrds would re-work the music and melody and turn it into a number one hit on the Billboard charts.) Seeger sang that America and the human race was at a time in history where we need to make a choice: do we want peace and love or do we want hate and war.

The first folk group with topical material to become popular among the radio listening and record buying public, since the success of the Weavers, was the Kingston Trio. With a polished sound, Bob Shane, Nick Reynolds, and Dave Guard, recorded the traditional folk ballad

181

"Tom Dooley." It reached number one in November of 1958, and remained on the charts for an amazing twenty one weeks. This hit sold 2.6 million copies and expanded the scope of traditional music more significantly than the Weavers. Their first album was also very popular and managed to stay on the charts for an astounding 195 weeks. The Trio's image was shaped to look middle-class and collegiate with a sound similar to the music of Tin Pan Alley. This so-called folk music extended the Weavers success to the next level. They made a conscious effort to use the interest in traditional songs to make a profit.

Many parents were convinced by the record industry that the Kingston Trio was a safe form of entertainment for young middle-class Americans. Many parents agreed that it was certainly better than rock'n'roll, which was gaining popularity among American youth. Many parents were opposed to rock'n'roll music because they believed it was an attempt by communists to infiltrate American society and corrupt American youth. The Reverend Jack Van Impe reinforced this fear when he professed that rock'n'roll music was "brought to the United States of America by the communist conspiracy to corrupt teenagers...." Some were opposed to rock'n'roll simply because it was rooted in African American culture, while others opposed it because it was laced with a multitude of sexual innuendoes.

While some people liked the Kingston Trio because of their non-offensive demeanor, others rejected them as a watered-down version of real folk music. People who thought of themselves as true enthusiasts of traditional American music believed that real folk music pointed out oppression and expressed protest. They rejected popular folk music because it contained none of the realism and history that traditional folk music conveyed. These strict interpreters of traditional music, represented by writers in Sing Out!, dismissed the Kingston Trio not only as a passing trend but also "an act of heresy" to the traditions of folk music.

While the Kingston Trio primarily performed non-controversial songs, one topical number they made into a hit was, "The MTA Song." It was written in 1948 when the Progressive Party endorsed the Mayoral campaign of Walter O'Brien. The song was a protest against rising subway fares in Boston.

The popularity and financial success of the Kingston Trio, regardless of their opposition, sparked a revival in traditional music that re-introduced songs of Seeger, Guthrie, and the collected works of John and Alan Lomax. They also inspired producers and singers to repeat the formula and put together singing groups with traditional material and a similar image. The producers wanted musical acts that would be able to reach other markets including the mainstream rock'n'roll record buyers.

One such group, Peter, Paul & Mary, had the same smooth harmonic style as the Trio, but an image that was a little more bohemian. With their beards and long hair, Peter, Paul & Mary, made a top ten hit out of Seeger's "If I Had a Hammer," and exposed some of his topical material to middle-class record buyers. This song was probably the first popular protest song of American youth and the first popular protest song that was totally unrelated to economics. Unlike the Trio's "MTA," or the Weavers' "Sixteen Tons," the topical song "If I Had A Hammer" was about freedom, equality, and justice not about economics or labor exploitation.

Following the success of Peter, Paul & Mary, the Kingston Trio recorded another of Seeger's protest songs called "Where Have All The Flowers Gone." Reaching its peak of popularity in April of 1962, this song was a clear protest against the death and sadness that accompanies war. It starts out pointing out that all the flowers have been picked by girls who get married and ends with the flowers being placed on the graves of soldiers who died in war. This song almost seemed like a warning to the nation that the Vietnam War was slowly approaching.

Joan Baez was another folk singer that sang Pete Seeger songs ("Where Have All the Flowers Gone"), protest tunes ("Last Night I Had the Strangest Dream"), and traditional material ("House of the Rising Sun") from America's past. Learning her craft in the coffee houses of Greenwich Village and Boston's Harvard Square, Baez became a popular performer of all kinds of American music. She is also known for introducing Bob Dylan to the Newport Folk Festival attendees in 1963. (More on Bob Dylan in the next chapter.)

Protest songs were becoming very popular among certain segments of American society because of the social strife building in the country. White Americans were intrigued by the struggle of southern black activists fighting for freedoms that every white youth took for granted. These civil rights activists were motivated by the history of black repression and an unbounded faith in their religious beliefs. Their main goal was no less than equal treatment under the Constitution. Many civil rights activists accepted the teachings of Mahatma Gandhi and Martin Luther King Jr. and set the stage for the coming decade of social and political protest. The thousands of black and white young people who participated in the social resistance of the decade used the traditions and tactics employed by the Wobbly strikers fifties years earlier, while incorporating contemporary thinking and strategy.

By the time both "If I Had A Hammer" and "Where Have All The Flowers Gone" were hits on the radio, U.S. law had changed regarding race relations. The major victories for minority civil rights began in 1954 when the United States Supreme Court declared in Brown vs. Board of Education that segregated schools were inherently unequal. As a follow up to this legal triumph, the Montgomery Bus Boycott was sparked by Rosa Parks and organized by Martin Luther King Jr. in December 1956. This action achieved legal integration for American blacks on Montgomery's public transportation system. In 1957 a piece of 1866 Civil War legislation was replaced with a new law authorizing the use of federal troops by the Executive Branch to enforce civil rights laws. And in September of the same year, a crisis in Little Rock, Arkansas required President Eisenhower to exercise this new law. He called on federal troops to protect black students attempting to enroll in the previously all white High School.

Three years later, the first sit-in for civil rights began on February 1, 1960 when David Richmond, Franklin McCain, Ezell Blair Jr., and Joseph McNeil took-on the old Wobbly tradition of sit-ins and challenged segregated lunch counters. Following the lead of the Southern Christian Leadership Conference, they demanded the same service as a white man. After their arrest, hundreds of blacks and whites joined them in support of their effort and the television exposed this struggle to white America. The violent images of blacks being beaten by police and dragged away to jail reached the living rooms of millions and shattered the image of American justice held by many complacent teenagers and college students.

Many of these young white northerners signed up for the Freedom Rides. Violence erupted on May 9th of 1961 when a brave Freedom Rider attempted to enter a segregated bathroom at a bus terminal in Rock Hill, South Carolina. Whites blocked the door and beat the Freedom Rider. Later in the day, when the bus was moving onto its next destination, it was run off the road and someone threw a fire bomb into a broken window. The riders were then beaten as they attempted to escape the smoke and flames. The young white Americans went home to the north with unique experiences and a new perspective.

Civil Rights activists had their own singing groups like the *Freedom Singers* of the Student Non-violent Coordinating Committee (SNCC) to help spread the message and be the musical backdrop to the movement.

Pete Seeger helped convince one of its leaders, Bernice Johnson, to form a group as he had done in the forties and fifties. Bernice recruited singers and activists like Rev. Charles Sherrod, Cordell Reagon, Bernice Reagon, Rutha Harris, and Bertha Gober. Their songs directly reflected their personal and communal experiences.

Pete Seeger also influenced one of the most prominent civil rights songs of the 20th Century: "We Shall Overcome." The song is actually a combination of two songs: "I'll Overcome Someday" and "I'll Be All Right." Charles Tindley wrote the first song around 1903 and the second is an old African American gospel song. It was around 1946 that a singer named Lucille Simmons learned the song. She reportedly performed it at a strike supporting the workers of the American Tobacco Company in Charleston, SC. She sang it very slowly and changed the word "I" to "we." Zilphia Horton learned it from Simmons who then taught it to Pete Seeger who then had it printed in Sing Out! with the title "We Will Overcome." Seeger then started singing the word "shall" instead of "will." SNCC then picked up the song for their meetings and the rest is history. "We Shall Overcome" has now become the best recognized song of the entire civil rights movement.

There were many other artists of the 1940s, 50s and 60s that protested racism, discrimination and economic inequality. Found especially within the jazz community, artists such as Lady Day, Charles Mingus, Max Roach, John Coltrane and Otis Redding had plenty to say about the civil rights struggle. Billy Holiday's rendition of "Strange Fruit" that condemned lynching was as masterful as it was haunting. First recorded in 1939, by the 1950s it became a jazz standard heard by many young people in clubs and on the radio. Charles Mingus' made a number of recordings with social commentary on his mind. An example of this was his "Fables of Faubus" which protested the 1957 events in Little Rock Arkansas where the struggle against segregation came to a head. In 1960 Max Roach dedicated an entire album to protest. Called We Insist! Freedom Now Suite, it included songs such as: "Freedom Day" and "Tears for Johannesburg." Even the album cover itself screamed: *PROTEST!* John Coltrane's 1963 song "Alabama" was an interpretation of Martin Luther King's speech at the memorial service for the victims of the Birmingham bombing. Otis Redding's 1964 "Change is Gonna Come," which was a haunting song about racism, discrimination and hatred, was as prophetic as it was moving.

One civil rights activist used his experience working against racism while with SNCC and the Southern Christian Leadership Conference to organize students to protest restrictions of free speech at the University of Berkeley. Mario Savio became the leader of the Free Speech Movement at Berkeley and started a campus protest that so dramatically symbolized the sixties era. Early in December, 1964, Savio reflected on his experience with SNCC to fellow protesters at a sit-in for the Free Speech Movement:

> Last summer I went to Mississippi to join the struggle there for civil rights. This fall I am engaged in another phase of the same struggle, this time at Berkeley. The two battlefields may seem quite different to some observers, but this is not the case. The same rights are at stake in both places- the right to participate as citizens in democratic society and the right to due process of law. Further, it is a struggle against the same enemy. In Mississippi an autocratic and powerful minority rules, through organized violence, to suppress the vast, virtually powerless, majority. In California, the privileged minority manipulated the University bureaucracy to suppress the students' political expression.

These students discovered the concept of passive protest and vocal opposition. Berkeley already had an outbreak of unrest in 1960 when students were arrested for protesting an anti-communism propaganda film promoted by the HUAC. In 1964 the campus erupted again in reaction to the Administration's banning of political booths to recruit volunteers and distribute literature. After one student was apprehended for not clearing the area, other students sat around the campus police car in which he was handcuffed, and prevented the police from taking him away. They made speeches and sang songs like "We Shall Not Be Moved" for almost 32 hours.

The following December, Savio gave a speech very reminiscent of the Wobbly speeches given to striking industrial workers fifty years earlier. Savio spoke in front of a cheering crowd of students. He said that the Board of Regents was acting like the Board of Directors of a company, the school president was acting like a company manager, and the faculty was acting like employees. He then called on the students to stop the running of the school and "put your bodies upon the gears and upon the wheels, upon the levers... indicate to the people who run it, the people who own it, that unless you're free, the machine will be prevented from working at all." Very much in the spirit of Wobblies singing during an industrial sit-down strike at the beginning of the century, Berkeley students sat and joined Joan Baez singing "We Shall Overcome" and "Oh my trials… soon be over..." The spirit of Joe Hill, Woody Guthrie and Pete Seeger was certainly present in the voices of those students that night. They were carrying on the tradition of using songs as a weapon in their struggle.

Throughout the 1960s Pete Seeger was a dedicated troubadour and troublemaker. He continued to travel and perform to all who would enjoy hearing him. He worked with others in the preservation and dissemination of all types of music: protest, international, traditional, and contemporary. In the 1960s he recorded a number of classic protest albums: Songs of Struggle and Protest in 1965, God Bless the Grass and Dangerous Songs in 1966, Waist Deep in the Big Muddy in 1967 and Pete Seeger Now in 1969. While Seeger was trying to make a living through performing and recording music, he was also transferring the tradition of singing protest songs to a new generation of musical minstrels on college campuses throughout the nation. Like a musical Johnny Appleseed, Seeger's music and attitude took off on a life of its own, growing and changing with the times. And the times sure were changing in the sixties. Before long there would be another troubadour and troublemaker who grabbed the topical songwriting mantel. He wrote and performed songs for a new generation of Americans dissatisfied with the state of American society and politics. His name was Bob Dylan.

Chapter Eight:
Bob Dylan & the 1960s: The Birth of Protest Rock

McCartney sings, backed up by a cello
And no one gets a pain in the belly
Why do folkies, then, get cramps
On hearing Dylan play with amps?

Unknown

Bob Dylan made a tremendous impact on the evolution of protest music in American culture. According to Israel Young from the <u>East Village Other</u>, Dylan was "the first singer-songwriter to incorporate contemporary psychological ideas into the form of the traditional ballad stanza." According to Betsy Bowden, "Dylan spoke directly to his peers, first in articulate words of protest accompanied by a few strummed guitar chords, then in songs that combine increasingly elaborate instrumentation with increasingly evocative lyrics." Dylan absorbed and adapted the musical style of Woody Guthrie and other traditional performers along with the emerging sounds of rock'n'roll, to form his own musical and lyrical style. He grew up watching movies about rebellious teenagers and identified with the images created by Marlon Brando and James Dean. He shared with other American youths the fear of nuclear war and rejected America's preparation for World War III. He grew up in the anti-communist hysteria of McCarthyism and reacted by adopting aspects of radicalism in his life and music. He also saw the repression of African Americans and reacted by writing songs filled with resentment toward white America. Dylan's music was a direct response to the conditions of American society and his own developing personality. Dylan's music made him the musical troubadour and symbolic leader for thousands of rebellious American youths dedicated to changing society. By the mid-sixties he not only contributed to the popularization of protest music, he also successfully incorporated elements of rock'n'roll into his songs. By mixing musical genres, Bob Dylan's musical troublemaking helped create a new form of protest music dubbed as folk-rock.

Bob Dylan was born Robert Zimmerman on Saturday, May 24, 1941, St. Mary's Hospital, in Duluth, Minnesota. In adolescence, the young Zimmerman reacted to films of the latter half of the 1950's as representative of his own developing self-awareness. *Blackboard*

Jungle was significantly influential because of its subject matter and accompanying musical score. The film was about the discontent of youth and student rebellion in neighborhood high schools. Zimmerman was reported to have said after viewing the picture, "This is really great: This is exactly what we've been trying to tell people about ourselves...." The significance of the movie was that rock'n'roll music, especially the title song "Rock Around the Clock" by Bill Haley and His Comets, was connected with youth rebellion. During the showing of this film, it was reported that young people "spontaneously jumped from their seats and danced in the aisles when it was played...." The young Zimmerman was heard saying of the song, "Hey that's our music... that's written for us." The song reached number one on the Billboard charts the week of July 9, 1955, and pushed the popularity of rock'n'roll into massive proportions among thousands of white and middle-class American youth. The rise of rock'n'roll should have been a clear indication to the nation that changes were encroaching American culture that would dramatically affect the status quo in the next decade.

Two other movies Zimmerman identified with were *Rebel Without a Cause* and *The Wild One*. The former was about a young man's struggle to find his own identity while disillusioned by his father's lack of will to stand up for his independence. The latter picture depicted a motorcycle gang terrorizing a small town and the rebellious lifestyle the clique represented. After seeing the exciting image of rebellious teenagers and tough bikers, Zimmerman went to a local clothing store and purchased garb similar to what Brando wore in *The Wild One*. The excitement of rock'n'roll and the rebellious images on the screen motivated Zimmerman to imitate this lifestyle. Zimmerman was not the only American reacting to these pictures. Many other youngsters acted as if "Harley and Davidson were the Lewis and Clark of the 1950's."

The artists at the center of this rock'n'roll phenomenon included: Bill Haley, Chuck Berry, Little Richard, Elvis Presley, Carl Perkins, and Jerry Lee Lewis. Millions of their records were sold between 1955 and 1958 to American teenagers. In 1955 alone, the sale of rock'n'roll records reached 277 million with teenagers buying forty-three percent worth. By 1960 rock'n'roll record sales had reached 600 million and seriously threatened the existence of the established popular music industry. The popularity of this new music challenged the traditional musical styles fashionable since the days of Tin Pan Alley.

Zimmerman's discovery of rock'n'roll convinced him to become a musician. Becoming a singer of traditional and protest songs was not even on the mind of this young teenager. He dreamed of becoming a rock'n'roll star. He began by figuring out piano chords to the songs of Little Richard and Jerry Lee Lewis. His first official performance was when he and some friends auditioned for a local college talent show that high school students could participate in. The committee rejected Bob's band when they heard his screeching versions of rock'n'roll tunes. Being turned down by the selection committee only convinced Zimmerman that the town of Hibbling was oblivious to the rock'n'roll capturing the nation's youth. This area of the country was described by Linda Fuller as a repressed and unimaginative community. She said Hibbling youth were "expected to think like their parents and be like their parents." Robert Zimmerman, on the other hand, had other plans. He followed the path of rebellion, non-conformity, and rock'n'roll.

An important part of Zimmerman's development as a rebel was changing his name. In 1958 he started using the name Bob Dylan (and by August 9, 1962, he officially changed it permanently). During many interviews with Dylan, he "never specifically acknowledged" that his adoption of the new name was a tribute to poet Dylan Thomas, but there are similarities to the styles of prose of the two men. Thomas "wrote poetry crammed with complex, surrealistic imagery based on sources as varied as social criticism, love, Christian symbolism, witchcraft, Freudian psychology, and personal myth...." Bob Dylan wrote complex poetry using symbolism and imagery, and put it to different styles of meter and rhythm. The messages of Dylan's songs were loaded with comments about violent human nature, social protest, psychological reactions to war, and the pain of relationships. Whether or not Dylan Thomas was an influence on Bob Dylan, both their work looked at the human condition in a similar fashion.

It was also during this period in the late fifties that folk music was popularized by the Kingston Trio and Peter, Paul, & Mary. While struggling to make it in rock'n'roll, Dylan recognized the rising interest in contemporary folk music. He saw the simplicity of the genre where one person with a guitar could record and perform traditional and contemporary songs, express personal opinions, entertain people, and make lots of money. While Dylan consumed all the folk music he could find, he discovered his potential with instruments and asked his friend Monte Edwardson to help him learn some basic chords on the guitar. Dylan spent hours perfecting songs he heard on the radio and old folk records. According to Dylan biographer Anthony Scaduto, "Bob listened to every conceivable popular music style, from jazz to hillbilly, studying and soaking up those that interested him, learning to imitate, to rework, to transform them into something his own."

It was at this absorption stage of his life that Dylan discovered Woody Guthrie. He spent hours listening to all his old folk records and devoured Guthrie's fictionalized autobiography, Bound For Glory. Dylan began to identify with Woody and imitate his musical style and persona. He interpreted Guthrie's songs of the Oklahoma Dust Bowl and The Great Depression. In fact, Dylan's interpretation became more important to Guthrie's mythologization than Guthrie's actual activities in the thirties and forties. Dylan interpreted Woody through his own personality and created a new modern version of the hobo image. Guthrie spoke of Dylan in 1961, distinguishing him from other performers in New York's folk community: "Pete Seeger's a singer of folk songs, not a folk singer. Jack Elliot's a singer of folk songs. But Bobby Dylan is a folk singer. Oh, Christ, he's a folk singer all right."

Dylan moved to New York emulating his hero Woody Guthrie while attempting to make it big in the Greenwich Village folk scene. He played at places like the Gaslight and Mike Porco's Gerde's Folk City at 11 West 4th Street. The audience didn't initially appreciate Dylan's style and imitation of Guthrie. They thought Dylan wasn't political enough to fit into the scene. As his own songwriting and personality developed, however, Dylan was not only accepted into the community, he became their primary spokesman.

The people Dylan surrounded himself with made a lasting impact on his personality and influenced some of his songs of protest. In seems that Dylan's first participation in politics, and thus his writing of political protest songs, stemmed from the interests of his friends. Dylan's roommate, David Whitaker, brought Dylan to his first political demonstration called Operation Abolition, organized to protest HUAC's promotion of a campaign to rid college campuses of communist infiltrators. Susan Rotolo, a full time secretary of the Congress Of Racial Equality (CORE), also influenced Dylan. She exposed Dylan to the civil rights struggle being waged by African Americans and progressive whites. He sang some songs of the movement such as "Many Thousands Gone."

Dylan identified with these struggles against censorship and racial injustice and came to realize certain realities of the United States. He wrote one of his first protest songs in support of CORE, called "The Death of Emmitt Till." It was about a young black boy from Chicago who was beaten and killed by two white men in Mississippi. The murderers were arrested, tried and then set free. Dylan told the story with frustration and contempt towards American injustice. The last two verses of the song challenged listeners to speak up and stop racial violence.

Dylan's first album was released on March 19, 1962 without much commercial success or artistic recognition from critics. In fact, the album only sold around three hundred copies before it was marked down and transferred to record-store overstock bins. The album had only two songs penned by Dylan, while the remainder was a tribute to traditional songs and Woody Guthrie. It was loaded with talking blues and country tunes that sounded original because of Dylan's distinctive voice and impressive guitar work.

An important aspect of this release, titled simply <u>Bob Dylan</u>, was the fact that Columbia, a major record label, signed this unknown performer. This stretch of the mainstream music industry contributed to the protest genre's evolution into popular music. The industry recognized the potential middle-class market for this urban style of folk music. Most other traditional and topical songs were usually released on minor labels such as Vanguard or Folkways. These smaller record companies had not been able to seriously penetrate the mainstream market.

Performers like Pete Seeger had always dreamed of reaching a massive audience with topical songs. Recording for Columbia made that dream possible; especially when his second and third albums became two of the most important recordings of protest songs in twentieth century America.

<u>Freewheelin' Bob Dylan</u> was his second record. It contained five songs of serious social and political protest and reflected Dylan's ability to respond to current events and write poetic songs. <u>Freewheelin'</u> was the album that started Dylan on the way to becoming an important symbol to various youth movements and civil rights struggles in sixties America.

The first song on the album was "Blowing in the Wind." When heard by Peter, Paul & Mary at one of Dylan's club performances; they instantly recognized it as a hit and recorded it for their third album. This cover version effectively introduced Dylan's songwriting abilities to thousands of record buyers and radio listeners who otherwise may not have discovered Dylan for years. In fact, within the first two weeks of its release, the Peter, Paul & Mary cover sold over 300,000 copies and became the quickest selling single in the history of Warner Brothers.

Jacques Vassal suggested that Peter, Paul, & Mary's popularization of "Blowing in the Wind" along with other performers singing it at civil rights marches and rallies, helped Columbia executives recognize that Dylan could be successful at recording his own songs.

"Blowing in the Wind" asked questions of the listener and motivated thought and anger about war and human injustice. Instead of focusing on the traditional themes of bad economic conditions and wage slavery, Dylan's song pointed out problems regarding racism, nuclear terror, and the hypocrisy of America's social structure. Unlike Pete Seeger in the fifties, who symbolized protest by using general ideas like freedom and injustice in "If I Had A Hammer," Dylan asked specific questions about problems in America. He then forced the listeners to formulate their own answers. Dylan's songs reflected concerns of new leftists while using imagery and lyrical suggestions to convey the message.

The questions he proposed were extremely relevant to problems of the day. Three of them were directly related to civil rights. Only one question is directed towards war in general (but could be related to contemporary society by replacing cannon balls with atomic bombs), and three deal with America's preparation for nuclear Armageddon. These questions made the listener think about looking for answers.

People criticized "Blowing in the Wind" because it didn't provide answers to the nation's social and political problems. I contend that the criticism is unfounded. Pointing out the problems in society should suffice. It is not the duty of topical singers to solve society's problems, but rather to influence emotions and motivate political and social activists. The problems in American society that Dylan pointed out existed long before he was born. Dylan was only attempting to find his own answers to these questions by writing and singing these topical songs. He was also telling others that their own answers will come in time and almost without warning. He sang that the "the answer (was) blowing in the wind." By using the wind as the carrier of the answers, he suggests that humans cannot control or even predict the answers. Dylan was quoted a few years later saying:

> There ain't too much I can say about this song except
> that the answer is blowing in the wind. It ain't in no book
> or movie or T.V. show or discussion group. Man, hip
> people are telling me where the answer is but, oh, I won't
> believe that. I still say it's in the wind....

The relevance of "Blowing in the Wind" and the whole Freewheelin' album, was amazingly reflective of the major social and political issues of the society. In 1962 American culture was being influenced by the strength of youth idealism. "Blowing in the Wind" was not only reflective of this youth spirit; it also encouraged many other northern songwriters to create music addressing the same problems. As civil rights struggles became a favorite subject for songs by so-called folk singers, the guitar toting protest singer became the symbol of discontented rebellious American youth.

Another protest song on the Freewheelin' album was the third cut entitled "Masters of War." It was a bristling and direct attack upon the manufacturers of war armaments. Dylan compared them to Judas of the bible and sang that they will never tell the truth as they inform the American public that America can be victorious in a nuclear war. The song painted a picture of people who are not concerned with human life and devoid of remorse towards war. It claimed that these people do nothing as the death toll due to war keeps rising. Dylan defended his attack with verses about generational differences towards war and a condemnation of the people he criticized. Dylan then ended the song with anger directed at the military industrial complex for all the death and destruction that they have caused.

"Oxford Town" protested the treatment of James Meredith, the first black man to attempt enrollment at the University of Mississippi in Oxford. The Governor of Mississippi, Ross Barnett, made a personal stand and prevented the student from enrolling. Eventually President Kennedy deployed federal troops to force the Governor to obey federal laws against segregation. The song told a story about the police using their weapons on the student only because he was a black man. Near the end of the song Dylan expressed frustration and concluded that participation in political demonstrations made no difference. He sang that after he and his girl was attacked by some tear gas, he decided to go home and forget about the whole thing. This could be considered an early indication that Dylan was not completely dedicated to social and political activism. It may also be an early sign that Dylan would eventually reject any leadership role in various youth movements.

Two of the songs on Freewheelin', "A Hard Rain's A-Gonna Fall" and "Talkin' World War III Blues," represented a new approach to writing protest songs. Dylan used images in his songs and successfully painted pictures in the minds of listeners with clear messages of protest. This distinguished Dylan from other protest writers of the past. Most traditional protest songs were clear condemnations of capitalists, scabs, rich politicians, or poor economic conditions. In the fifties, Seeger toned down the protest and sang vague songs of freedom and justice. Dylan, however, intensified the genre by using words and phrases to create clear images of social and political protest.

"Hard Rain" was Dylan's vision of the world involved in its own destruction. Some critics say that Dylan reacted to the Cuban Missile Crisis and wrote "Hard Rain." Others have pointed to evidence that the initial version of the song was written before the crisis occurred. Regardless of where the inspiration came from, the song is clearly a convincing cry to American society that we were on the brink of Armageddon. Throughout the song Dylan asked four basic questions: "where have you been," "what have you seen," "what did you hear," and "what'll you do now." In each verse he responds to the questions with metaphors. Many of these have several possible meanings while still succeeding to convey the main theme of protest. Dylan painted many frightening images.

Individual listeners need to use their own memories and personal experiences to interpret the images in the song. It is very possible for each mind to see different things. One image a listener could have when Dylan sang "ten thousand talkers," was of Cold War politicians and their endless talking about peace without having the courage or willingness to prevent world-wide nuclear Armageddon. Another image could be that of a television or radio newscaster telling lies to the American people about what's really happening. The meaning of one single line could create multiple images in each listener's mind and still be unlike the original Dylan imagined. Years later Dylan commented on the meaning of the term "hard rain."

> It's not atomic rain though. Some people think that. It's
> just a hard rain, not the fallout rain, it isn't that at all. The
> hard rain that's gonna fall is in the last verse, where I say
> the 'pellets of poison are flooding us all,' I mean all the
> lies that people are told on their radios and in the
> newspapers, trying to take people's brains away, all the
> lies I consider poison.

"Talkin' World War III Blues" was an anti-war song performed in the Guthrie-style talking blues. "Talkin' War" was about man's psychological reaction to the national preparation for nuclear destruction. Dylan expressed fear of being alone after the nuclear war. As the narrator of the story, Dylan told how he visited his doctor to get rid of dreams about life after World War Three. The specialist called it a "bad dream" and believed Bob was "insane." The doctor told him to sit on the "psychiatric couch" and tell his story. Bob proceeded to detail the dream starting with a flash of "lights," and then an attempt to get food at a "fallout shelter," only to be shot at. When he went over to someone at a "hot dog stand," the man ran away because he thought Bob was a "communist." After suggesting to his concocted female companion that they "go and play Adam and Eve," and after he attempted to call an "operator" for someone to talk to, Dylan got nervous about his situation. While explaining this story, Dylan was interrupted by the doctor who told him that he was having similar dreams; the only difference between the two dreams was that in the doctor's dream, he was alone. Dylan explained in the song that everybody was having the same dream and he even invites others to join him. What a bizarre song.

"Hard Rain" and "Talkin' War" illustrate how Dylan protested conditions in society by suggesting images and telling abstract stories to convey messages of protest. In "Hard Rain" Dylan tried to frighten listeners away from destroying humanity by creating unpleasant images poetically linked together with guitar licks and rhyming words. In "Talkin' War" Dylan pointed out the stupidity of preparing for nuclear war by using humor and anxiety in a traditional talking-blues style. These two songs, as well as the rest of the Freewheelin' album, signaled a turning point in the evolution of topical songs sung in the traditional style. Instead of direct attacks on a particular institution, person, or group, Dylan obscured his target with art and poetry using complex language and intricate musical arrangements. Phil Ochs, (although a great topical songwriter in his own right), was still using the same conventional forms of topical song-writing.

Another interesting aspect to the Freewheelin' album was the hazy suggestion that Dylan's roots lay in rock'n'roll. Information about two (non-protest) songs in the liner notes indicate that other players performed with Dylan. The liner notes mention that a guitar, bass, piano, and drums accompany Dylan on "Don't Think Twice, It's All Right." After listening to this song many times, I could only hear Dylan's voice, accompanied only by his own guitar and harmonica. I faintly heard some guitar accompaniment, but the other instruments mentioned are completely inaudible. In "Corrina, Corrina," the liner notes also list the same instruments. In this recording, however, the drums are clearly keeping the beat and there is another acoustic guitar at work beautifully mixing with Dylan's. At certain times in the song, when the harmonica performed solo, a bass guitar could be heard, but still no piano. It is apparent that at some point certain instruments were eliminated from the recording. Even Robert Shelton mentioned in No Direction Home that "essentially the same studio band" that performed on the single "Mixed Up Confusion" accompanied Dylan on both of these songs.

"Mixed Up Confusion" is additional evidence that Dylan was into rock'n'roll well before he was a protest folksinger. The single was released six months before Freewheelin' and was recorded with a complete rock'n'roll band. The flip-side of the single was an "electric version" of the traditional song "Corrina, Corrina," and apparently recorded at the same session as "Don't Think Twice" with the same accompanying musicians. According to Scaduto, this single "was felt to be a mistake" because it was "not in keeping with Dylan's growing image as a protest writer and singer." It failed to generate the sales that Columbia expected and was taken out of print. If this single had been circulated more widely, Dylan may not have been exclusively known as a guitar strumming, protest folksinger. There may also be other rock'n'roll songs that Dylan recorded unknown to music researchers and Dylan fans. According to Betsy Bowden, the sessions for Freewheelin' had at least seventeen songs that were not included on the album.

Between the release of Dylan's second and third albums, he witnessed the realities of American society, and wrote some of his most potent civil rights songs. Dylan participated in a voter registration drive in Greenwood, Mississippi, and saw first-hand the poor conditions of the homes and communities of American blacks. He did not learn about American society through politics; he learned about politics through experiencing American society. Wilfred Mellers believes that Dylan was motivated to write civil rights songs because of his social conscience not the desire to identify with a political group or social movement. According to Dylan himself, his songs were only a reflection of the times. He said, "The songs are there. They exist all by themselves just waiting for someone to write them down. I just put them down on paper. If I didn't do it, somebody would."

On May 12, 1963, Dylan was scheduled to appear on the Ed Sullivan show. One of the numbers he planned on singing was "Talkin' John Birch Paranoid Blues," a satirical attack on the conservative right-wing group who investigated people accused of being communist sympathizers. In the third verse Dylan suggested that the organization supported Adolf Hitler.

The producers of the Sullivan show believed that the song would insult certain members of the audience and told Dylan not to perform it; apparently they didn't want to incite a defamation lawsuit. Even though the lyrics appeared in the first issue of <u>Broadside</u> in February of 1962, and was performed in the clubs of New York, the producers did not want to take any chances. Instead of submitting to the condition set up by the network, Dylan refused to perform and left the studio. Unfortunately, after CBS television refused to allow the song on their program, Columbia Records decided to take the song off Dylan's new album, even after some copies were already released to the public. The song's message of protest was increased by the actions of CBS censorship and Dylan's refusal to submit to their terms. "Talkin' John Birch" became not only a protest of right-wing paranoia, but also a protest of censorship in America that Pete Seeger had struggled so long to overcome. Ed Sullivan said later that he "couldn't understand why" the John Birch Society was given special consideration. He said the broadcasters "understood and sympathized with our viewpoint, but insisted they... couldn't take the subject into entertainment."

A primary factor in Dylan's popularity was his performance at the 1963 Newport Folk festival. At the start of the festival, he was only one performer among many. By the end of the weekend, he was transformed into an "eclectic poet-visionary-hero." By this time in Dylan's career, he had still not broken into mainstream recognition. His songs were known primarily because of Peter, Paul & Mary and Joan Baez, who made recordings of them. But Dylan himself was not popular until he closed the Friday night show of the festival. The day of his performance, Dylan was seen "outside the park where he just sat on the green -unrecognized- and sang to a few friends informally." By the end of the evening, however, Dylan would be surrounded by crowds of adoring fans looking to him as their leader. At what Robert Shelton called "a dress rehearsal for the Woodstock Nation," Dylan was at first only "an underground conversation piece," but by the end of his performance on Friday night, he had become the hit of the festival. Dylan's recognition reached explosive proportions when he accompanied Joan Baez on Sunday night. At this point Dylan crossed the threshold and became "a star." According to one spectator:

No matter what the people at the festival saw or heard or said, they felt the presence of Joan Baez and Bob Dylan. These two great artists left deep impressions on festival goers as they sang by themselves and together.

These festivals traditionally gathered performers and enthusiasts of folk songs and tried to ignore big names that usually attract crowds of spectators. By the time of the '63 festival, however, a new phenomenon developed which Serge Denisoff called the "star system." People were more interested in seeing certain performers, than learning about home-grown music or ideas about social change and traditional radicalism. The workshops attended by someone like Joan Baez were filled to capacity, while other workshops with obscure performers had sparse attendees.

Once Dylan gained the recognition of these new fans of topical music, he simultaneously shied away from any role of leadership. Instead of being a concerned folklorist leading young people in protest, in the vein of Pete Seeger, he rejected the spokesman title and insisted that his songs were personal feelings and not words of wisdom. When asked questions at the '63 festival about his protest songs, he said:

> I just have my own thoughts and I get the words down on paper and these are my songs.... I'm not writing folk songs, protest songs, freedom songs or for any other category. I have certain things that just have to be said. People can judge my songs in whatever way they want and get out of them, whatever they see in them. These are just the thoughts that are honest and real to me.

Dylan's third album, The Times They Are A-Changin', was released early in 1964 to waiting record buyers and critics. The title itself was a message of protest. Change is against the status quo, so promoting a message of change is also conveying a message of protest. The title cut of the album was geared specifically to express the communication problems American youth were having with their parents. Dylan accused older generations of not knowing enough about their own children to help them mature into adulthood.

The first verse of the title song, "The Times They Are A-Changin'," created an image of a giant wave of change coming over the people, inevitable and unavoidable. The song almost seemed to be a follow-up to "Blowing in the Wind." In this song, however, Dylan made specific statements instead of asking general questions.

The second verse was an attack on journalists, reporters and authors who try to pick the winners and losers in society. Dylan sang that they were disconnected with the changes coming to America. It will not be long, he sang, before the people on the top of society were going to switch positions with those on the bottom.

The third verse was a direct attack on politicians not serious enough about the problems in American society. Dylan expressed the feeling that social and political evolution in American society is unstoppable and unavoidable and only the youth can lead the way. He told American leaders that if they did not join the revolution, then the people would force it upon them. This verse is very similar to the old saying: if you're not part of the solution, you're part of the problem.

The fourth verse was an attack on parents who could not understand their children. It pointed out that parents did not understand aspects of flowering youth culture including: rock'n'roll, communal lifestyles, radical political activism, and the developing counterculture.

The last verse of the song was a revolutionary comment on the division between the old and the young. The message confronted the future with the past and challenged people to accept the new value system developing among the younger generation.

Another significant song of protest on the album was "With God On Our Side." It condemned the preparation for nuclear war and people's rationalization of violence by using the phrase: we did it "in the name of God." The song pointed out the reality of war in which the victor always claims that God supported their cause. Throughout American history the United States has defended its military actions using the excuse that it was a battle of good versus evil. This song examined this phenomenon by pointing out different wars in American history that were supposedly fought for the good of the nation and in the name of God.

The first verse introduced the narrator of the song and the area of the world he came from. Dylan challenged the conventional wisdom that American youth cannot make substantial contributions to society. The verse also set up the narrator as a law abiding citizen reminiscent of the conservative fifties.

The second verse began a general survey of wars in American history. It reminded people that the Native Americans were slaughtered by white men because of manifest destiny, national imperialism, and economic expansion.

The third verse reminded the listener that the United States fought each other in the Civil War and then the Spanish at the turn of the century. Instead of learning from the pain, suffering, and death of war, survivors celebrated their victory by believing they had done it in the name of God.

The fourth verse continued this historical survey by looking at the First World War. This war was unlike others in human history, for in WWI the reason for fighting was unclear to the soldier. Between 1914 and 1918 over thirty million people died. Some by running into rifle and machine gun fire, others were exploded by mortar fire, or killed by toxic gas; and many died from the influenza virus. The war was fought along more than 12,000 miles of trenches from Belgium to Switzerland; sometimes the trenches were within a stone's throw of each other. All this was precipitated by the assassination of Archduke Francis Ferdinand. As the fighting dragged on for years, soldiers realized that war was not about glory, honor, land, money, or freedom, but death and destruction. In fact they had no idea why they were fighting. The First World War started the human race on the road to destroying the false myths, romance, and glory of war.

The fifth verse points out that even after fighting an enemy acquainted with evil, given time, friendship is possible. It makes the listener wonder how the United States and Germany switched from being enemies to being friends so quickly, especially considering the hatred and genocide perpetuated by the Nazi's in the Second World War.

The final verses contained Dylan's comments on contemporary conditions of the cold war world and America's preparation for a nuclear conflagration with the Soviet Union. The song also pointed out that God condemns killing.

The next two protest songs on the album dealt with civil rights in America. The first was "Only A Pawn In Their Game." This number protested the same murder that Phil Ochs sang about in "Too Many Martyrs" (more on Phil Ochs in the next chapter). One of the song's most powerful statements had Dylan condemning the rich and powerful southern whites who controlled the poor communities. White politicians used political power and influence over poor whites to oppose political equality for black Americans. Dylan sang about white "southern politicians" taking advantage of the "poor white" population by telling them that they should be grateful being "white" and not "complain." Dylan doesn't condemn the poor white man for allowing himself to be manipulated; he placed the blame on the politician. The poor white man is "only a pawn in their game." Dylan sang about the exploitation of poor whites in keeping the blacks at the bottom of the southern social structure.

The final protest song on the album was The "Lonesome Death of Hattie Carol." It was another attack on the American system of justice that is based more on money than truth. It was an attack on the injustice in American law when people of power confront people of color. The song described the murder of a black woman by the child of a person who had significant political influence in government and the legal system. After Dylan describes the killing he sang in the first chorus that we should not cry for the person murdered.

This chorus changed over the course of the song as the story developed. The song described the murderer who had well connected and affluent parents who were able to provide legal protections for their son. When Dylan sang that the murderer was released on bail "in a matter of minutes," he was protesting the American bail system where someone with money goes free while someone without money stays in jail until the trial. After the case finally came to trial William Zanzinger received "a six month sentence." Dylan sneered at this diminutive punishment as compared to the crime. He ended the final chorus with a request that now we should cry. Dylan didn't ask the listener to cry over the death of the woman, but to shed tears for government negligence in bringing justice to the criminals.

In an interview with Frances Taylor of the Long Island Press, Dylan was quoted as saying, "I never wanted to write topical songs." He explained, "In the Village there was a little publication called Broadside and with a topical song you could get in there." Dylan continued, "I wasn't getting far with the things I was doing... but Broadside gave me a start." Broadside built on the tradition created by the IWW with their songbook "to fan the flames of discontent" and continued with Pete Seeger and his Peoples Songs Bulletin and Sing Out!. The main purpose of the Broadside publication was to revive traditions of radical topical singers and give newcomers somewhere to start. This publication gave many writers, including Bob Dylan, the chance to see their songs in print.

Just because Dylan used every means available to spread his music, including Broadside, it does not mean that he was ingenuous about the songs he wrote. Some music critics denounced Dylan for not really believing in what he sang about. The people who were around him during his best years as a protest singer attest to his sincerity. Joan Baez defended Dylan's commitment to the causes: "I think he was involved with much more that he would ever like to say." Dave Van Ronk said, "He was no opportunist. He really believed it all. I was there." Phil Ochs continued Dylan's defense: "He definitely meant the protest. At one point he was definitely a left-winger, a radical, and he meant every word he wrote. He was just going on to bigger things when he started denying it, that's all." Dylan's best defense, however, came from the producer of his first two albums, John Hammond:

> When he first came here he was thinking and talking about justice, and about social problems. Bobby really wanted to change things. He was uptight about the whole setup in America, the alienation of kids from their parents, (and) the false values.

Dylan was viewed as someone who was singing about current events as they happened. He came of age at a time when young Americans were creating their own leftist politics in contrast to the radicalism of the thirties and forties. Dylan's songs reflected these changes. Carl Oglesby, prominent one time leader of Students for a Democratic Society (SDS), described Dylan's relationship with the student and civil rights movements as synonymous:

> Dylan's early songs appeared so promptly as to seem absolutely contemporary with the civil rights movement. There was no time lag. He wasn't a songwriter who came into an established political mood, he seemed to be a part of it and his songs seemed informative to the Movement as the Movement seemed informative to the songwriter. This cross-fertilization was absolutely critical in Dylan's relationship to the Movement and the Movement's relationship to Dylan. He gave character to the sensibilities of the Movement.

Dylan's fourth album, Another Side Of Bob Dylan, showed a distinct change in his musical style and lyrical content. Dylan began to take a more personal approach towards his songs and returned to his roots of rock'n'roll. According to Nat Hentoff, Dylan's album "appeared to express his current desire to get away from 'finger pointing' and write more acutely personal material."

The messages conveyed on his second and third album were so relevant to the maturation of the sixties generation that young people viewed Dylan as their national spokesperson of protest. For many young people his songs were a guide to understanding American society. Many viewed Dylan as their political guru and sought guidance from him. Dylan rejected this role of generational leadership and only wanted to make music. This movement away from radicalism is apparent in "I Shall Be Free No. 10."

Dylan continued this theme of rejecting leadership with "My Back Pages." He sang about "politics" and "professors" who "deceived" him "into thinking" that he had "something to protect." At the end of each verse he sang that he "was so much older then... (but) I'm younger than that now." He seemed to convey that as we get older we seem to have more questions and less answers.

Dylan ended the album with "It Ain't Me Babe." This song has been interpreted by people to contain multiple meanings. The most obvious is about a man who rejected the love of a woman whose expectations were too high. A second meaning could have been Dylan sending a message to fans that he was abandoning movements of social change and concentrating on his own life. The most popular protest singer in twentieth century America seemed to be rejecting a position of leadership given to him by thousands of fans and opted instead to sing about personal feelings mixed with social/political images.

The 1964 folk festival was a showcase for his new anti-political songs from Another Side. The festival should have been a signal to protest-song enthusiasts that Dylan was evolving as a singer-songwriter. Robert Shelton described Dylan's performance at the festival as uneventful and uninspiring. The two songs he sang at the Topical Song Workshop on Friday afternoon were completely non-political: "It Ain't Me, Babe" and "Mr. Tambourine Man." You can see Pete Seeger in the video documentary *Festival*, sitting behind Dylan tapping his feet and wondering exactly what "Mr. Tambourine Man" was actually about.

During his solo performance Sunday night, Dylan did not perform any of the protest songs he was known for. He concluded his performance by singing a duet with Joan Baez on "With God On Our Side." Irwin Silber wrote an open letter to Dylan in Sing Out! as a response to his new album and performance at the '64 folk festival. He criticized Dylan for writing non-political songs, thus selling-out his radical comrades for popularity.

You seem to be in a different kind of bag now.... You said you weren't a writer of 'protest' songs. Well, okay, call it anything you want. But a songwriter who tries to deal honestly with reality in this world is bound to write 'protest' songs. How can he help himself? Your new songs seem to be all inner directed now, inner-probing, (and) self-conscious....

Another Side also signified another trend in the development of topical music. While Dylan was rejecting songs of protest and moving toward introspective songs of subjective personal feelings, he was also moving back to his roots of rock'n'roll. Two songs on Another Side had a rhythm and blues feel to them. Even though Dylan is the only performer on these recordings, he created an obvious beat that could easily be accompanied by drums and a bass. The two songs that stand out on the album as having a rock sound are "Black Crow Blues" and "I Don't Believe You." In Song and Dance Man Michael Gray wrote that the album's rock sound should have been a clear signal to listeners that Dylan was not committed to being a protest folksinger.

People who saw Dylan as a singer of protest songs performed in the traditional style did not realize that his true musical inspiration always remained in American rock'n'roll. According to Anthony Scaduto, it was the Byrds rock version of "Mr. Tambourine Man" that convinced Dylan to take his musical and lyrical talent back into rock'n'roll. Dylan also saw Eric Burdon and the Animals as an exciting development in folk music. Dylan heard Burdon's electric version of "House of the Rising Sun" in 1964 while touring in England and reacted similar to the way he responded to seeing *Blackboard Jungle*. "My God," Dylan said, "ya oughta hear what's going down over there! Eric Burdon and the Animals, ya know? Well, he's doing 'House of the Rising Sun' in rock. Rock! It's fuckin' wild! Blew my mind!" Die-hard folkies considered Burdon's electrified version of the song blaspheme against folk tradition. Others saw it as a wonderful combination of the different musical genres of folk and rock. Some consider it the first folk-rock song ever released and very important to the development of a new musical phenomenon.

Dylan also recognized the genius and relevance of the Beatles' contribution to the development of rock'n'roll.

I knew they were pointing the direction of where music had to go... you see, there was a lot of hypocrisy all around, people saying it had to be either folk or rock. But I knew it didn't have to be like that. I dug what the Beatles were doing.... Their chords were outrageous, just outrageous, and their harmonies made it all valid.

The relationship between the rock'n'roll and folk communities changed when Dylan played an electric guitar at the Newport Folk Festival in July of 1965. By the time of the festival, Dylan had become the accepted leader in the performance and recording of topical songs. Many of Dylan's fans who expected him to stay with the same style and form were shocked when Dylan electrified his performance with members of the Paul Butterfield Blues Band. The band rehearsed only three songs for the rock performance: "Maggie's Farm," "Like A Rolling Stone," and "It Takes a Lot to Laugh, It Takes a Train to Cry." "Like a Rolling Stone" was a prime example of Dylan's ability to be vague while still expressing feelings of youth discontentment. The chorus itself was in the same spirit of Woody Guthrie looking for truth in Bound for Glory or Jack Kerouac searching for his own destiny in On The Road. The chorus described the feelings of many American youths who were dropping out of society and searching for an answer to all their gut wrenching questions.

During Dylan's first electric number at the festival, people reacted in different ways to what was becoming the combination of two genres of music. Some say people from the audience were yelling because they couldn't hear the words, others contend that the booing was a reaction to the fact that it was amplified electric guitars and not topical music in the traditional style. With Mike Bloomfield's electric guitar blazing, the drums and bass pounding away, nobody could hear Dylan singing. Pete Seeger was seen backstage visibly upset, threatening to cut the sound cables with an ax. (In a recent reflective interview, Pete acknowledged that he was upset at the sound levels, but now describes what Dylan did that night as "great.")

After "Like a Rolling Stone," boos and catcalls were an obvious accompaniment to the applause and cheers. Some people yelled "get rid of the band" and "play folk music." Dylan and the band played one more number before they left the stage. As the crowd became more unruly, Pete Yarrow moved out onto the stage to calm the situation. Realizing that the crowd could become dangerous, he basically begged

Dylan to come back to the stage. Dylan returned with an acoustic guitar and called for an E harmonica from the crowd. After dozens were thrown onto the stage, Dylan performed "Mr. Tambourine Man" and "It's All Over Now, Baby Blue" in his traditional style. Dylan was visibly shaken by the festival's reaction to his musical transition back into rock'n'roll. Rick Sullo took a close up photograph of Dylan that shows his emotional reaction to the audience. The photo seems to show what looks like a tear running down Dylan's left cheek.

Some saw his innovation as a welcome expansion to the festival's music that was becoming stale and impotent. Reporting the festival in Sing Out!, Paul Nelson felt Dylan's electric set was a breath of fresh air. He wrote that the people who booed Dylan's performance "chose the safety of wishful thinking rather than the painful, always difficult stab of art...." He described Dylan's electric presentation as an inspiration:

> The only one in the entire festival who questioned our
> position was Bob Dylan. Maybe he didn't put it in the
> best way. Maybe he was rude. But he shook us. And that
> is why we have poets and artists.

Over the years of teaching music history in high schools, colleges, libraries and senior centers and talking to many people who were there at the 65 Newport Folk Festival, I have come to the conclusion that perception and preconceptions of what is aesthetic to the ear and mind had a great influence on how people remember that day. I have spoken to people who thought what Dylan did that night was "amazing," "excellent," and even "inspiring." Others have a completely different impression. Some attendees believed Dylan "insulted" the crowd by playing loud and "unintelligible" music. They though it was "noise" that belonged to the rock'n'rollers of the decade. In an interview with Robert Shelton for the New York Times in August of 1965, Dylan said, "I know in my own mind what I'm doing. If anyone has imagination, he'll know what I'm doing. If they can't understand my songs they're missing something." I guess a lot of people that evening were definitely "missing something."

Bob Dylan's transition from folk to rock was part of a widespread trend in mid-sixties American musical culture. Rock music was becoming a relevant and accepted form of social and political expression in American society. The aggressiveness of the music could be seen as a signal that the nation was about to go through a period of unprecedented violence and youth rebellion. Dylan's use of rock music with electrified instruments to express protest poetry about society was a sign that the culture itself was on the verge of being rocked off balance. Bob Dylan was a musical troubadour significant to the development of three very important trends in American protest music: he used imagery to express messages of protest, he helped solidify the symbolic connection between American youth and protest songs, and he used rock music to carry his messages of protest. Dylan did not lead this evolution in American music, but his musical troublemaking was integral to its development. His lyrical talent and innovation not only made him nationally popular among American youth and their symbolic leader; his musical gift also contributed to the birth of a new form of music called protest rock.

Chapter Nine:
Phil Ochs & the Protest Songs of American Youth

One good song with a message can bring a point
more deeply to more people than a thousand
rallies.

Phil Ochs

Phil Ochs was a troubadour and troublemaker who reflected the evolution of American youth from idealism to fatalism. We can learn a lot about the demise of youthful idealism in the late sixties and early seventies by examining the politics and music of Phil Ochs. The four major events that rocked the world of both Phil Ochs and that of America's politically active youth were the assassination of President John F. Kennedy in 1963, the murders of Senator Robert Kennedy and Reverend Martin Luther King in 1968, and the events at the Democratic National Convention in Chicago of the same year. Phil loved the traditional folk medium that was famous because of the work of people like Woody Guthrie and Pete Seeger. But as the tastes of American music consumers changed, so did the style of Phil Ochs. As the war in Vietnam dragged on and the peace movement failed to change the direction of the electorate in 1968, Phil Ochs became as disillusioned as the movement. As the decade wore on, and the nation seemed destined to explode from within, the songs of Phil Ochs ominously reflected the idea that the youthful idealism of the Kennedys was all a fantasy. And by the end of the decade, Phil was as broken and depressed as the anti-war movement was in those dark days of August 1968. What he left behind was a wealth of protest songs that reflect that age and the ideals of its activists.

Born in December of 1940 in Texas, and raised in New York, Ohio and Virginia, Ochs was brought up like many kids in the baby boom generation. He was a big fan of American movies, especially the heroic depictions of cowboys and war heroes created by John Wayne and company. Phil also loved the vibrancy and sexuality of Elvis Presley. Phil loved what Elvis had done: combine country music with rhythm and blues using his own voice and personality to create a new form of rock'n'roll music. While fascinated with American cinema and American music, Phil's real love was journalism and the idea that there is truth in the world. He believed in the existence of truth, it only needed to be found and reported.

Phil's love of current events and journalism encouraged him to attend Ohio State College where he also continued his passion for writing and music. While taking classes in journalism, Phil honed his writing skills and developed his political views. Writing for the two school papers The Lantern and Sundial, Phil showed his radicalism, which eventually became too much for the publications. After being pushed out of the paper he started to send his pieces to local rags as letters to the editor or commentary pieces. He even started his own short lived newspaper he called The Word. Phil also learned how to play guitar at Ohio State from a friend of his, Jim Glover. At one point the two of them formed a duo they called the Singing Socialists. In Phil's mind, he was following in the footsteps of Joe Hill, Woody Guthrie and Pete Seeger. They eventually changed the name of their group to the Sundowners, a name that Phil lifted from a movie starring Robert Mitchum.

It was when Phil moved to New York that his career would get a jump start. It was there in Greenwich Village that he would interact with some of the greatest influences of his career. People like Jim Glover, (who had gone to New York earlier) who was already his onetime musical partner; Alice Skinner, who became his wife and the mother of his child; Bob Dylan who became his competitor; and Pete Seeger who became his mentor.

It was Pete who brought Phil to a little known publication called Broadside. Phil's first song appeared in Broadside #13 and according to Michael Schumacher "Phil had a song in every one of the magazines biweekly issues." Pete Seeger recalls being with Phil and Bob Dylan at the offices of Broadside and thinking that he was in the presence of the two greatest songwriters ever. The magazine did a cover on Phil in issue #36 and added two of Phil's songs to their newly pressed record Broadside Ballads, Volume I, which was the first time he had a song of his own on record.

It was also at Broadside that Phil was able to express his position on the power of music in any political or social movement. Fifty years after Joe Hill wrote "A pamphlet, no matter how good, is never read more than once, but a song is learned by heart and repeated over and over…." Phil put it in his own words in an article he wrote for Broadside #22 titled "The Need for Topical Music." Released March of 1963, he wrote "one good song with a message can bring a point more

212

deeply to more people than a thousand rallies." Phil certainly understood the power of song; just as the troubadours and troublemakers who preceded him.

It was Phil's songwriting ability that made people in the folk community take notice. He was invited to play the 1963 Newport Folk Festival at one of the songwriting workshops. He was so excited on his way to the festival in Rhode Island that he ended up in a hospital with severe headaches and had to be medicated. Finally making it to the festival, Phil delighted members of the pro-civil rights audience with three of his newest numbers: "Too Many Martyrs," "Talking Birmingham Jam" and "Power and Glory"

While providing material to <u>Broadside</u>, Phil was able to get a recording contract with Electra Records. His first album, <u>All the News That's Fit to Sing</u>, released in 1964, addressed many of the issues that concerned college students including civil rights, free speech and American imperialism. Even the album cover seemed to be a message to college students. It pictured Phil sitting on his guitar case reading the newspaper. Dressed in a colorless jacket and holding a cigarette, Phil is intently concentrating on reading the news of the day. His message to the youth was to stay informed about what is going on in the world.

Of the fourteen songs on the record (fifteen on the re-release), eleven had themes of protest. Five of those were direct protest songs very different from Seeger's vague "If I Had A Hammer" and "Where Have All the Flowers Gone." Two of the eleven, "Power and Glory" and "Bound for Glory," attempted to evoke the memory of Woody Guthrie as the historic troubadour of protest songs. "Power and Glory" was similar to Guthrie's popularized version of "This Land is Your land." It provided a positive emotional feeling while describing the people and beauty of America. "Bound for Glory" was a direct tribute to Guthrie by reminding listeners of his travels, music, and dedication to the poor and destitute of America.

The opening song on the album, (and probably one of the most chilling) was "One More Parade." It created the image of the parade that marches young men off to war. He ridiculed the idea of sacrificing human life in war. The image that Ochs created was that of mindless drones following orders that nobody really understands.

He followed "One More Parade" with a song called "The Thresher." Pulled right out of the newspaper, the song is about a horrible tragedy aboard a U.S. Navy submarine. At 9:18 a.m. on April 10, 1963, 129 men perished in what has been described as an implosion. According to

National Geographic, "the most likely explanation is that a piping joint in a sea water system in the engine room gave way. The resulting spray shorted out electronics and forced an automatic shutdown of the nuclear reactor." Like the title of the album, Ochs was able to grab a headline out of the newspaper and create a song like the olden days of the colonial Broadside Ballads. He was showing that news can still be presented in the form of a song.

Another number on the album, "Automation Song," was similar to what Guthrie and Seeger used to sing. It evoked memories of traditional protest songs that came from industrial workers, farmers, and miners. Ochs' message was similar to "Sixteen Tons" and "Brother Can You Spare a Dime" recorded by the Weavers and other folk outfits. "Automation Song" protested the problems people must face when confronted with advancing technology. Automation does increase production but it also decreases the labor needed to accomplish the same work. It puts laborers out of work and makes it harder for them to find similar jobs.

"Ballad of William Worthy" directly addressed a problem that concerned radical American students. Many rebellious youths, especially intellectuals and leftist radicals, saw Fidel Castro and Che Guevara as heroes to their own people for their revolution to free Cuba from American influence. The US government, on the other hand, saw them as enemies to national security. Many radical students believed that democracy and freedom were more important than economics, and rejected the US government's anti-Castro position. Phil spent many hours studying the situation in Cuba. His onetime singing partner said: "Phil knew more about Castro and Cuba than" anyone he knew, including his own father. In "Ballad of William Worthy," Ochs sang about a man who went to Cuba several times but started having trouble traveling when the Cubans took control of US companies operating in Cuba. William Worthy became an enemy of the state because of his travels to a country that the US government considered off-limits. At the end of each verse, Ochs sang that since we live in the "free world" we can't leave; almost as if Americans were prisoners of their own government's anti-Castro policy.

Two songs on the album that may appear not to have a protest theme but still promote subtle revolutionary ideas were: "Celia" and "Knock on the Door." The song "Celia" while appearing to be a love song, contains themes of protest. It was about Celia Mariano who served time in a Filipino prison for revolutionary activities. Worldwide protests finally forced the Philippine government to release their prisoner. She was eventually able to re-connect with her American husband in London after a ten year separation. "Knock on the Door" on the other hand, is a general warning of fascism. Ochs reviews the history of modern civilization by using examples of totalitarianism from Rome to Nazi Germany. Bringing the song to modern times, Ochs reminds the listener of the millions who died in Soviet Russia, especially during the reign of General Secretary Josef Stalin, when it was not safe to speak out against the government. The main point of both songs is to warn of the dangers of despotic governments that could form anywhere.

The album contained two songs dedicated to the African American civil rights struggle. "What's That I Hear" was very uplifting and similar in spirit to many of the Freedom Songs of the movement. The number also might remind the listener of Seeger ringing the bell of freedom in "If I Had A Hammer." The second civil rights song, "Too Many Martyrs," was more of a direct protest song in the spirit of Woody Guthrie than the Freedom Songs of the civil rights movement. Ochs portrayed feelings of anger and sorrow rather than feelings of hope and love. "Too Many Martyrs" protested the June 1963 murder of Medgar Evers, the leader of the NAACP Mississippi state chapter.

Two of the most direct and satirical protest songs on the album were "Talking Cuba Crisis" and "Talking Vietnam." These two songs were Ochs' way of commenting about two very important developments in the early sixties: the Cuban Missile Crisis and the growing US involvement in the Vietnam War.

"Talking Cuba Crisis" was a description of the several days in American history when the world seemed on the brink of nuclear holocaust. The song began by introducing the President of the United States while implying absurdity by telling the American people to pause for a commercial break. It then ridiculed politicians who squabbled while the future of civilization balanced on the brink of destruction. The song contained references for the folk crowd like mentioning Gerde's Folk City (a popular club in Greenwich Village) and Republicans going insane. The way the song was somewhat spoken while being somewhat sung, sounded like the combination of a talking blues number with a comedy sketch. It was similar to Bob Dylan's "Talking World War III Blues."

"Talking Vietnam" was written in the same satirical style as "Talking Cuban Crisis." It compared the struggle in Vietnam to the struggle in Birmingham, USA. In both places people were fighting for freedom and justice. After a helicopter full of trainees was shot down by the Viet Cong, Ochs sang, that the communists don't ever "fight fair." At the end of the number, Ochs told America that "Diem democracy" is "rule by one family" and an army of US Soldiers. Ochs protested the growing conflict in Vietnam by questioning the reasons for fighting. If the United States is supposed to support freedom and democracy, then how can it rationalize sending young men to die protecting a third world dictatorship?

Phil's second record was titled I Ain't Marching Anymore, and was just as pointed as his first collection of topical songs, but also included an element of Phil's growing disillusion about the promise of America. One music critic called the record "one of the finest albums of topical music available," while another wrote "Don't be fooled by the title. Mr. Ochs is still marching, against war, against intolerance, against the south, and nearly everything else that troubles people today." Of the fourteen songs on the record, eight had a direct theme of protest, two were about JFK, two were Guthrie-esque and two were adaptations of poems.

Even the cover of the album was laced with protest. This time Phil was without his guitar, cigarette or newspaper. He is sitting on the ground with his legs stretched out with crossed ankles. His hands are in his pant pockets and he is leaning up against a wall plastered with old political and advertising posters. Phil is looking off in the distance with a very serious emotion on his face. Directly behind him is a "Goldwater for President" sign that has been partially torn down and a black peace sign painted on the wall. The title of the album is in quotes as if making a statement in a newspaper.

The title song of the album, "I Ain't Marching Anymore," was part of the anti-war theme of the record. It sounded like a follow-up to the song "One More Parade." The song surveyed the different wars that Americans had been involved in and focused on the soldier who fought them. He suggested that it is the soldier who should decide when fighting is worth the cost. Ochs tried to convince the listener not to march in any more parades to any more wars.

The other antiwar song on the record was "Draft Dodger Rag." This number was a good showcase of Ochs' use of wit to oppose the war in Vietnam. It was a whimsical list of excuses young people used to avoid the draft. He sang to the draft board that he would be willing to fight if there was no blood or killing. Pete Seeger loved this song and would perform and record it throughout the sixties.

There were three songs on the album that dealt with Civil Rights: "In the Heat of the Summer" dealt with the riots in Harlem in 1964; "Talking Birmingham Jam" was about segregation and the fight for equal rights; and the album closer was "Here's to the State of Mississippi."

The language of "Here's to the State of Mississippi" makes it the most serious protest song on the album. At the end of each verse Ochs sang that he wanted Mississippi to leave America and join another nation. Each verse was an attack on different parts of the state. He sang that if you drained all the rivers in Mississippi, only "nameless bodies you will find..." and even the "people" of Mississippi "can't wash the blood from their hands." He compared the people running the state with "criminals" and "clowns." Ochs also protested the "laws" of the state which betray the meaning of the constitution by treating black people as second class citizens without the same rights as white people. He even attacked the police of the state, by singing that they are nothing but "murderers."

There were two songs on the album that dealt with the plight of the worker in American society and the need for people to unify and fight for better jobs and conditions: "That's What I Want to Hear," and "Links on The Chain." Both songs emphasized that only through unionization and solidarity can unemployed Americans improve their lot.

The first song was a call to action to those people who have been thrown out of work because of automation. It was also a condemnation of those who complain about their situation but do nothing about it. In the final verses Phil reiterated the point of the song that only by joining with others can workers win more rights and better conditions.

In "Links on The Chain" Phil sang about the importance of maintaining togetherness among all working people. I believe the most poignant verses of the song actually condemn the unions for their lack of support for the Civil Rights Movement. He pointed out that when African Americans were fighting for equal justice and access to American society, the unions did not back them up. The Civil Rights movement actually received push back from certain union members and some unions themselves. Phil's main point was that all struggling people are links in the chain regardless of ethnic background. In order for the chain to be strong we must support all the "links," including blacks who are fighting for the same rights that union men have fought for in the past.

The song "Iron Lady" described the process of someone being put to death in the electric chair. The Iron Lady is the chair itself. Phil condemned the concept of an "eye for an eye" because that is how the culture of death in society continues. He sang about the mistakes people make in life, and how we should be given a second chance. He also pointed out the mistakes in the justice system that condemn innocent people to death.

One song dealt with the struggle Phil went through following the assassination of John F. Kennedy. Titled "That Was the President," Phil clearly expressed his sadness over JFK's death. He had high hopes for the President who represented a new generation of Americans in a post-World War II world. He sang that part of his world ended when "the bullets of the false revenge have struck us once again." He conjured up the memory of seeing Kennedy in an open car driving through Dallas, but then sang about the despair and loss of hope that ended on that fateful day in 1963 with so many promises unfulfilled.

"These Are the Days of Decision" was a subtle attack on elected officials and politicians who knew there were problems in society but did nothing about them. He referred to war and the civil rights struggle affecting America (specifically the murders of three civil rights activists in Mississippi: James Earl Chaney, Andrew Goodman, and Michael Schwerner), while politicians sat by and did nothing. Phil sang that, "the cost" of doing nothing is "most dear." In the liner notes to the album, Phil was more direct.

> The American politician has developed into the gutless master of procrastination with a maximum of non-committal statement and the barest minimum of action. This moral vacuum is exceeded only by the apathetic public who allows him to stay in power. How feeble is the effect of a song against such a morass, but here it is.

Two songs on the album contained the spirit of Woody Guthrie: "Hills of West Virginia" and "Ballad of the Carpenter." "Hills of West Virginia" was a feel-good song about the beauty of America, while the other was a cover originally written by Ewan MacColl. "Ballad of the Carpenter" was clearly about the life of Jesus Christ while converting him into a working man who is fighting for laborers and farmers. Phil

218

explained in the liner notes of the record why he decided to record a cover song for his album.

> The State Department has a nasty habit of blocking the entrance of Ewan MacColl into this country, and undoubtedly one of the reasons is songs like this. All political considerations aside, if you take a serious look at the quality of culture in America, you can see that the State Department can ill afford such a tactic.

Ochs' third album, titled <u>Phil Ochs in Concert</u>, was a collection of recordings he made during performances in Boston and New York during the winter of 1965-66. All the songs on the album were new and not yet recorded. Of the 11 songs on the album, seven had clear messages of protest, one had a subtle message of revolution and three were more introspective in nature. On the back of the album, Phil displayed seven poems written by Mao, the communist leader of China. Following the poems, Phil wrote, "Is this the enemy?" In his own introduction to the song "Cannons of Christianity," Phil related that it is not really a protest song but more of an "anti-hymn." Phil said, "It's the first anti-hymn folks," to great applause.

The opening song on the record dealt with the many differences between the generations. Titled "I'm Going To Say It Now," it was a general protest number written for college students assembling on America's campuses for unrestricted freedom of expression. As the song progressed, Ochs pointed out the political differences which divide the school administration and the students. One example of this division was the University's support of Nationalist Chiang Kai-shek while many students supported China's communist revolution led by Mao Zedong (Mao Tse-tung). Demanding the constitutional right to free speech, Ochs sang that he felt less free than those in other countries. This song protested those in power whose desire was to control every aspect of the student's lives and reminded those in control that power can be acquired with large numbers of people.

The second song on the record, "Bracero," was about immigrants in America who are exploited by the economic system that uses their cheap labor without concern for their health or well-being. This song reminds me of the Woody Guthrie songs, "Deportees" and "Doe Re Me." Phil is obviously singing for the plight of migrant farm workers in America just like Guthrie did twenty five years earlier.

There were three anti-war songs on the record. The first was "Is there Anybody Here," a criticism of soldiers marching off to war to find "glory." He reminded the listener of the lessons learned from the Nazi war crime trials in Nuremburg that soldiers cannot use 'following orders' as an excuse for committing war crimes. The second anti-war song, "Cops of the World," protested the use of the United States military as an international police force. He used an analogy of a woman being sexually violated to describe how the US treats Third World countries in maintaining global interests and multinational profits. The third anti-war song, "Santo Domingo," protested the United States invasion of the Dominican Republic on April 28, 1965, when 400 marines landed in Santo Domingo after the country's leader resigned.

Of the two songs protesting the older generation's criticisms of American youth, "Love Me, I'm a Liberal" is probably the most pointed. Phil made fun of liberals who maintained a distance from political activism. Ochs attacked liberals who objected to school integration by singing about people who want blacks and whites to live together but 'not in their backyard.' In the last verse he provided an excuse for liberals who turned their back on the New Left: they are now older and wiser. (wink wink!) The song was dripping with sarcasm.

Phil was even able to express protest while introducing his songs in concert. In the introduction to "Ringing of Revolution," Ochs mocked California Governor Ronald Reagan and President Lyndon Johnson and then said "this song is so cinematic that it's been made into a movie.... Frank Sinatra plays Fidel Castro, Ronald Reagan plays George Murphy, John Wayne plays Lyndon Johnson, and Lyndon Johnson plays God." The audience laughed and applauded as Ochs concluded, "I play Bobby Dylan, the young Bobby Dylan." In his introduction to another song, "Cannons of Christianity," Phil says that he heard the voice of God and responded: "You're putting me on of course Dylan," and the crowd laughed and clapped again. This showed that many young people saw Bob Dylan as their political leader.

Of the three songs dealing with more introspective issues, there was one on the album that some people did recognize. "There But for Fortune" was recorded by Joan Baez with some mild success. It reached number eight on the British charts and number fifty on the American Billboard charts. It was about how fate can be the most powerful force in the universe. In the song Phil asked why some people are poor and others rich and why some people have opportunities to succeed while others don't. Phil's response after every verse was the same: it's all just a matter of fate.

The final song on the album is a haunting number about accomplishing as much on this earth as possible before we die. The fact that Phil was already singing about being gone after only his third record tells us that he had a feeling of the future. "When I'm Gone" explains to Ochs fans that there will be a time when he will no longer be singing. He expressed his understanding that when he's gone he won't be able to participate in politics, social movements or singing songs; and therefore it is important for him to do it all while he's still alive.

While popular music was changing, Phil's music was also changing. He was inspired by Dylan's movement into rock with <u>Highway 61 Revisited</u>, the Beach Boys' experimentation in the studio with <u>Pet Sounds</u> and the Beatles' inspiring collection of folk rock style recordings on <u>Rubber Soul</u>. This new style of songwriting and recording was showcased in Phil Ochs' <u>Pleasures of the Harbor</u>. While containing only eight songs, four of them clocked in over seven minutes, two were over five minutes long and the final two were about three minutes in length. At the time, the album was "one of the longest running single disk pop albums in history." Only one of the songs could be considered a protest song: "Outside a Small Circle of Friends." The song was about how not a single person tried to stop a murder that took place in New York while people watched. The other songs on the record were more personal than political; more introspective than topical. Many considered the final song on the record, "Crucifixion," a complete disaster, while others cherished the song as Phil's finest masterpiece of lyrical talent.

<u>Tapes from California</u> was a way of Phil combining the sound of his first three records that had the traditional folk style, with the production complexities of <u>Pleasures of the Harbor</u>. This latest record was a lot more haunting than the previous album. With this collection of songs, Phil continued down the road of depression and disillusionment regarding American ideals of justice and equality. The album does achieve many musical accomplishments. For example, Phil threw out all songwriting conventions and recorded a 13 minute song titled, "When in Rome." He also wrote a seven minute biographical song about the IWW troubadour Joe Hill. Without a chorus, Ochs was able to capture the mythos of Hill's entire life into one song.

The two songs of direct protest on the record were: "White Boots Marching in a Yellow Land" and "The War is Over." The first verses of "White Boots" set up the war in the air where American pilots were bombing North Vietnam. Phil sang that the generals and politicians were more interested in the casualty reports of the enemy than the value of their own soldiers. Phil also referred to the candy that many soldiers were known to give Vietnamese children. The third verse pointed out that all the training in the world cannot match people who are fighting for their own land. Phil pointed out that this was a civil war, and there was nothing we could do as a nation to solve their internal conflict. The fourth verse dealt with the manner in which the American army was interrogating prisoners. If the point of the war was to win over the hearts and minds of the enemy, then creating more enemies by torturing some of the captives is not the way to do it. In the final verse Phil could be referring to the USO and the recruitment drives that the military are always involved in. As the young men volunteer to go off to war, they are really only preparing themselves for their own death.

"The War is Over" was Ochs' expression of disillusionment with the idealism that dragged America into the war in Vietnam in the first place. It was written for a rally that was planned for June of 1967. He sang it at a number of rallies in 1967 and 1968 and also in a public rally when the war was finally over in 1975. America first began its involvement in Vietnam following WWII as the Cold War was beginning. We assisted the French in maintaining their colonization of the region and then slowly involved ourselves in their conflict. You can hear Ochs condemning films that portray war as glorious and adventurous while the nation's citizens send their children to die in a war while their own civilization crumbles around them. Phil was able to use cinematic imagery to declare a simple statement: "The War is Over."

Phil's experience in Chicago during the 1968 Democrat Presidential Convention had a dramatic influence on his song writing. The Youth International Party (Yippies), led by Jerry Rubin and Abby Hoffman, advertised that Lincoln Park in Chicago would be a gathering of the tribes just like the be-ins of San Francisco and the Monterey Pop music festival held in the summer of 1967. Rubin and Hoffman used the popularity of rock music in an attempt to motivate people to attend political rallies. There were a number of organizations that attended the convention for different reasons. While the Students for a Democratic Society (SDS) wanted to change the Democrat Party and a group that called themselves the Motherfuckers wanted to see massive disruption in the streets, people like Allan Ginsburg and David Dellinger were there to try and prevent violent confrontations.

While a number of musicians were asked to be a part of the event, Phil Ochs, along with John Sinclair and MC5s, were some of the few musicians present in Chicago during the convention. Phil performed at an indoor concert that was dubbed as an 'Un-Birthday party for LBJ' where he performed many of his protest songs as some attendees burned their draft cards. On August 28, the day Humphrey was nominated, Phil performed at a rally and once again sang his now signature song "I Ain't Marching Anymore."

He was an official member of the McCarthy campaign so Phil was able to get in and out of the Conrad Hilton Hotel; Where McCarthy's Headquarters were located. There he was able to watch the events of the convention unfold on his television; whether it was in the hall or out on the streets. He had hoped that the Democratic Party would listen to the disparate voices coming from the protesters, but the reality was different. Inside the convention hall, the forces of Humphrey prevailed in the nomination fight, and outside the hall the police forces of Mayor Daley were beating the living hell out of protesters and journalists alike.

Phil was spared any police brutality but he was arrested during one of the many political theatre events that the Yippies sponsored. This time they were nominating a pig for president. (Yes, they nominated an actual pig!) The radicals met in an alleyway near the Civic Center and then worked their way out onto the street. Causing a mess in the traffic and without permits, Phil, the pig and others were promptly arrested while Jerry Rubin delivered the pig's nomination speech. While visually effective, this type of political theatre actually accomplished nothing to stop the war, nominate Eugene McCarthy, or adopt the peace platform at the convention.

According to Jerry Rubin, the violence in Chicago was the exact response the Yippies wanted from Mayor Richard Daley and the Chicago Police.

> We wanted to create a situation in which the Chicago
> Police and the Daley Administration and the Federal
> Government and the United States would self-destruct.
> We wanted to show that America wasn't a democracy,
> that the convention wasn't politics. The message of the
> week was of an America ruled by force.

Rubin and Hoffman may have wanted violence, but Phil wanted to see changes. He left Chicago emotionally depressed, physically exhausted and politically wounded.

Phil reacted to his experience in Chicago by writing and recording Rehearsals for Retirement. Released in late 1968, there were many songs signaling his disillusionment with American politics. Of the ten songs on the album, three had direct messages of protest while many of the others expressed Phil's sadness and prediction that American civilization was on the brink of destruction. Phil described this point in his life as transformative: "I no longer feel any ties of loyalty to the present American society... I've gone from being a left social democrat to an early revolutionary mentality...."

Even the cover of the record showed Phil's growing sense of disillusionment. The picture on the cover was of a tombstone with Phil's image carrying a gun, standing in front of an American flag. The inscription under his picture read:

Phil Ochs
(American)
Born: El P, Texas 1940
Died: Chicago, Illinois 1968
Rehearsals for Retirement

On the back cover Phil had printed a poem he wrote after leaving Chicago. In part it read:

> This then is the death of the American
> Imprisoned by his paranoia
> And all his diseases of his innocent inventions
> He plunges to the drugs of the devil to find his gods...
> And I realize these last days these trials and tragedies
> Were after all only
> Our rehearsals for retirement

Of the three direct songs of protest, the first was an attack on the police in Chicago and the whole mindset of opposition to the anti-war movement. Titled "I Kill Therefore I Am," it began by introducing the listener to the Chicago police coming in on a "pale pony" to save the American people from the anti-war hippies. He was describing the lines of police on their horses trying to clear the streets and parks of protesters. Phil then blamed the police for racism and violence. Phil saw firsthand the way southern police treated blacks protesting and marching for their civil rights in the fifties and early sixties. In Phil's mind, the Chicago police were treating the anti-war protesters in the same fashion as the civil rights marchers a decade earlier. One verse showed how the police didn't care what the protesters had to say. Their only concern was maintaining law and order, even if that resulted in maintaining a fascist state. The final verse clearly exhibited the way Phil saw the police. In Phil's mind, the police saw the students as gangsters whose only concern was breaking the law. The police saw a revolutionary with a gun and assumed he was fighting for hate. In Phil's mind the revolution to end the war was not about hate, but love and brotherhood.

"William Butler Yeats Visits Lincoln Park & Escapes Unscathed" is an eerie song that sets a musical stage allowing the listener to almost smell the tear gas as it's being thrown into the crowds of protesters. The smoke from the tear gas bellowed through Lincoln Park and the rest of Chicago by the convention center and the Conrad Hilton. The flames in the eyes of young people that Phil referred to in the second verse could be the result of the tear gas. He even referenced the "Robespierre robes" of the French revolution when Robespierre was the head of the Committee of Public Safety that put tens of thousands of French citizens to death because they opposed the rule of the revolutionary committee. The song is sad and depressing. It shows Phil's downward spiral into fatalism and the difficult situation the anti-war movement was in.

Throughout the song Phil referred to a "young maiden" he met. After the horror of the police brutality, Phil sang that he went looking for her but she now "lies in stone." I listened to this song a number of times and I believe the young woman he is referring to is liberty. It was the desire for liberty and peace that motivated Phil to go to Chicago. It was liberty that was lost in the tear gas, the beatings and the nomination of a pro-war plank with Hubert Humphrey. I am convinced that Phil believed it was American liberty that died in Lincoln Park that fateful week.

After a few seconds of silence on the record there is a short 30 second song fragment in which expressed Phil's disgust at those who talk about revolution and their desire to change things, but never put their actions with their words. Phil had the right to criticize others who sang for money but didn't sing for causes. In fact, Phil was known for turning down paying gigs so he could perform at a rally.

225

While "The World Began in Eden But Ended in Los Angeles" was not about Chicago or the war in Vietnam, the song makes a poignant comment on the cultural rot taking place in America. In the first verse Phil sang that we came to America for a new beginning. In the second verse he pointed out that some Americans constructed "highways" and "homesteads" while others continued migrating to the new western lands. It was in the third verse, however, that Phil's most profound comment is made when he sang about being outside on the open road only to "breathe the air of ashes." He seems to be predicting the demise of America and a coming environmental catastrophe or nuclear holocaust.

The final album of original material released in his lifetime was erroneously titled, <u>Phil Ochs Greatest Hits</u>. It was a collection of forgetful songs. The last song on the album, however, was a frightfully visionary number titled "No More Songs." It begins with an apology to his fans for not having any more political songs to write and then uses imagery to say goodbye.

While Phil continued to perform when he could, such as the 'Un-birthday party for President Johnson', or the 'War is Over Rally', and participate in whatever political rally he could, after Chicago he was never the same. He began to drink heavily and stopped making new music. While Phil's chronic alcoholism was destructive, his mental illness probably had more to do with his demise than anything else. He told friends that he suffered from manic depression. Joan Baez was worried for him in the mid-1970s because his health was so bad. Phil stopped bathing, drank heavily and acted differently every day. In fact, at one point Phil announced that Phil Ochs was dead and he was now John Train. And John Train was not a pleasant person to be around. It got so bad that Phil eventually took his own life. According to his brother Michael:

> He flirted with suicide a number of times. You can see it
> in the lyrics of his songs for at least the last three
> albums…. My last conversation with him I'll never
> forget. It was like 'I'm really gonna kill myself Michael'
> and I said 'Yea Phil (Phil loved food) Yea, give up food
> Phil?' and he cracked up laughing. He said 'OK good
> point' and the next week he kills himself. The next week
> he hangs himself.

The legacy of protest that Phil left behind was tremendous. Even though his life ended a lot earlier than it should have, he left behind a legacy of songs and activities that still has an impact today. His songs were sung in the 80s, 90s and into the 2000s. His signature song "I Ain't Marching Anymore," was even revitalized by many singers during the protests against the war in Iraq which started in 2003.

Billy Bragg adapted the famous tune, "I Dreamed I Saw Joe Hill Last Night," (written by Earl Robinson and made famous by the great singer Paul Robeson) in honor of Phil Ochs. You can see him singing "I Dreamed I Saw Phil Ochs Last Night" at the very end of the documentary about Ochs' life called <u>There But For Fortune</u>.

Songs have been written using some of Phil's melodies. For example, the song "Here's to the State of Mississippi," has been adapted to oppose President Bush and the war in Iraq. More recently, a song was written by Robert Thomas using the same melody to attack President Barack Obama. It is printed here with permission of the author.

Here's to the state of Barack Obama
The taxes are so high and the debt is too great
We go to the pump and pay the highest freight
Off to the store as we see our pay degrade
We know it's his fault, but elect him anyway
Oh, here's to the land you've torn out the heart of
Barack Obama, find yourself another country to be part of

Here's to the state of Barack Obama
Health Care imposed on the people as we wait
He spends all our money on projects that are waste
Stops an oil pipeline for favors lying in wait
When promises he made lay lingering in state
Oh, here's to the land you've torn out the heart of
Barack Obama, find yourself another country to be part of

Here's to the state of Barack Obama
We go to our job and find it cut to 29
Off to the bank to find what we're worth this time
Then to the pump to pay 4 and a dime
And all he can say is: It's not my fault this time
Oh, here's to the land you've torn out the heart of
Barack Obama, find yourself another country to be part of

Here's to the state of Barack Obama
He finds a war in Libya just to fit his time
He thinks he's got Egypt following in line
He left Iraq a mess, which one is next in line
They gave him the peace prize; they said it was his time
Oh, here's to the land you've torn out the heart of
Barack Obama, find yourself another country to be part of

Here's to the state of Barack Obama
They failed to pass the dream act – he does it anyway
He sends guns to Mexico - then hides it all away
He plays with our security – in Benghazi and LA
He plays us like the fools we are – just ask the N.S.A.
Oh, here's to the land you've torn out the heart of
Barack Obama, find yourself another country to be part of

Phil Ochs was a troubadour and troublemaker who had a tremendous impact on the protest music of the later sixties and early seventies. He was a contemporary of Bob Dylan who made his best effort at maintaining his integrity and honesty in an industry that is brutal in its criticism and as unforgiving as any business whose priority is to make profit. While Phil's songs never made it to the top of the charts, they were heard on college campuses, in dorm rooms, at anti-war meetings and rallies, civil rights marches, concerts, and song festivals. The themes of his songs: pro-labor, pro-unionism, free speech, anti-war, anti-colonialism, anti-interventionism, civil rights, and immigrant rights continued to be addressed in songs throughout the decades that followed his peak in the mid-1960s. Phil Ochs not only represented American youth, but a growing political leftist movement that embraced radicalism, anarchism, and extreme libertarianism. While most of his music style was based in the folk medium, his influence was strongly felt in the rock'n'roll arena. The rock bands and artists of the 1960s adopted the same themes that Phil promoted; only they put their words to a different form of music. While the folk style was the vehicle of protest in the fifties and early sixties, by 1965 it was rock'n'roll that carried the messages of protest.

Chapter Ten:
Rock'n'roll: A New Vehicle for Protest Songs

You brought us up to care about our brothers.
You brought us up not to run away from injustice
but to recognize it and fight it and destroy it. And
now you castigate us. You castigate us because
we think and we care. You demean our
consciences for which you are largely
responsible. And you insult us by describing
protest as our social fun.

Pat Stimer

The troubadours and troublemakers of protest-rock combined the radical traditions of America's past with contemporary national issues and used the language of rock'n'roll to carry the message. When rock'n'roll started in the 1950s, its message was simple: let's have fun. It didn't matter what color you were or what church you went to, what was important was that everybody had fun. But by the 1960s, rock'n'roll evolved into a new form of music that adopted the youthful idealism of Woody Guthrie, the energy of Pete Seeger, the poetic diversity of Bob Dylan, the honesty of Phil Ochs and the language of Chuck Berry and the Beatles. Rock musicians were popular entertainers who protested social and political conditions in America. Unlike earlier protest minstrels who sang about economic exploitation and unjust wage slavery, these rock'n'roll performers protested government control, racism and war while making money as performers in a popular musical medium.

Rock'n'roll in the 1950s was considered fun by its adherents but dangerous to its objectors. To the youth of America, rock'n'roll represented a new form of expression that encompassed the entire body. Just like the swinging youths of the 1930s and 40s these kids also danced to the music they listened to. The song could be "Great Balls of Fire" or "Tutti Fruti," it didn't matter. The kids would create dances to go along with the music. Some of these dances were more risqué than the dances of yore. But of course that's what the adults of the 1930s said of the various swing dances being created to go along with Benny Goodman, Glenn Miller and Cab Callaway.

Rock'n'roll critics also saw it as some kind of conspiracy. Some blamed communists or Soviet spies for infiltrating the youth of the country. Others condemned the music as representative of African culture. Some people didn't like it because it was loud, amplified and usually with a fast rhythm. The popular music of the time (except for bebop jazz) was easy listening music with a singer that could be simply understood like Frank Sinatra or Pat Boone. So when the screeching guitars of Chuck Berry or the banging piano of Little Richard came over the radio or record players, parents reacted with a collective: *"turn that down!"*

The origin of rock'n'roll can be traced to the Honker bands of the 1940s. During World War II, many jazz bands had to shrink because of economic reasons. Government rationing and war time shortages led many bands to shake off extra musicians and instruments. Eventually leaving only vocalist, drums, piano, standup bass, saxophone, and sometimes a rhythm guitar. In this format the saxophone was the lead instrument and carried most of the melody. These bands were known as Honker bands and they could be considered the first rock'n'roll outfits.

One of these Honker bands was Jackie Brenston and His Delta cats. They had the typical Honker band set-up with piano and sax leading the melody. One of their greatest hits could also be considered the first rock'n'roll song in American history. Written by James Cotton, "Rocket 88" could also be considered a double entendre song like the blues, jazz, folk and spirituals of the past. As people heard the lyrics they may have wondered what Jackie Brenston was singing about; his automobile or his sex life.

The Honker bands changed in sound when the sax was replaced with the electric guitar. The electric guitar was already being used in the blues community with many great artists such as BB King and Muddy Waters. But when Chuck Berry took the Honker band setup, added his electric guitar and then sang about growing up in America, a new musical form was born. This music was fast, rhythmic, danceable and meaningful. While Berry's lyrics were not laced with protest, it certainly represented the immediate concerns of teenagers: school, dating and cars. Songs like "School Days" and "Roll Over Beethoven" not only spoke their language, it also gave them something to dance to.

Little Richard was able to excite American teenagers just like Chuck Berry. While Little Richard's instrument of choice was the piano instead of the guitar, they both brought their instruments to new heights. In fact Richard usually didn't even sit down during his performances they were so full of vitality and excitement. With his virtuoso piano progressions, unique vibrant yell and poetic lyrics, Little Richard inspired many young Americans to use the piano lessons they got as children and apply those skills to rock'n'roll. "Tutti Frutti" and "Good Golly Miss Molly" were such big hits that record companies scrambled to find white artists to cover the songs and take advantage of this great songwriter.

It is important to mention that this growth of rock'n'roll coincided with the civil rights movement. The 1950s was an amazing time for the advancement of civil rights. Some of the visible victories for civil rights in the fifties where: the Brown vs. Board of Education decision which started the process of de-segregating schools across America; the Montgomery Bus Boycott that achieved legal integration for American blacks on Montgomery's public transportation system; a piece of 1866 Civil War legislation was replaced in 1957 with a new law authorizing the use of federal troops to enforce civil rights laws; and in September of the same year President Eisenhower exercised this new law by calling on federal troops to protect black students attempting to enroll in the previously all white High School. While American blacks were fighting for the same rights as white Americans, suburban teenagers were absorbing this new rock'n'roll music coming from the very same people who were being discriminated against.

When Elvis Presley came onto the scene, there was now no way to resist this music. While Jerry Lee Lewis was popular and Buddy Holly had his fans, it was Elvis that truly made rock'n'roll a household name. While the topics of his music was innocuous and in no way a form of protest, his physical presence itself was a threat to the adults in America. The way he danced and the way he moved his hips excited girls and boys alike but outraged the older generation. Those that swung their way through World War II were now offended by Elvis and his erotic interpretation of 1950s popular music.

While Elvis was very popular throughout America, a new form of music was flourishing that challenged the consumer conformity of most of the country: Surf Music. Represented first by Dick Dale and his relaxed beach lifestyle and rip-roaring guitar licks, this new music showcased a bohemian beach lifestyle that many in the traditional mainstream consumer culture found to be aberrant to the American way of life. The Beach Boys were also an exciting new band that exemplified this lifestyle and became hugely popular on the west coast and eventually in the whole country. While the songs and music of Dick

Dale and the Beach Boys were not full of protest messages, the lifestyle they represented and the new style of music that they performed and recorded in itself was a form of protest to the popular forms of music at the time, such as Roger Williams, Dean Martin or Perry Como.

When the Beatles arrived in the United States, American youth were still in a state of shock following the assassination of President John F. Kennedy. Some suggest that young people were waiting for something exciting to happen after the horror of Kennedy's assassination left them empty and depressed. By the spring of 1964, six Beatles' songs had reached number one on the Billboard charts. By April, five of the top fourteen songs in America were by the Beatles. Throughout their career, the Beatles had at least one number one hit every year ending in 1970 with "Let It Be" and "The Long and Winding Road." In total, the Beatles had twenty number one hits on the Billboard charts, the highest of any group or musician at that time. Their success in the United States can be attributed to a combination of outstanding talent and brilliant marketing. They blended the best elements of British skiffle groups, white rock'n'roll stars like Elvis Presley and Bill Haley, and the black rhythm and blues musicians like Chuck Berry, Fats Domino, and Little Richard.

Beatles' music engulfed US airwaves with a pop-idol frenzy that surpassed all expectations. By the end of 1963, two Beatles songs, "She Loves You" and "I Want To Hold Your Hand" had already reached 2.5 million in sales in Britain alone. When they arrived in the United States in February 7, 1964, thousands of kids were going wild for them at the airport. It was a reception none of them had expected. John Lennon's first wife recalled that when they touched down in New York, they "all thought the screaming was the screaming of the jet engines, but in fact it was the screaming of the fans."

At first, the lyrics to Beatles songs were simple themes of boy meets girl, developing relationships, and the pain of losing a loved one; but by December 1965 with the release of Rubber Soul their art was changing. The musical arrangement of the songs became more complex and the themes were more personal. Songs like "Norwegian Wood (This Bird Has Flown)," and "In My Life" displayed the personal and emotional development of John Lennon from a writer of simple popular songs into a songwriter exposing the inner emotions of a confused and tormented rock star. George Harrison expressed opposition to the British Tax system in "Taxman" using the same language of imagery developed by Bob Dylan. Harrison sang about every possible thing people could do like take a walk or a drive and how the government was ready to put a tax levy upon the activity. Except for this song, the Beatles didn't enter the realm of protest music until the late sixties when John Lennon deliberately dedicated himself to peace and various causes of protest.

A major significance of the Beatles to American music was their influence on other musicians. Bob Dylan was convinced that he could make money by writing, recording, and performing rock songs. He followed the success of the Beatles with his own expansion into rock'n'roll with Bringing It All Back Home, Highway 61 Revisited, and Blond On Blond. Charles Kaiser suggests in 1968 In America that there was a very competitive and healthy rivalry between Dylan and the Beatles. However they did it, the Beatles and Bob Dylan affected the rest of American music, resulting in young people forming rock bands all over the US. In fact, Ringo Starr credits Bob Dylan with introducing marijuana to the Beatles!

The year 1965 was very important for the development of protest rock. On September 25, 1965, "Eve of Destruction" hit number one on the Billboard charts. This was the first popular protest song of the rock era. Written by Philip 'Flip' Sloan and Steve Barri, and recorded by Barry McGuire, the song addressed many national and international problems. The song protested war, injustice, and the older generations' expectations of their children. "Eve of Destruction" also pointed out the deadlocked politics in Washington, DC while injustice prevailed across the nation. The song set the tone for the sixties generation of protest songs and opened up the market for bands that wanted to record topical material of their own. McGuire sang "Eve of Destruction" with a strong raspy voice that really conveyed a feeling of helplessness and anger.

After the success of "Eve of Destruction" Philip Sloan wrote another protest song called "Let Me Be." Recorded by the Turtles, this song reached its peak of popularity in November of 1965, about four months after Sloan's previous hit. "Let Me Be" was aimed at young people who wanted to follow their own lifestyle, career, and family obligations. It protested society's negative reaction towards people that dress, act, and live differently than mainstream culture. "Let Me Be" was a protest against the last remnants of fifties' conformity.

Another contribution to the protest of 1965 was "Laugh at Me" by Sony Bono. This was an obvious protest song against conformity and the older generation's desire for traditional values. American youth by 1965 were looking for their own direction in clothing and lifestyles.

Also in 1965 was a song recorded by the Seeds and written by Sky Saxon called "Pushing Too Hard." It was a criticism of those who attack the young for dressing different, acting different, and having a different set of values.

Another 1965 protest song (released in January of 1966) titled "Its Good News Week" was recorded by the Hedgehoppers Anonymous. This song protested the threat of nuclear war, the dangers of atomic testing in the atmosphere, the lies and distortions broadcast on the evening news, and the destruction of Chinese traditions taking place in Communist China (called the Great Proletarian Cultural Revolution).

1965 also saw the success of the Byrds. In Los Angeles the previous year, folksingers David Crosby and Jim McGuinn (who later changed his name to Roger McGuinn) joined with Gene Clark, Michael Clarke and Chris Hillman to form the Byrds. They were inspired by the innovative musical talents of Bob Dylan and the Beatles and sought to imitate their style. Throughout 1964 they worked hard to gain followers and succeed in the music business. They wanted to play rock music and make lots of money. In April of 1965, even before Dylan picked up the electric guitar in Newport, and before the release of "Eve of Destruction," the Byrds mixed rock music with serious lyrics with the release of "Mr. Tambourine Man." Fans and critics heard this new sound and were amazed by the bright crisp interpretation of Dylan's hazy suggestive song. Producers Terry Melcher and Jim Dickson were uncertain of the Byrds' musical ability and hired studio musicians to play almost all the instruments for the recording except for the vocals and Jim McGuinn's 12-string Rickenbacker. Within two months "Mr. Tambourine Man" reached number one on the Billboard charts. The Byrds contributed to the development of two important trends in sixties rock; the interpretation of Dylan's protest songs with rock music and the use of topical lyrics in popular rock songs.

The Byrds covered many other Bob Dylan songs with their rock sound, especially on their first album, Mr. Tambourine Man, released in June of 1965, and their second album, Turn Turn Turn, released in December of 1965. Some of Dylan's songs they recorded were "Chimes of Freedom," "All I Really want To Do," "Spanish Harlem Incident," "Lay Down Your Weary Tune," and "The Times They Are A-Changing."

The third single the Byrds released was even a bigger hit than the first. "Turn, Turn, Turn" was released as a single in October of 1965, reached number one by the first week in December, and stayed there for three weeks. Pete Seeger adapted this song from his favorite part of the Bible: the Book of Ecclesiastes. In the words of Fred Bronson, Billboard compiler, "Turn Turn Turn" was "the number one single with the most ancient lyrics." The language of the song was similar to the kind of words that Seeger used in "If I Had A Hammer." "Turn Turn Turn" called on a generation to make a new world with the time they had. The song told people that now is the time to make a better world for everyone. The words of this song had an important relevance to the generation coming of age in the sixties and a glimpse of the social upheaval only a few years away.

The Byrds were also developing their own song-writing style. Some of David Crosby's best songs with protest messages were: "Renaissance Fair," "Everybody's Been Burned," "Lady Friend," and "What's Happening?!?!" Other excellent songs by Crosby not released until the late 1980s were: "It Happens Each Day," "Psychodrama City," and "Triad." One of these songs caused friction in the group because of its delicate subject matter. "Triad" was originally recorded by the Byrds in August of 1967 but shelved by McGuinn. Crosby gave the song to the Jefferson Airplane to record for their Crown of Creation album in 1968. Crosby eventually released the song in 1971 on a live Crosby, Stills, Nash, & Young (CSN&Y) album titled, 4 Way Street. "Triad" protested sexual taboos that existed in American society. It was Crosby's way of questioning his lovers' hesitation towards a three-way relationship while also challenging society's restrictions on sexual freedom.

"Triad" was very reflective of American youth's changing attitudes towards sex and contemporary family structure. Young people rejected the family unit as the main living arrangement and created their own with friends and lovers. This new communal living arrangement adopted values in opposition to those of mainstream society. Abbie Hoffman attempted to describe the new attitude towards the family unit in his book Revolution For The Hell Of It. He used the Beatles to explain the structure of the new family unit in America's counter-culture.

> They are organized around the way they create. They are
> communal art. They are brothers and, along with their
> wives and girlfriends, form a family unit that is
> horizontal rather than vertical, in that it extends across a
> peer group rather than describing vertically like
> grandparents-parents-children. More than horizontal, it's

circular with the four Beatles the inner circle, then their wives and kids and friends. The Beatles are a small circle of friends, a tribe. They are far more than simply a musical band. Let's say, if you want to begin to understand our culture, you can start by comparing Frank Sinatra and the Beatles. It wouldn't be perfect but it would be a good beginning. Music is always a good place to start.

A direct anti-war song written by Crosby, while still with the Byrds, was "Draft Morning." It was recorded in August of 1967 and released in January of 1968 on Notorious Byrd Brothers (an album released after Crosby left the group). The song used a few simple words to protest the military draft. It told a story of a young man who awoke in the morning knowing that it was his last day as a civilian. After a few verses the music blended with gunshots, machine gun fire, explosions, yelling and even louder explosions, only to fade back into the music. The listener is brought into a fierce battle and then returned back to the song. In the last verse Crosby pointed out that to serve in the military during war meant killing another human being. The song asked the basic question of humanity: why do we kill each other?

The Byrds second album in 1966 included a McGuinn song protesting the murder of President Kennedy. "He was a Friend of Mine" was a solemn tribute to a man who inspired many young people in the United States. Many American youth identified with him because of his young family and idealism. The abrupt end of the Kennedy presidency shocked millions and inspired Roger McGuinn to write the song.

Throughout the remainder of the 1960s protest songs became prevalent and popular. In 1967 the Youngbloods released "Get Together" with a message of peace. In 1968 another rock'n'roll protest song was released called "People Got to Be Free" by the Rascals. It was written by Felix Cavaliere and Eddie Brigati, two members of the band. The song was a clear condemnation of any traditions, laws or mores that treated someone different just because of who they may be. They were mostly speaking for the growing counter-culture movement in the mid-sixties, but it also applied to the Civil Rights movement that had taken a new turn with the assassinations of Malcolm X, Martin Luther King Jr. and Bobby Kennedy. In fact, the song was written as a reaction to these assassinations. The song reached number one on the Billboard charts the week of August 17 1968 and stayed at the top for five weeks.

Another song written to protest the assassination of Martin Luther King Jr and Bobby Kennedy was "Abraham, Martin and John." It was written by Dick Holler and recorded by Dion DiMucci. In December of 1968, it reached number four on the charts and expressed the sorrow and despair of the nation. This was not a rock song but certainly contained the spirit and sadness of the times felt by American youth.

The Temptations added their own song to the protest genre titled: "Ball of Confusion." It was a smorgasbord of all the major issues facing America nearing the end of the 1960s such as racism, police brutality, discrimination, segregation, violence and a whole list of problems facing modern American society.

"War" recorded by Edwin Star and written by Norman Whitfield and Barrett Strong was a direct protest song against all forms of war. This was a powerful song that pulled no punches in its condemnation.

Authoritarianism was another issue addressed by the rock genre. The song "Signs" by the One Man Electric Band reached number three on the pop charts in May of 1971. It was a comment on the ever intruding control that institutions had on people. The song protested all kinds of signs. Whether it was a sign telling you to wear a shirt and shoes or a no trespassing sign; the song screamed out in protest against it.

The song, "Fresh Garbage," by Spirit was an attack on the consumerism that leads to waste. The issue of environmentalism was growing strong in America in the early seventies, and this number reflected the desire of people to start cleaning up our streams, rivers and lakes.

Even though the Doors were not a political band and more representative of psychedelic music, they did add some protest songs to the genre. "The Unknown Soldier" was written as a protest against war and the resulting death. Another Doors song that made a comment on American society was "Peace Frog." This was a protest against what happened in Chicago during the 1968 Democratic Convention where Mayor Daley's police beat protesters senseless while the DNC nominated Hubert Humphrey for President of the United States on a pro-war platform.

"Time of the Season" by the Zombies was written by Rod Argent. It was a statement to the nation that love and brotherhood was the only way to live. Just like the messages of the Beatles from "Love Me Do" to "All You Need Is Love" and Pete Seeger's "I Have a Hammer,"

"Time of the Season" was telling America that the time for peace and brotherhood was now.

"In the Year 2525" was written by Rick Evans for his own band Zager and Evans. It took only three weeks for the single to reach number one on the charts the week of July 12, 1969 and it stayed there for six weeks. They made one thousand copies of the record themselves, calling their company Truth Records and personally "distributed the single… to radio stations and record stores." While the song does not directly protest a particular social condition or legal barrier to equality, it has a message of protest against the direction of the human race. The song begins by suggesting that the human race will lose control of its individualism and be drugged by the government as described in the dystopian novels Fahrenheit 451, 1984 and Brave New World. The song then predicted that we will turn food into a pill and won't need our arms or legs because technology will supply all society's needs. It goes on to envision a time when people are having babies in test tubes forcing God to cast final "Judgment" on the human race. In the final verses, the song wondered whether we as a species are worthy of survival.

The 5th Dimension's "Age of Aquarius/Let the Sun Shine In" was an adaptation of a song from a very popular Broadway show called *Hair*. It was another song that represented the younger generation. It became a number one hit April 12, 1969 and remained on the top of the charts for 6 weeks. One of the key lines in the song is near the end when they sang about opening "your heart" to the people of the world.

Rock festivals of the 1960s, and the artists that performed at them, represented a new cultural spirit of peace and love. The Monterey Pop Festival and Woodstock were two events in the late sixties that represented the idealistic drive for the utopian dream of ultimate freedom. The performers and audience were united in trying to make "a new society in the shell of the old" just like the Wobblies sixty years earlier.

The Monterey Pop International Music Festival was very important to the expansion of music developing in California and across the nation. The counter-culture communities in the Haight-Ashbury area of San Francisco and the Sunset Strip in Los Angeles joined together to spend a weekend in June 1967 filled with "Music, Love, and Flowers." Approximately 200,000 people attended this festival on June 16, 17, and 18, that launched a number of successful rock careers and funded various music education causes. "It was a time of enormous optimism," remembered Derek Taylor, the festival's publicist. "We were going to change the world by smoking marijuana and taking LSD. There would be no more wars, and we would celebrate this by getting all these peaceful people to Monterey, as audience and as artist." According to Lou Rawls, (who performed the Friday evening show of the festival):

> The people at Monterey Pop were not only rock'n'rollers, they were also socially conscious and politically aware musicians. They were the people that made the world become aware of exactly what was going on; be it radical political, or environmental. Monterey Pop was like a forum, a stage, a place where they could speak their piece, say what they had to say, and the message would get across. You could equate it to a seminar. People were not only there for the music, but also for the commentary being made through the music.

Many of these musicians believed in the same social philosophy. "If you are in a position of influence, you should do something about it," said Cass Elliot of the Mamas and the Papas. "Not necessarily inflict your opinion on other people, but if you really think you're right, you should tell it." David Crosby also felt that the music festival was very important to the counterculture's expression of their values. "What happened at Monterey was the flowering of an entirely different set of values." Crosby explained, "We were just blowing ourselves loose from the fifties and had a whole different entire value system... one that values life and creativity and freedom and equality and civil rights...." Another hippie commented to an interviewer: "We struggle in our own humble way to destroy the United States." This counter-culture revolution was defined well by Warren Hinckle in a Ramparts article in 1967.

> Hippies have a clear vision of the ideal community... communal life, drastic restriction of private property, rejection of violence, creativity before consumption, freedom before authority, (and the) de-emphasis of government and traditional forms of leadership.

Monterey Pop was a musical tribute to the living philosophy of America's counter-culture, just like the Pageant of the Paterson on June 7, 1913 was a celebration of worker heroism and labor solidarity. Both these events were a cultural representation of their peers while exposing themselves to the rest of society. The striking workers in Paterson in 1913 wanted others to see their strife and support them with money and general strikes. The hippies in Monterey were trying to have a cultural event that would express their philosophy of life through music and create a new community based on their value system of sex, drugs, and rock'n'roll.

Both events were also conceived to raise funds to benefit people who agree with their philosophy. Money made at the Pageant of Paterson was intended to help striking workers. Profits made from Monterey Pop helped struggling musicians in different communities. Just like in the Paterson festival, Monterey Pop had its financial troubles. Fortunately it was still able to help many community programs. The groups that benefited from Monterey Pop included a Harlem Musical Instruction program, San Francisco Free Clinics, the Sam Cooke Scholarship, Los Angeles Public Television, the San Francisco Earthquake Relief Fund, Romanian Angel Relief, and the Rhythm and Blues Foundation. Although separated by fifty-four years, both the Pageant of the Paterson and Monterey Pop had similar intentions and used art and music to communicate protest and community solidarity.

David Crosby made a very strong statement of political protest about the Kennedy assassination at the Monterey Pop Festival. When introducing "He Was A Friend Of Mine" to the audience, Crosby pointing out that the festival was being filmed and his statements would probably be censored. With this preliminary attack on the establishment out of the way, Crosby spoke his mind about Kennedy's death and the Warren Commission Report that rejected the idea of a conspiracy.

> When President Kennedy was killed, he was not killed by one man. He was shot from a number of different directions by different guns. The story has been suppressed, witnesses have been killed and this is your country...

This direct political statement was strong coming from a rock star. Crosby's approach towards the Kennedy assassination was a blatant defiance of the Warren Commission and the official position of the U.S. government. It is very probable that Crosby's use of the stage and the studio to express social and political protest angered others in the band.

In 1970 David Crosby told <u>Rolling Stone</u> that his statements were fairly strong. "Now, admittedly that's a little extreme for an artist to get into those areas at all.... But I was pissed about it...." Al Kooper, one of the musicians who performed at the festival, could see the Byrds falling apart: "You could see them breaking up on-stage, sort of, at Monterey. There was tremendous tension between McGuinn and Crosby." Even Crosby knew it was the end of the Byrds:

> We were very close to the end of the Byrds. It might
> have been one of the last gigs we did together. Stephen
> Stills and I had started to sort of hang out with each
> other and play music together. And at that point
> [Buffalo] Springfield was reaching its demise also,
> because Neil Young had left just before the Monterey
> Festival. Steven asked me (to) take his place. So I was in
> both bands there.

For some of the bands at the festival it was one of the last time they performed as a group. Both the Byrds and Buffalo Springfield broke up soon after the festival and Crosby joined Graham Nash (of the Hollies), and Stephen Stills and Neil Young (of the Buffalo Springfield), to form one of the first super-groups: Crosby, Stills, Nash & Young (CSN&Y).

Buffalo Springfield was already known at the time of Monterey Pop because of their song: "For What it's Worth." It was written by Steven Stills and reached number seven on the <u>Billboard</u> charts in 1967. It was a statement of protest against people being beaten and arrested for exercising their right to free speech. "For What It's Worth" became a rallying cry for the American counter-culture in California.

The origin of the song goes back to 1965 when the Byrds were playing at a club on the Strip in Hollywood called Ciro's. As they became more popular, unusual looking people flocked to their shows to dance and listen to the music. Other bands with similar new sounds arrived, including the Lovin' Spoonful, and the Mamas and the Papas. By 1966, the area became a haven for artists, musicians, and enthusiasts of a new flowering counter-culture. Early in 1967, these people banded together in protest when an eviction notice was given to Pandora's Box, a coffee house at the intersection of Crescent Heights and Sunset Boulevard. They marched in the streets holding signs with sayings like "Give Us Back Our Street" and "Protest Not Riot." Jim Dickson, the Byrd's producer, remembers the young people peacefully protesting the community development project that would close down Pandora's Box: "The kids hadn't done anything evil enough to bring out big crowds of police, whole platoons with billy clubs and helmets just beating people up. They arrested 300 people one night and it never made the papers...." After releasing "For What It's Worth," Buffalo Springfield performed the song for the Smothers Brothers Show in 1967 and it became a hit.

For The Who and the Jimi Hendrix Experience, the Monterey Pop Festival was an abrupt and revolutionary introduction of them to American audiences. When The Who destroyed their instruments on stage and Hendrix lit his guitar on fire, they performed acts of theatrical violence that expressed rebellion. Eric Burdon remembers, "The climax of the show was just like a terrorist attack, with the bombs and the smoke. It was just shocking."

The festival was very important to the expansion of alternative bands that were flowering in California. Some groups were offered record contracts because of their performance at the festival. Most prominent of these were the Grateful Dead, Quicksilver Messenger Service, The Steve Miller Band, and Big Brother and the Holding Company with Janis Joplin. According to Eric von Schmidt, "The Monterey Pop festival was the first union of what was becoming the new American pop music."

The Grateful Dead were already well known in San Francisco among the participants of Ken Kesey's *Trips Festivals*. The Dead were known for their ability to improvise in very long jams. They recorded only one protest song for their first album in 1967 titled "Morning Dew." Originally written by Bonnie Dobson, a singer on the Canadian folk circuit, this song took place after an imagined nuclear holocaust. It was inspired by the novel On the Beach written by Nevil Shute. When I first listened to the song as interpreted by the Grateful Dead, in my mind, I heard the suffering of war veterans after returning from Vietnam. The song created an image of a soldier waking from a horrible dream while a companion attempted to console him. With an eerie sound, the Dead conveyed the fear and anxiety felt by the soldier when he heard "a baby cry" and then a "young man run." I imagined that the soldier was reliving his horrific experiences from Vietnam through his dreams. At one point in the song he was terrified because all his friends were gone and his companion tried to console him, "You never see those people anyway," she said. The people he was imagining could have been his buddies from Vietnam. The Grateful Dead created dreamy images with electrified instruments and words to convey a message of despair and horror. Whether it was the horror of nuclear war or the hell of the jungles of Vietnam, the song created images of protest as envisioned by people who listened to it.

Another band to receive a record contract resulting from a performance at Monterey Pop was Quicksilver Messenger Service. They were also from San Francisco and known for long jams of rock music fused with the sounds of blues and jazz. One of the first protest songs they released was "Pride of Man." Pressed on their self-titled album, "Pride of Man" was a warning to American youth that the cold war between the USA and the USSR would only lead to nuclear destruction.

Another song they recorded on a later album was "What About Me." This composition was a protest dedicated to all the people who adopted the communal lifestyle and anti-establishment social behavior. The first verse was a direct attack against industrial pollution and the desecration of the earth. Following each chorus the song continued to attack the establishment by pointing a finger at newspapers and the negative things people wrote about hippies. The third and final verse expressed the skeptical feelings that some people had about American society.

Another important contributor to Monterey Pop's element of protest against mainstream culture was Country Joe and the Fish. This group was formed by Joe McDonald in the Berkeley area as a comical protest of the United States' war in Vietnam. Their first release was a 45rpm record pressed especially for a march on the induction center in Oakland. The record was titled "Songs of Opposition" and included "I-Feel-Like-I'm-Fixin'-to-Die Rag" and "Superbird." "Country Joe and the Fish were the left wing band from Berkeley!" Steve Miller remembered, "These guys were political commentators in a pop/rock arena, and they did it with humor." "I-Feel-Like-I'm-Fixin'-to-Die Rag" was a comical song which made the whole Vietnam War feel like a game.

The first version they recorded was in the traditional folk style, but by the Monterey Pop Festival they were into rock'n'roll. In the second verse, McDonald protested against leaders of the military industrial complex who live only to fight war and prepare for the final battle with the Soviet Union. The song's third verse was an attack on the money manipulators on Wall Street. McDonald pointed out that armed conflict meant profits for people who manufacture weapons of war. The final verse was a message of draft resistance aimed at parents who have children at the draft age. No mother really wishes her son to die, but the simplistic image McDonald portrayed, was based more in reality than the glamour and heroism that is conveyed to young people about war. Some young Americans did choose to resist rather than fight.

"An Untitled Protest" was another anti-war song that told the story of a Vietnamese girl who survived the bombing of her country from American planes. Using finger cymbals and an organ, the song transported the listener to the rice paddies of Vietnam. The listener could feel the pain and suffering caused by the war through images of death and destruction. After the images, it is implied that those who "send cards and letters" instead of stopping the war were just as guilty as those fighting it. McDonald also provided an image of an inexperienced soldier meeting his end.

The Jefferson Airplane was also very important to the expansion of the hippie message of anti-establishment, anti-society, peace and love. By the time of Monterey Pop, the group had a number five hit with "Somebody to Love," a number eight hit with "White Rabbit," and their album Surrealistic Pillow reached number three on the Billboard charts. These songs contained messages of love and the hippie ethic of the communal lifestyle promoting freedom and drugs. Grace Slick, a major songwriter and driving force of the band, viewed Monterey Pop as a symbol of the special relationship between the audience and the musicians. "I didn't think of anybody as celebrities." Slick remembers, "Nobody was really famous. We were just all doing this 'thing' and all that separated the performers from the audience was the physical fact of the stage."

It wasn't until a couple of years later, with their release of Volunteers and their performance at the Woodstock festival, that the Jefferson Airplane became more political in their music. The bass player of the group, Jack Cassidy began to notice the beginning of their change at Monterey Pop: "We were also making a departure with our material due to Paul's (Kantner) desire to write about what's going on around him.... Paul would write about news events...."

The events in the year 1968 were cataclysmic to the notion of peace, love, and flowers so prevalent at the Monterey Pop Festival. The assassination of Civil Rights leader Reverend Martin Luther King Jr. on April 4, 1968, produced a wave of nationwide violence in 110 American cities. The assassination of presidential candidate, Senator Robert F. Kennedy on June 5, 1968, produced national despair and hopelessness among anti-war and youth activists culminating in the confrontation with police outside the Democratic National Convention in Chicago.

David Crosby wrote a protest song in reaction to Robert Kennedy's murder called "Long Time Gone." He recorded it with Steven Stills and Graham Nash for their self-titled debut album: <u>Crosby, Stills & Nash</u>. According to Crosby:

> It was written the night Bobby Kennedy was killed. I believed in him because he said he wanted to make some positive changes in America, and he hadn't been bought and sold like Johnson and Nixon - cats who made their deals years ago with the special interests in this country in order to gain power. I thought Bobby, like his brother, was a leader who had not made those deals. I was already angry about Jack Kennedy getting killed and it boiled over into this song when they got his brother, too.

"Long Time Gone" was not only a statement of anger aimed at the senseless murder, it was also an expression of frustration against the political system that ignored the wishes of its people. Crosby expressed the frustration of all the various groups who wanted to stop the war, promote peace, and bring about social change in the nation. He used the length of someone's hair as a symbol of the cultural barrier between the generations as well as youth's unified cry for peace and love.

After all the madness of 1968, a festival was held at White Lake in the town of Bethel, New York the following year. The Woodstock Music and Arts Festival reinforced to the nation that peace, love, and cooperation was still possible. The original intention of the festival came from an idea to create a retreat in Woodstock, New York, where musicians could go and record their music in a groovy setting. Michael Lang, John Roberts, Joel Rosenman, and Artie Kornfeld joined together to create a music festival in the spirit of Monterey Pop that would make a profit for their company called Woodstock Ventures.

The actual organization of the event was a disaster. Not enough food, water, sanitary facilities, or first aid was available for the large number of people who arrived. The predicted 50,000 people turned into an estimated crowd of 400,000. These people seriously tapped the available facilities of what was dubbed by Abbie Hoffman as "Woodstock Nation." The farm that Max Yasgur rented to Woodstock Ventures for $50,000 had by Friday morning of August 15, 1969, become a cultural Mecca for the American counter-culture, radical activists, rock enthusiasts, and fascinated youth. The first newspaper reports were negative, but the ability of almost a half a million people to survive -*with a little help from their friends*- without major problems, amazed the nation and created the symbol of a generation in a violent time.

There have been many things said about this festival, but I think the man who put it best was Max Yasgur on Sunday afternoon August 17. He started to speak to the crowd by saying: "I'm a farmer." After the crowd roared their approval, Max continued by pointing out the difficulty of bringing water and food to such a large group of people. He continued by reflecting on the historical importance of the weekend:

> I don't know how to speak to twenty people at one time let alone a crowd like this, but I think you people have proven something to the world…. This is the largest group of people ever assembled in one place…. The important thing you have proven to the world is that a half a million kids… can get together and have three days of fun and music, and have nothing but fun and music. And I God bless you for it!

Max made it possible for people in the crowd to feel they had connected with someone in the older generation.

The political statement of Woodstock was that hundreds of thousands of kids could get together with almost unlimited freedom and listen to music without violence or serious trouble. It also told mainstream America that rock music was a serious form of communication that spoke to a whole generation of Americans. Woodstock has remained a symbol of that generation with meaning that goes beyond the music itself. It is remembered more for the media images created after the festival than for the actual event itself. According to Tom Law, an important member of the Hog Farm (who helped with food, first aid, and security):

> The event was so much bigger than the music. It was a phenomenon…. And it was also the most peaceful, civilized gathering that was probably happening on the planet at the time….

The first performance of the festival made a lasting statement. Richie Havens opened up the festival with energy and inspiration. The only reason why he went first was because the organizers were not even ready for performances and there were already over one hundred thousand people in the audience. Since Richie Havens' music was mostly acoustic, he was the lucky choice to go on first. Richie Havens was already known in folk circles and the burgeoning folk-rock scene for performing songs like "The Klan" which was an attack on the KKK.

Besides performing a number of Beatles tunes such as "With A Little Help From My Friends," "Strawberry Fields Forever" and "Hey Jude," Havens performed one of his protest songs called "Handsome Johnny." It was a lyrical review of some of the struggles of the America people. Starting with the Battle of Lexington and Concord, the song moved onto the Battle of Gettysburg in the Civil War, the Battle of Dunkirk in World War II and then the Korean and Vietnam conflicts. The song ends with the struggle in Birmingham; not a war against another country but a civil rights struggle within our own nation.

It was his final song that made history at the festival. He closed his set with a song called "Freedom" which was based on the song "Motherless Child." The promoters wanted Havens to keep playing and occupy the audience until the next act was ready. Havens remembered it well:

> I did about four or five encores 'til I had nothing else to sing and then 'Freedom' was created right there on the stage.... It was what I thought of; what I felt -the vibration which was freedom- which I thought at that point we had already accomplished.

The performers and the audience at Woodstock represented a generation of Americans who believed the promises made by teachers and parents regarding freedom, independence and equal justice. They represented Americans who believed that recreational drugs should be available just like alcohol; they endorsed openness in sexual relations and believed that society should fulfill its constitutional promise of freedom and equal justice for all. Political radical, Abbie Hoffman, described the message of Woodstock as an example to the world.

> There was a concept that when you were at Woodstock, the world was watching and you wanted not just too show them that you were O.K. You wanted to show

249

them that there was some model here, some ideas that could be used to save the planet.

Following Richie Havens' performance was the band Sweetwater. They started their set with "Motherless Child" and ended it with "Let the Sunshine In" and "Oh Happy Day." Their song choices epitomized the beginning of the weekend: love and flowers.

After Bert Summer, Tim Hardin, Ravi Shankar and Melanie, the two individuals who closed the first day of the festival were the son of a legend (Arlo Guthrie) and a folk singer who was known as "one of Woody's stepchildren" (Joan Baez). Arlo represented a new generation of folk singers who were born after World War II and didn't have the same experiences as those who lived through the Great Dustbowl and the Great Depression. One of Arlo's choices to sing was: "Coming Into Los Angeles." This song represented the growing recreational drug culture in America.

Joan Baez started her set with another version of "Oh Happy Day" to sum up the feel of the first day. Her rendition of "Joe Hill" was haunting especially after she explained that it was an organizing song. By singing "Joe Hill" in front of a quarter million people she carried the torch from the Wobblies to the Hippies. Joan Baez not only sang songs in protest against the Vietnam War, but on October 16, 1967 she was arrested with 123 others for blocking an entrance to the Oakland, California Induction Center during anti-war demonstrations called: "End the Draft Week." Her husband David also served time in a federal prison for avoiding the draft. "Something is disastrously wrong when our nation pursues an unjust war..." said Baez. "Young boys are being asked to fight and die. We are repeating the errors of yesterday when we try to solve our problems by killing...." Baez ended her set with the slave spiritual "Swing Low Sweet Chariot" and the civil rights song "We Shall Overcome." By singing the songs of slaves, civil rights activists, and a tune dedicated to an executed labor martyr, Baez was connecting the sixties counter-culture with other protest movements of the past, especially the Wobbly idea of creating a "new society within the shell of the old."

Saturday started with the band Quill, followed by Country Joe McDonald. After taking the stage, he performed a half dozen songs and ended his set with his already famous "I-Feel-Like-I'm-Fixin-to-Die Rag." He completed a few verses and then stopped to address the audience: "Listen people I don't know how you expect to ever stop the war if you can't sing any better than that, there are about three hundred thousand of you fuckers out there, I want you to start singing, come on..." The audience sang as hard as they could but still couldn't stop the war. Country Joe performed this protest song again with his band, Country Joe and the Fish, the following morning; but still couldn't stop the war.

Following Santana, John Sebastian (of the Lovin' Spoonful), the Keef Hartly Band, the Incredible String Band, Canned Heat, Mountain and the Grateful Dead, Creedence Clearwater Revival took the stage. Even though they performed no direct songs of protest during the festival they personified the hippie ethic and lifestyle. Within a year they would record one of the strongest arguments against the Vietnam War. "Fortunate Son" was an attack on the draft system used for the Vietnam conflict. If you went to college or got a position in the National Guard you probably wouldn't end up in Vietnam. The problem was who was getting the college deferments and the Guard positions: the fortunate sons of the rich, the powerful, and the politicians.

Following what many believed to be a lackluster performance by Janis Joplin, Sly and the Family Stone took the stage. They were considered to be one the great successes at Woodstock. Bob Spitz wrote in his excellent biography on the festival called Barefoot in Babylon that Sly Stone's set was "the most outstanding performance of the entire festival." Two of their songs have direct elements of protest: "Stand" and "Don't Call Me Nigger Whitey." After singing "Everyday People," "Dance To The Music," "Music Lover," "I Want To Take You Higher" and "Love City," Sly's band tore into their big hit "Stand!" It reinforced the idea that the only way to maintain your freedom is to stand up for what you believe in. The song was vague enough so that you could be thinking of any movement or cause you believe in when singing or listening to this song. Although not performed at Woodstock, "Don't Call Me Nigger, Whitey" was a call to both white and black people to stand together for freedom and peace.

Following The Who's Sunday morning's outstanding sunrise performance, the Jefferson Airplane took the stage. They performed their hits "Somebody to Love" about the hippie non-monogamous lifestyle and "White Rabbit" promoting drug use. They also performed the song written with David Crosby "Wooden Ships" about the end of the world and their protest song "Volunteers." The Jefferson Airplane personified the Haight-Ashbury communal lifestyle and the spirit of radical social and left-wing political protest. "Woodstock had been a joy of new rebellion," Grace Slick remembered. "The radicals were going to take over and everybody in the bands and audience was equal...." Paul Kantner's song "Volunteers" tried to inspire this revolutionary spirit among American youth.

"We Can Be Together" was another Kantner song that responded to the developing war between young radicals and the establishment. Although not performed at Woodstock, the song was released on the album Volunteers in November of 1969, only three months after Woodstock. "We Can Be Together" tried to unite the counter-culture in American society against the establishment, just like Ralph Chaplin's "Solidarity Forever" tried to unify Wobblies against the industrial capitalists. The aggressive language of "We Can Be Together" clearly conveyed the frustrated attitude of American youth.

Jimi Hendrix was the highest paid performer at Woodstock and probable the least seen. By the time Hendrix started his set, there were only about thirty thousand people left on the festival grounds. People started moving out of the area late the previous evening. What was left behind by the multitudes of hippies was garbage and mud. While the songs Hendrix performed at Woodstock cannot be considered as protest music, one piece he did perform did carry a message of rebellion. From the first notes of the "Star Spangled Banner" to the screeching transformation into "Purple Haze," Hendrix was making a comment about the state of America. We were at war abroad in Vietnam while in a continual state of crisis and conflict with the Soviet Union and Communist China. African Americans, student protesters and counter-culturists were being harassed, beaten and arrested for speaking out against the insanity of war and racism. It seemed like Hendrix was using the song to make a statement about the condition of the American dis-union!

One of the biggest events of Woodstock was the inspiring performance of David Crosby, Steven Stills, Graham Nash and Neil Young (CSN&Y). By the time they came onto the performing stage it was early Sunday morning before sunrise. Their music was very introspective of their personal emotions regarding social and political opinions. Graham Nash remembered the late sixties as a time when their music became more political.

> The message in the music began to change drastically.
> We began to talk about what was happening to us as
> people, as artists, as performers, as viewers of the

society of in which we were operating. We began to talk about the Vietnam War, we began to flip out our record companies and our managers who said 'wait a second... come on, let's get happy again here, nobody's going to buy these records, your talkin' about deep stuff here, this is not going to sell...' well, we didn't care.

Joni Mitchell wrote "Woodstock" for CSN&Y to record for the movie about the Woodstock festival. Also released on CSN&Y's second album Déjà Vu, "Woodstock" told the story of the festival in a very symbolic manner. It was as if the singer was a person meeting others on the way to Woodstock.

The most interesting thing about this song was that its writer never made it to the concert. The song captured the spirit of the festival with the author never stepping one foot on Max Yasgur's farm. "The deprivation of being stuck in a New York hotel room and not being able to go provided me with an intense angle on Woodstock," Joni Mitchell remembered.

I was one of the fans. I was in the position of being a kid who couldn't make it. So I was glued to the media.... Woodstock, for some reason, impressed me as being a modern miracle.... For a herd of people that large to cooperate so well, it was pretty remarkable and there was a tremendous optimism. So I wrote the song "Woodstock" out of these feelings....

Crosby, Stills, Nash & Young became famously connected with Woodstock because of their excellent performance, the song they recorded written by Joni Mitchell and the fact that Woodstock introduced their new musical collaboration to the nation. They went on to write some very poignant protest songs, especially between the years 1969 and 1971. Crosby, the most rebellious musician of the group, gained this reputation while in the Byrds and his presence at Monterey Pop. Crosby's songs on CS&N's debut album included "Long Time Gone" about the Robert Kennedy assassination and a number called "Wooden Ships" that he wrote with Steven Stills and Paul Kantner of Jefferson Airplane.

"Wooden Ships" (performed by both Jefferson Airplane and Crosby, Stills & Nash at Woodstock) was a frightening story about people who escaped from a nuclear holocaust into the sea. The song starts with a line that symbolizes the whole philosophy of the hippies. It explains that smiling is the one form of communication that crosses all language boundaries. The song then addressed the issue of war by bringing together two soldiers from opposite sides, both asking the same question: "who won the war?" After pointing out that it didn't matter what side of the war someone was on, the theme of brotherhood was continued in the third verse where they share food. The lyrics endorsed the utopian ethic of sharing everything. This philosophy, incidentally, is very similar to that which the Wobblies and American communists endorsed. The final verses of the song protested the possibility of nuclear war and symbolized the wish of American youth to escape this destruction with a lover.

"You Don't Have To Cry," written by Steven Stills made a statement against the middle-class work ethic of a 9 to 5 job. In "You Don't Have To Cry" Stills told listeners that even though they were living a life they didn't like, they didn't "have to cry," they only had to change their life. He asked people in contemporary society to question what some have described as a rat race. The song concluded with the listener knowing that the singer once lived in the business world of schedules and bosses, but now has the "time to cry" because he left to pursue a life with less worries and obligations.

Crosby, Stills & Nash's second album entitled Déjà Vu, included the work of Neil Young. A few of the songs carried messages of protest without any blatant finger pointing or name calling. The album itself tried to connect with the people of the "Woodstock Nation." "Teach Your Children" had a message of reaching out to the older generation for understanding and learning. It was followed by "Almost Cut My Hair" which told others to "let their freak flag fly." These songs set the tone for the first side. The second side of the record opened with "Woodstock" and its message of unity and jubilation. This was followed by the title song where Crosby wondered what was really "going on" in the nation. Little did he know that less than a few months later the National Guard would open fire on college students at Kent State in Ohio.

In May of 1970, college campuses were full of unrest primarily due to Nixon's announcement on April 30, 1970, that American and South Vietnamese forces invaded Cambodia to destroy North Vietnamese and Vietcong bases of operations. The next day students at Kent State held a burial ceremony for the US Constitution. On the evening of May 1, the downtown area witnessed property damage and arrests. On May 2, students tried to burn down the campus ROTC building. Only two hours later, over a thousand National Guard troops arrived at the campus. Neither the presence of the National Guard or Governor Rhodes' condemnation decreased the tension. That evening there was more destruction and arrests. On Monday morning while many students were returning from home and going to class, others gathered in the main commons area of the campus. The National Guard read the riot act and students responded with rocks and the Guard's own tear gas canisters. At around 12:30 the Guard fired into the crowd, killing four people and wounding nine.

Neil Young wrote a song of protest about the murders at Kent State. "Ohio" was released as a single in June 4, 1970; only a month after the shootings stunned the nation. Graham Nash loved the song as soon as he heard it. "It floored us," Nash told Rolling Stone. "We went into the studio the next night and it took us an hour and a half to cut it. And we really meant it. Take that for whatever you feel, but we meant it."

David Crosby was with Neil Young when the song was written. Crosby remembered:

> After National Guardsman fired on students at Kent State and killed people, I watched Neil Young see, really see, that famous picture of the girl kneeling over the dead kid, looking up as if to say, 'Why?' I handed him the guitar and watched him write the song.... I got on the phone and called the guys in LA and said, 'Book the studio, man. This is it. Get the studio time tonight. I don't care where. This is important.' I got Neil to the airport and we got on a plane and we flew down. We recorded it that night with "Find the Cost of Freedom" on the back side of it. Gave it to Ahmet Ertegun... and the record was out within days. It was on the street within a week of the event. With a finger pointed right where the guilt lay: Nixon and the warmongers. At that point, we were powerful. We affected the world...

In between touring and recording, CSN&Y went off to record their own solo albums. In 1970 Steven Stills recorded his self-titled LP which included "Love the One You're With" promoting the counter-culture lifestyle. In the same year Neil Young recorded After the Gold Rush which included his second major song of protest, "Southern

Man." This song attacked racism and discrimination and condemned the "southern man" for perpetuating this hatred. It was such a powerful song that it invoked a response from Lynyrd Skynyrd with their "Sweet Home Alabama."

David Crosby kept busy with If I Could Only Remember My Name released in February of 1971. The album included Young, Nash as well as Jerry Garcia and Phil Lesh of the Grateful Dead. The first song on the record was "Music is Love" which summed up his philosophy that music was the way to freedom and peace. "Laughing" was Crosby's way of telling his fans that nobody knows all the answers to all the serious questions about American society. "What Are Their Names" was Crosby's statement against the power structure in America. "I don't dig politics," Crosby told Rolling Stone in 1970. "I don't think politics is a workable system any more. I think they gotta invent something better.... It's really not happening for me to live in a country where they gun people down in the streets just for that, for saying they don't dig it that way." In the lyrics to "What Are Their Names," Crosby clearly expressed his dissatisfaction with American leadership.

Graham Nash's first solo album titled Songs for Beginners, released in May of 1971, contained two very specific songs of protest: "Military Madness" and "Chicago/We Can Change the World." "Military Madness" protested the military influence in people's lives. In 1971 the war in Vietnam was still raging and the nation's colleges were in chaos resulting from Nixon's policy of expanding the war into Cambodia. Nash reacted to this environment of chaos: "You could say from a very early age I've been aware of the absurdity of war. There is always one side that wins out economically and industrially because they were the ones who manufactured the war and weapons. It's happening today and it is no different." In "Military Madness," Nash sang about his significant memories of war that remain in his past. He also questioned American involvement in Vietnam.

"Chicago" was Nash's top ten hit that protested the treatment of those on trial for inciting a riot outside the 1968 Democratic National Convention in Chicago. The defendants included: Tom Hayden and Rennie Davis of SDS, Abbie Hoffman and Jerry Rubin of the radical Yippies, Black Panther Bobby Seale, and anti-war activist Dave Dellinger. Crosby, Stills, Nash & Young were invited to make an appearance at a benefit concert for those on trial. Nash and Crosby wanted to perform but Young and Stills did not. Nash said, "I wrote this song to Neil and Stephen and to everybody that I thought might want to hear about the fact that what was happening to the Chicago Seven (sic) wasn't fair." During the trial Bobby Seale demanded that he be allowed to defend himself but was denied that right. When he continued to address the court, the judge told Seale that he would be restrained if necessary. The next day the judge had Seale "gagged and chained" to his chair. Nash sang about the trial and called on everyone who believed in freedom and justice to come and lend a hand.

Nash went on to write other good protest songs with his friend David Crosby and on his own. Two that really stand out are "Immigration Man" released on <u>Graham Nash/David Crosby</u> in April 1972 and "Prison Song" released on <u>Wild Tales</u> in January 1974. "Immigration Man" was Nash's protest against the constraints and red tape used by the government to keep people out of the US. Nash sang about trying to get in and out of the country. "Prison Song" was a protest against US marijuana laws where he pointed out the unbalanced privileges given to the affluent and the unfair system of bail that keeps the poor in jail while letting the rich go free. Nash sang about how rich people get away with things that poor people do not.

In the summer of 1970 Steven Stills incorporated his old hit "For What It's Worth" into a CSN&Y tour. He adapted the song, "49 Bye-Byes," by combining the lyrics of "'For What It's Worth" and new words that were relevant to the problems of the time. Released on <u>4 Way Street,</u> the recording was titled "America's Children." The song was like a talking protest blues performed with a piano instead of a guitar. It even compared American non-violent revolutionaries with Jesus Christ.

While Crosby, Stills, Nash & Young believed in the causes they sang about, they did not let the issue of protest dictate their music. Graham Nash tried to explain his topical material: "What we've been trying to do as musicians is to entice people to think more, to find out more information, and to figure out something they can do. Everyone here can make a difference...." While making music about issues that truly affect their lives, these musicians believed that topical songs are only one aspect of a musician's repertoire. David Crosby believed that limitations exist between topical material and a musician. He explained:

> The only time that songwriters... should react to what's going on is when they are absolutely moved to do so. When it just smacks them in the face and they gotta react. I don't think you oughta go out and look for

causes, in order to have a cause, or because it's hip this week. I don't think you should take a political stance. I don't think it has anything to do with making music at all.

The protest-rock music of the late sixties and early seventies represented a new generation of troubadours and troublemakers that developed in the midst of the civil rights movement, the anti-war movement, political assassinations and the urban riots of the sixties. The issues they addressed were different from those of the revolutionaries, settlers, slaves, soldiers, abolitionists, miners, unionists, Wobblies, okies and folkies but their spirit of protest was the same. The musical protest minstrels of the sixties rock era expressed messages of opposition against social repression, war, and racism. The called for individuality, freedom, peace and civil rights for everyone. They protesting for free speech, free love and even a free lunch. These new troubadours and troublemakers created a distinctive style of music taken from the roots of jazz and blues in order to carry their new messages of protest. The artists of protest-rock were entertainers' first and social commentators second. They did not lead the sixties movement for social and political change in the United States, but they certainly mirrored society's will to protest the undesirable conditions in their country and to search for solutions. Arguably the most popular troubadour and troublemaker of the rock era was John Lennon.

Chapter Eleven:
John Lennon: A Minstrel of Radical Protest

The war is over. If you want it.

John & Yoko

While most writers and performers of protest songs in the late sixties and early seventies were entertainers who communicated messages of dissent, John Lennon was a rock star who evolved into a minstrel of protest. After leaving the Beatles, Lennon dedicated his life and music to causes of protest as Joe Hill did three generations earlier. Lennon used his rock-star image as a former Beatle to express messages of protest about the society he lived in. His music and politics were built on the traditions of protest developed by generations of troubadours and troublemakers before him, while taking on his own audience and issues. Out of all the singer-songwriters and groups discussed in the last chapter only John Lennon became a troubadour and troublemaker of protest music like Joe Hill, Woody Guthrie, Pete Seeger, Bob Dylan and Phil Ochs before him. When Lennon stopped writing topical songs, he marked the symbolic end to an era of popular rock-protest songwriting representing the politics of the American counter-culture and the New Left. He wasn't the last troubadour and troublemaker, he was only another link *in the chain* in the evolution of American protest music.

John Lennon started his career as a rebellious rock'n'roll musician in the clubs of Liverpool and Hamburg. Lennon was influenced a great deal by youth culture developing in fifties' America. Similar to Bob Dylan, Lennon reacted to the three American movies, *Rebel Without a Cause, The Wild One,* and *Blackboard Jungle.* He was fascinated by the rebellious nature of the teenagers and the excitement created by the music. During this period, he was also obsessed with the music and persona of Elvis Presley. This fixation with rock and rebellion led to the formation of the Quarrymen, the Silver Beatles, and then the Beatles. As young musicians in Liverpool and Hamburg, the Beatles embodied what Lennon always wanted to be; a rebellious rocker. When John Lennon, Paul McCartney, George Harrison, and Ringo Starr hired Brian Epstein as their manager, however, they accepted certain restrictions on their appearance, personal lives and political opinions. Epstein marketed the Beatles as the 'good boys' of rock'n'roll and expected them to keep up certain public appearances. Lennon was reprimanded whenever he expressed any aspects of protest, and he usually capitulated to the demands. In his 1980 interview for <u>Playboy</u>, Lennon reflected on the control the Beatles ceded to Epstein:

> For years, on the Beatles tours, Brian Epstein had stopped us from saying (anything) about Vietnam or the war. And he wouldn't allow questions about it. But on the last tours, I said, 'I'm going to answer (questions) about the war. We can't ignore it.' I absolutely wanted the Beatles to say something about the war.

After becoming a massive pop star with the Beatles, Lennon began to speak out about controversial subjects. By 1965 and 1966 the war in Vietnam was growing in scope and producing reverberations within American society. "We think of it every day," Lennon said. "We don't like it. We don't agree with it. We think it's wrong." This opposition to the Vietnam War did not create as much of a firestorm as when Lennon said, "the Beatles are more popular than Jesus...." This statement was Lennon's way of protesting youth's pre-occupation with rock'n'roll. Lennon used the term "Beatles" to symbolize the rock "scene" in America and Britain. From his point of view, the frenzy created by the presence of the Beatles meant that American and British teenagers were more excited by Beatles music than anything else.

Drugs were a major influence on Lennon's musical development and counter-culture persona. In fact, Lennon attributed the Beatles' discovery of marijuana to Bob Dylan. "He first turned us on in London," Lennon recalled the evening at the St. Regis Hotel in 1964. "He thought 'I Want To Hold Your Hand,' when it goes 'I can't hide'- He thought we were saying 'I get high'- so he turns us on, and we had the biggest laugh all night... We've got a lot to thank him for." Many of Lennon's songs have been attributed to the influence of LSD and marijuana. The most notable were "She Said, She Said," "Doctor Robert," "Tomorrow Never Knows," "Strawberry Fields Forever," "Lucy In The Sky With Diamonds" and "I Am A Walrus." However introspective or musically complex the songs were, Lennon didn't express a political opinion in his songs until 1968 when the Beatles were very near the end of their partnership and protest-rock was already accepted among mainstream record buyers.

"Revolution," on the flip side of the enormous hit "Hey Jude," was the first Lennon song that expressed a political position. By August of 1968 when "Revolution" was released, the United States and Europe were engulfed in waves of student protests against the Vietnam War, civil injustice and restrictions on free speech. Both Martin L. King and Bobby Kennedy were dead and the American Left was splitting on the tactics needed to stop the war. When Lennon saw on British television the demonstrations outside the American Embassy in London, he was inspired to write the song "Revolution." The young people Lennon saw were protesting England's support for United States actions in Vietnam. "Revolution" was a statement against the use of violence in the pursuit of social and political change. Even though Lennon and the Beatles were important symbols to the ideas of revolution, they still believed that love and flowers were the best way to change the world.

The first verse of "Revolution" exhibited Lennon's indecision about supporting violence in the name of peace and justice. In the version released as a single, Lennon sang that he wanted to be "out" of the destruction. In the version released on the two record set dubbed the White Album, Lennon suggested that he might be getting "in" the revolution. This indecision signified his fragile dedication to non-violence. Lennon spoke about the song in 1971:

> There were two versions of that song, but the underground Left only picked up on the one that said 'count me out.' The original version which ends up on the LP said 'count me in' too; I put in both because I wasn't sure.

In the second verse, Lennon showed the world that he was serious about the need for revolution. He sang his support for change as long as a good plan existed that everyone could follow. He also rejected the funding of radical causes that promote violence and hatred.

The third verse exhibited Lennon's opinion about how to go about the revolution. Instead of changing the US Constitution or its institutions directly, Lennon wanted to revolutionize peoples thinking and the way they live. He also rejected the revolutionary principles of certain American Marxists who followed the course laid out by Mao Zedong. Lennon reflected on the meaning of the song in his Playboy interview.

The lyrics still stand today. There're still my feeling about politics: I want to see the plan. That is what I used to say to Jerry Rubin and Abbie Hoffman. Count me out if it's for violence. Don't expect me on the barricades unless it is with flowers. As far as overthrowing something in the name of Marxism of Christianity, I want to know what you're going to do *after* you've knocked it all down. I mean, can't we use *some* of it? What's the point of bombing Wall Street? If you want to change the system, change the system. It's no good shooting people.

The song is almost anti-revolution, especially when he criticized radicals who believed communism was the way to freedom, justice, and equality. Lennon said in 1971:

I didn't really know that much about the Maoists but I just knew that they seemed to be so few and yet they painted themselves green and stood in front of the police waiting to get picked off.... I thought the original communist revolutionaries coordinated themselves a bit better and didn't go around shouting about it.

When "Hey Jude" reached number one on the Billboard charts, with "Revolution" on its flip side, pictures of the violent clashes between protesters and Chicago police were in magazines, on television sets and on the minds of many Americans. In August of 1968 Soviet troops invaded Czechoslovakia and almost a quarter of a million Mexican students protested the Presidency of Gustavo Diaz Ordaz. It really seemed that the world was in revolution.

Two months after "Revolution" entered the airways, John and Yoko released Two Virgins. Recorded the night they first made love, the album was the most avant-garde recording of Lennon's career. The most controversial aspect of the album was the photograph on its cover. John and Yoko appeared nude, standing, holding hands, and looking into the camera. The reverse side was the couple standing with their rears to the camera. By appearing nude on the album cover, Lennon had accomplished two substantial things; one was the expression of protest against society's sexual norms and the other was a challenge to mainstream concepts of art and pornography. By making the ultimate protest against American standards of decency, Lennon damaged his popularity with mainstream society and alienated himself from the working class of America. The idea of someone posing nude for an album cover, in itself, was a revolutionary statement coming from a pop star. The album also sparked an interest by the FBI, for J. Edgar Hoover investigated anyone that looked like a part of radical America.

The use of nudity to protest society's mores was also a component of a rock musical on Broadway called *Hair*. It began as an experiment in "free-form" theater on October 17, 1967, at the Public Theater in East Village New York. After limited success in East Village, a producer was found and *Hair* opened on Broadway April 29, 1968. It ran for over seventeen hundred performances but finally lowered the curtain on July 1, 1972. The play was an examination of Claude, the main character, as he decided between going to war in compliance with the draft, or avoid it by escaping to Canada. The position of the American counter-culture on Vietnam was well represented with marching slogans like "Hell no we won't go" and "What do we want / Peace / When do we want it / Now." After the cast celebrated in a simulated be-in and burned their draft cards, Claude still couldn't decide whether to burn his card. Following a song by Claude, some of the cast rose from behind the stage (with dimmed lights) in the nude. In the second act, the cast tried to persuade Claude not to go to war. They sang about the "dirty little war" and all the "weapons (used) to kill." In the end Claude chose to leave his counter-culture friends and enter the jungles of Vietnam. The play ends with the cast singing "Let the Sun Shine In," celebrating their own life, and mourning Claude as a war-time casualty.

Hair was the first popular rock musical to convey a message of protest against the Vietnam War and traditional American society in general. The nudity and harsh language was directed at mainstream American society's attitude toward alternative lifestyles and hippies in general. It opened only one month before John and Yoko photographed the cover of Two Virgins. Lennon protested the social mores of American culture with Two Virgins, as *Hair* protested mainstream culture and the war in Vietnam. Lennon may not have been an American, but he certainly was in touch with American hippie culture.

After Two Virgins, John and Yoko continued their protest activities with their "bed-ins" for peace. Designed as a strategy to gain public recognition of their peace campaign, John and Yoko got married on March 20, 1969, in Gibraltar and then went to Amsterdam to begin their bed-in. In 1980 Lennon told Playboy magazine, "We knew our honeymoon was going to be public anyway, so we decided to use it to make a statement.... In effect, we were doing a commercial for peace instead of a commercial for war." In the late seventies, Lennon remembered:

> Who could forget the sight of half the world's press pushing and trampling each other at the door of our bedroom in the vain hope of seeing the Beatle and his nigger doing it for peace in the Amsterdam Hilton's honeymoon suite? Or the sighs of disappointment when it dawned on them that there was to be no sex and we weren't even naked!

After the Two Virgins record cover, many reporters probably expected them to shed their clothing and pose for the cameras.

Lennon was so excited about his marriage and the important message of the bed-in, that he wrote a song called "The Ballad of John and Yoko." He went into the studio with Paul McCartney on April 22, 1969, and recorded the song. It became number one in Britain and number eight in the United States, remaining on the US charts for a total of nine weeks. This song was a new form of songwriting for Lennon. Instead of creating images by connecting words and sentences that create meaning, Lennon wrote a story about his life and his views on certain contemporary issues. "The Ballad of John and Yoko" started him on the way towards writing more straight-forward songs of protest.

Following the success of "The Ballad of John and Yoko," Lennon tried to take his bed-in campaign to the United States. Since US Immigration denied Lennon a visa, he held the event in Montreal because of the easy access to the American press from Canada. Along with Yoko Ono, Timothy Leary, Tommy Smothers, Mick Jagger, George Harrison, and a cast of many others, Lennon recorded "Give Peace a Chance" with an eight track portable tape recorder. The song was released in the US on July 7, 1969. "Give Peace a Chance" was not only a demand for world peace; it was also a protest of political "isms" as destructive to human relations. Lennon also told everyone to cheer "for the Hippies and the Yippies" and "come together, all together."

After reaching number two in Britain and fourteen in the United States, "Give Peace A Chance" became an anthem for the American anti-war movement. On November 15, 1969, Pete Seeger led a half a million anti-war demonstrators at the Washington monument in singing "Give Peace a Chance." Lennon reacted after seeing the use of his song at the demonstration: "I saw pictures of that on British TV, with all those people singing it, forever and not stopping. It was one of the biggest moments of my life." Lennon described the bed-ins for peace as another important moment in his life.

> They were great events when you think that the world
> newspaper headlines were the fact that we were a
> married couple in bed talking about peace. It was one of
> our greater episodes. It was like being on tour without
> moving, sort of a big promotional thing. I think we did a
> good job for what we were doing, which was trying to
> get people to own up.

Lennon's peace campaign was interrupted by McCartney who wanted to go back into the studio with George Martin and produce a new album. Abbey Road was the last album they recorded as the Beatles (although Let It Be had a later release). The last song to be recorded for Abbey Road was the first on the record. John's "Come Together" was originally written for Timothy Leary's aborted California Governor Campaign. "Come Together" was also written for the counter-culture and the anti-war movement. Lennon sang that everyone must be free.

John and Yoko continued the peace campaign with their "War Is Over" advertising endeavor and a performance at a UNICEF benefit on December 15, 1969, at the Lyceum in London. They performed with George Harrison, Eric Clapton, Billy Preston, and Keith Moon. The Lennon's followed the benefit by purchasing billboard space in New York, Hollywood, Toronto, Paris, Rome, Berlin, Athens, and Tokyo. In London alone John and Yoko bought two thousand posters to proclaim their simple message of peace; large dark letters spelling "WAR IS OVER" and underneath, in much smaller print was "If You Want It, Happy Christmas from John & Yoko." John Lennon was using his popularity and wealth to help end the war just as Phil Ochs used his protest songs and pointed political commentary to do the same.

The Lennon's followed their peace campaign with the release of the single "Instant Karma" in February of 1970. Reaching number three in America, it made a positive comment about people, comparing them to astronomical objects such as the "moon...stars and the sun." Even though "Instant Karma" was not a direct protest song, it did make some socially relevant comments and certainly helped recruit more activists to their anti-war cause.

Lennon's first solo album since the breakup of the Beatles was <u>John Lennon/Plastic Ono Band</u>. It was released on December 1, 1970, after the violence at Kent State, Jackson State, and the growing militancy of the American New Left. "Working Class Hero" was the most protest oriented song on the record. Lennon used his childhood experiences to identify society's manipulation of the working masses from school age through adulthood. He also used the F-word to convey his distaste for society's expectations.

The only other song on <u>Plastic Ono Band</u> that had a message of protest was "Well Well Well." It was a brief song about the activities of John and Yoko as peace activists. "Well Well Well" was also a signal to Lennon's fans that he would be soon diving into the cause of women's liberation.

The next protest song that Lennon wrote was "Power to The People." In this song Lennon sang about the exploitation of the worker and in support of women's liberation. This number was an example of Lennon's attempt to identify with the traditional audience of protest songs: the working class. "Power to the People" was probably Lennon's most successful direct protest song. It reached number eleven in the United States and number six in Britain. In 1971 it was played on popular radio stations for over nine weeks and sold over a million copies around the world.

It was written after Lennon completed an interview with Robin Blackburn and Tariq Ali for <u>Red Mole</u>, a radical magazine in London. Lennon stated that he was giving interviews and writing protest songs to motivate people to change the world. "What I'm trying to do is to influence all the people I can influence," Lennon said.

> When I started, rock'n'roll itself was the basic revolution
> to people of my age and situation. We needed something
> loud and clear to break through all the unfeeling and
> repression that had been coming down on us as kids.

This interview in <u>Red Mole</u> clearly exhibited Lennon's growing political radicalism in favor of the working class. He stated that there can only be a revolution "by making the workers aware of the really unhappy position they are in, (and) breaking the dream they are surrounded by."

Lennon's second solo album was <u>Imagine</u>. Released on September 9, 1971, this record was another example of Lennon's increasing contribution to the protest music genre. It was his most successful album of the seventies, reaching number one in both the US and the UK. With the album on the top of the <u>Billboard</u> charts for three weeks, the title song surprisingly only reached number three in the US. "Imagine" is clearly the song that Lennon is known for around the world. It was his musical vision of the perfect society that the counter-culture had always tried to promote. "Imagine" also defined the same society that Joe Hill, Woody Guthrie, and Pete Seeger had tried to promote with their songs years before. While economic in context, "Imagine" was also the ultimate song of utopia for many non-radicals troubled by civil strife. It suggested that we eliminate the parts of human nature that cause division, hatred, and mistrust.

The other two protest songs on the album were "I Don't Want to Be a Soldier" and "Give Me Some Truth." The first song clearly set Lennon against the Vietnam War. He sang that to die was preferred to being a soldier and death was better than being a lying lawyer. The second number was an attempt to rhyme the song's words while making references to aspects of Lennon's life. He made clear attacks on American and British elite he called "uptight short-sighted narrow-minded hypocrites" and "neurotic-psychotic pig-headed politicians." Lennon made an obvious reference to the New Left's arch enemy, Richard Nixon, when he sang, "yellow bellied son of tricky dicky." Lennon also protested the lies that politicians use to remain in positions of power. Although clearly a topical song against society, it lacked a specific target for its message of protest.

Three months after Lennon recorded <u>Imagine</u>, John and Yoko went into the studio to record a Christmas song that contained their message of peace, love and protest. "Happy Xmas (War is Over)" was released in the US on December 1, 1971 and was a direct protest song against war.

In August of 1971, a month before <u>Imagine</u> was released, John and Yoko moved to America's Greenwich Village. This move caused a dramatic shift in Lennon's politics. Before leaving England, Lennon was involved in the traditional themes of protest that minstrels (pre-Dylan) traditionally engaged in; worker exploitation and censorship. While still in Britain, John and Yoko supported the striking workers in Scotland at the Upper Clydeside Shipbuilders plant. They also helped <u>OZ</u>, a radical underground magazine put on trial for contributing to the delinquency of children. Lennon acknowledged the importance of the working class in a revolution in the interview published in the Red Mole in March of 1971. "We should be trying to reach the young workers because that's when you're most idealistic and have (the) least fear," said Lennon. "Somehow the revolutionaries must approach the workers because the workers won't approach them."

After John and Yoko moved to the US in August of 1971 in search of Yoko's daughter, his politics and music moved away from the issues of the workers and towards the issues of the American Left. He met with representatives from America's radical organizations in New York: Yippies, Black Panthers, feminists, and underground radicals. All of Lennon's music from the time they moved into the United States until the re-election of Richard Nixon in November of 1972 was geared exclusively toward disseminating messages of protest for the radical American Left.

One individual from New York who influenced Lennon's music was David Peel. Peel played rock music for free in East Village, New York. Peel's radical politics were expressed in songs like "The Pope Smokes Dope" and his album Have a Marijuana. Lennon met David Peel and Jerry Rubin on Second Avenue and Ninth Street in East Village to hang out and enjoy the afternoon. They started singing "The Pope Smokes Dope" with others joining in. The police quickly appeared and made the radicals move on. Lennon wrote the song "New York City" from the experience.

The first significant American musical and political event that Lennon participated in was the John Sinclair benefit concert called *Ten for Two* on December 10, 1971. John Sinclair was a radical, political-poet who lived the counter-culture lifestyle. "Our program is Cultural Revolution through a total assault on the culture through rock'n'roll and sex in the streets," said Sinclair. "We will use every tool (and) every media we can get our hands on. We are totally committed to the revolution... (and) Rock'n'roll is the spearhead of the attack." He was arrested for giving two joints of marijuana to an undercover policeman and received a ten year sentence for his crime.

The *Ten for Two* benefit was held at the University of Michigan Chrysler Arena in the name of the John Sinclair Defense Fund. A total of sixteen thousand people listened to political speeches in favor of changing marijuana laws, in opposition to the Vietnam War and in protest against social injustice. The speakers were Rennie Davis, Dave Dellinger, Ed Sanders, Bobby Seale and Allen Ginsberg. The benefit included music by Phil Ochs, Stevie Wonder, Archie Shepp, Commander Cody, Bob Seeger, David Peel and John Sinclair's own MC5.

Sinclair's MC5 had a revolutionary philosophy for their songs. At the beginning of MC5's first record, the lead singer yelled to the audience:

> I want to hear some revolution out there brothers.... The time has come for each and every one of you to decide what you are going to be, the problem or whether you are going to be the solution....

John Sinclair also had a political purpose behind his management of the MC5.

> With our music and our economic genius we plunder the unsuspecting straight world for money and the means to revolutionize its children at the same time.... We don't have guns because we have more powerful weapons-direct access to millions of teenagers is one of our most potent, and their belief in us is another.

By the time John and Yoko arrived in Ann Arbor for the benefit, it was three o'clock in the morning. Lennon and Ono were accompanied by three acoustic guitar players and Jerry Rubin on the congas. They opened their portion of what Jerry Rubin called a "political Woodstock," with their new song about the tragedy at the Attica State Penitentiary simply titled "Attica."

On August 24, 1971, George Jackson was shot to death in Attica State Prison in New York. Following the death, about one hundred prisoners took over the facility and captured hostages. On the fifth day of the occupation, the State Correction Facility Task Force attacked the compound with helicopters, tear gas, and massive gunfire. The prisoners that survived the onslaught were stripped naked, forced to crawl in the mud, and then beaten by the institution's officers. What happened at Attica left 39 dead from gunshot wounds, 89 seriously wounded, and 3 stabbed to death (and another corrections officer later died due to complications from his wound). 10 of the 43 dead were hostages, and 8 of those 10 hostages were killed by the guns of the attacking police force.

Lennon's song about the event, "Attica State," protested this brutal attack against the prisoners and hostages and took a very unpopular stand. The song clearly blamed Governor Rockefeller for the killings and called on people to join the movement fighting for justice and civil rights.

The second song John and Yoko performed at the Sinclair benefit was Yoko's "Sisters, O Sisters," a feminist song about freedom and wisdom. They followed that with Lennon's "Luck of the Irish," a song he wrote for the thirteen civil rights' protesters in Northern Ireland who were killed by British troops.

"John Sinclair" was the final song of the evening. It was Lennon's new number written especially for Sinclair and the *Ten for Two* performance. It accused the US government of corruption and demanded Sinclair's freedom. Before performing the song, Lennon made a plea for revolution: "We came here not only to help John (Sinclair) and spotlight what's going on, but also to show and to say to all of you that apathy isn't it, and that we can do something. Oh, so flower power didn't work, so what, we start again." He was conveying to his audience that more aggressive actions may be necessary to bring about the revolutionary change the hippies and Yippies have been advocating.

In January 1972 John and Yoko were guests on the *David Frost Show*. After Lennon played "Attica State" for the television audience, he initiated discussion of the song: "I understand that society hasn't worked out what to do with people who kill and violent people. But there are a lot of people in jail who aren't violent, who don't kill, and they're in there for no reason at all, then they go mad in Jail." The audience's reaction was mixed as a heated discussion raged between Lennon and the television audience. He summed up his position when he said, "Let's make it human for them while they're in there."

Also on the *David Frost Show* Lennon performed a rendition of his new song for political radical Angela Davis. She was a highly intelligent student who graduated Phi Beta Kappa from Brandeis University. She went on to study at Sorbonne University in Paris and the University of Frankfort. Davis eventually went back to California and became a protégé of the famous Professor Marcuse at the University of California in San Diego. After being labeled a communist and terminated from the University, she challenged mainstream society and worked for various radical causes including the Soledad Brothers Defense Committee. On August 7, 1970, four heavily armed African

American convicts took five hostages, including the state District Attorney and a judge, for the release of the Soledad Brothers. Their plan was interrupted by the police who attacked the van. The result was the judge and three of the kidnapers died. The guns used in the kidnapping were traced to Angela Davis. Apparently she had purchased the weapons and was at the scene of the crime. While Davis was awaiting trial, George Jackson was killed while trying to escape jail. Lennon sang for Angela Davis, her dead lover and other political prisoners of the world.

John and Yoko continued to keep busy with causes of protest by performing music, protesting government policies and speaking to television audiences. In February of 1972, they demonstrated in New York against British policy towards Northern Ireland. A week later, the Lennon's then co-hosted the popular *Mike Douglas Show* for an entire week. Lennon introduced his own hand-picked guests and performed his protest songs for the TV audience. Lennon brought on Yippie Jerry Rubin and Black Panther Bobbie Seale, two very controversial figures from radical America. Lennon also performed with Chuck Berry on his two tunes "Memphis" and "Johnny B. Goode." On other days he performed "It's So Hard," "Imagine," "Attica State," and "Luck of the Irish." That week of New York television was probably the height of Lennon's public communication of protest messages. By singing his new protest songs to a television audience that would probably have never heard him otherwise, Lennon spread his rock-protest songs even further than his "pop" audience. By performing protest songs and initiating conversation about the messages they contained, Lennon combined two mediums to protest American society: music and television.

Lennon committed himself to the cause of women's liberation with his song "Women is the Nigger of the World." The ABC network attempted to ban the song from being performed on the *Dick Cavett Show*, but instead forced Cavett to read a disclaimer directed at their "black audience." Lennon then performed the song for the first time to the American public.

Following the performance, Lennon read a statement to the audience written by U.S. Representative from California Ron Dellums, the chairman of the Congressional Black Caucus. It defended the use of the word "nigger" in the song.

> If you define 'nigger' as someone whose lifestyle is
> defined by others, whose opportunities are defined by
> others, whose role in society is defined by others, the
> good news is you don't have to be black to be a nigger in
> this society. Most of the people in America are niggers.

The song was released as a single and barely made it to number fifty-seven.

Lennon released <u>Some Time in New York City</u> in the United States in June of 1972 to bad critical reviews and low record sales. Compared to his success as a Beatle, and his recent <u>Imagine</u> album, <u>Some Time</u>, was a failure. It only reached number 48 on the charts. It included all the political songs John and Yoko had been performing at their appearances: "Woman is the Nigger of the World," "Sisters, O Sisters," "Attica State," "Born in a Prison," "New York City," "Sunday Bloody Sunday," "The Luck of the Irish," "John Sinclair," "Angela," and "We're All Water." The record reviewer for <u>Rolling Stone</u> called it an attempt at "artistic suicide" and described the songs as "awful." It was obvious that even the counter-culture's own rock magazine was turning away from Lennon's protest music when the review said, "The tunes are shallow and derivative and the words are little more that sloppy nursery rhymes that patronize the issues and individuals they seek to exalt."

Lennon defended his music as a natural progression of his art displaying the same message in different forms. "People always talk about my music as if it's some new craze I'm into," Lennon said. "Really it's been a natural evolution from 'All You Need Is Love' to 'Give Peace A Chance' to 'Power to the People' to 'Attica State.' It's the same evolution that a lot of people have been through."

Lennon's last rehearsed concert performance was at the *One to One* benefit organized by Geraldo Rivera for mentally handicapped people at the state owned Willowbrook hospital. He played his latest biographical song, "New York City" as well as "Mother" and "Cold Turkey." The protest songs he performed included his latest single "Woman is the Nigger of the World," and "Imagine." Lennon added new anti-war significance to "Come Together" when he sang "Come together / Stop the war / Right now / Over me...." The show ended with a look at his roots with "Hound Dog." As an encore, Lennon led the band in soft reggae sounds while Yoko read a speech:

> The streets of our country are in turmoil. The
> universities are filled with students rebelling and rioting.
> Communists are seeking to destroy our country. Russia
> is threatening us with her might and the Republic is in
> danger. Yes, danger from within and without. We need
> law and order.

John interrupted her written speech with a chant "Law and Order."
Yoko continued, "Without law and order our nation cannot survive."
After reading this statement (which sounded a lot like something
Richard Nixon said during the 1972 Presidential Campaign), Yoko told
the audience that the speech was written in 1932 by Adolf Hitler.
Lennon then led the crowd in singing "Give Peace a Chance" mixed
with his chants: "No more war. No more four more years. No more
nothing. We don't need it." While Yoko compared Nixon to Hitler,
Lennon used "Give Peace a Chance" to protest Nixon and his policy of
fighting the Vietnam War. Segments of the performance were broadcast
on ABC television on December 15, 1972, shortly after Nixon was re-
elected President by every state in the union except Massachusetts.

The *One to One* concert was Lennon's last serious statement of
protest using his music. The performance raised money for a cause that
was difficult for conservatives to argue with. Mentally handicapped
people who are abused usually gain sympathy with mainstream
America. The politics around the *One to One* concert was very different
from the politics of bringing radicals Jerry Rubin and Davis Seale on
the *Mike Douglas Show*. Jon Wiener believes the *One to One* concert
was Lennon's effort to improve his image with the American public.

Some Time in New York City exhibited Lennon's inability to
successfully write protest songs the way Phil Ochs and Bob Dylan did
so masterfully. After its commercial failure, Lennon seemed to abandon
the concept that songs should directly reflect the radical news of the
day. He abandoned music collaboration with Yoko and concentrating
on more personally reflective songs. By avoiding 'finger pointing'
songwriting, Lennon's next album was well-received, while still
conveying messages of protest and youth solidarity.

Mind Games (which he originally intended to name it "Make Love
Not War") was released in the US November 2, 1973 and by the end of
the month reached number nine on the charts. The "Mind Games"
single, released a few days earlier, only reached eighteen on the charts,
but was a signal of Lennon's new approach to political songwriting.

"Mind Games" reminded Lennon's fans that John and Yoko had "planted (the) seeds" of revolution by their activities with American radicals. It also reinforced his original message as a Beatle and peace activist that "love is the answer." The song seemed to signal a less aggressive approach toward political activism.

Included with the <u>Mind Games</u> album was a small book that contained information about creating a new nation called "Nutopia." The last song on the first side was a three second cut called: "Nutopian National Anthem." It was three seconds of silence. In the spring of 1973 Lennon held a press conference to announce the creation of a new nation:

> We announce the birth of a conceptual country, Nutopia. Citizenship of the country can be obtained by declaration of your awareness of Nutopia. Nutopia has no land, no boundaries, no passports, only people. Nutopia has no laws other than cosmic. All people of Nutopia are ambassadors of the country. As two ambassadors of Nutopia, we ask for diplomatic immunity and recognition in the United Nations of our country and its people.

The two other songs on <u>Mind Games</u> that contained messages of protest were "Only People" and "Bring On the Lucie (Freda People)." "Only People" was similar to the theme in "Mind Games" in that it urged other people to change the world through peace and cooperation. Lennon reminded the movement that everyone must work together to force change. He sang that people cannot depend on organizations or governments to improve human relations and increase personal freedom. "Only People" called on all men and women to fight together against the Orwellian totalitarian controls of the American state that repressed its own people and conducted a war against other peoples. "Bring on the Lucie (Freda People)," was a direct attack on President Nixon. It also displayed Lennon's anger over his growing problem with the US Immigration Service. In March of 1973, the Immigration Service told Lennon that he must leave the country or face deportation. "Bring on the Lucie" is clearly a protest against these hassles throughout 1973 and into 1974. Without mentioning him by name, Lennon clearly identified Nixon as guilty of crimes against humanity in Vietnam and warned him that "da people" will ruin his Presidency.

It turned out that Lennon was completely correct when he said that the US government was watching him and tapping his phones. Following a lengthy battle with the FBI, investigator Jon Wiener finally received John Lennon's "confidential" FBI files. As documented in his book, Gimme Some Truth: The John Lennon FBI Files, Wiener showed that Lennon was under surveillance from at least December 1971 through May of 1972. The FBI believed that Lennon was a dangerous revolutionary that needed to be stopped. In one document released to Wiener, the FBI included the entire lyrics to the song "John Sinclair" as an example of sedition. The FBI considered protecting the Nixon presidency more important than the 1st Amendment's guarantee of free speech.

In 1974 Lennon recorded his first number one hit since the beginning of his solo career. "Whatever Gets You Thru the Night" reached the top on November 16, 1974. That same year also marked Lennon's last concert appearance when he performed with Elton John at Madison Square Garden on November 28, 1974. It was a bet between the two musicians that Lennon's song would reach number one on the Billboard charts. Elton John won the bet and Lennon reluctantly agreed to make the guest appearance.

By 1975 Lennon traded in his political activism and music career for domestic life at the Dakota in Greenwich Village with Yoko and their new son Sean. In October, Lennon finally received a reprieve from his four year battle with the United States Immigration Service. The judge in the case, Irving Kaufman, sided in Lennon's favor and said, "Lennon's four year battle to remain in our country is testimony to his faith in the American dream."

With his permanent residency established, Lennon was finally able to relax and enjoy his new home in America. He concentrated on raising Sean while living a solitary life without recording music or making public performances. After five years of musical silence, however, Lennon went back into the studio with Yoko and recorded a new collection of songs. On December 8, 1980, less than a month after they released Double Fantasy, Lennon was shot outside his home in New York City. The world was rocked by the senseless murder. The man who sang that "happiness is a warm gun" died by the hand of a madman with the help of a *warm gun.*

The protest music of John Lennon can be summed up with words written by Paul Hodson: "Lennon's political songs were not an instrument for change, just an expression of the need for it." His protest music did not change society; it only reflected some of its problems. "Attica State" did not free any prisoners or change the penal system; "Angela" did not influence the outcome of her murder trial; "Women is the Nigger of the World" did not change men's attitude toward women; and "Imagine" did not create a utopia where people can live together in peace and harmony. Lennon did not change the world, but he expressed the counter-culture's desire for peace, and the New Left's radical demand for political and social change.

Similarities exist between the legend of Joe Hill and the memory of John Lennon. Both men immigrated to the United States to live in peace, with liberty and freedom. They both found problems in America and tried to fix them. Hill objected to the economic exploitation of the working class and sought to overthrow the capitalist system, while Lennon protested political oppression, the war in Vietnam and mainstream social mores. By adopting positions against the American government, both men were looked upon as enemies of the state and labeled traitorous. Hill's trial and execution was seen as synonymous with the repression of the Wobblies and Lennon's deportation case was a direct by-product of the US government's fighting back against the radical New Left.

An interesting irony also exists when the circumstances surrounding the death of these two men is compared. Joe Hill was executed during a wave of political oppression directed against the IWW and symbolized government repression of radical labor. Lennon, on the other hand, was not killed by the authorities but by one of his fans. It was one of the millions of people who helped make Lennon a rock star, who took away the gift of life and ended the musical career of a brilliant artist. Even though Hill and Lennon died for different reasons and by different hands, both men symbolized musical protest to the people they sang their songs for.

While both Hill and Lennon were from Europe and writers of American protest songs, their message, audience and genre of music were different. Where Hill protested economic exploitation and promoted the destruction of capitalism, Lennon sought to stop a war in Vietnam and protest social and political restrictions in American society. While Hill identified with exploited industrial workers, Lennon's main audience was students and political radicals. Where Hill adapted his songs from religious hymns and Tin Pan Alley pop tunes, Lennon wrote his own material in the style of rock music. The similarities and differences between Joe Hill and John Lennon symbolize the twentieth century evolution of protest music in American culture from focusing on economics to concentrating on individuality. Where Joe Hill focused on economic injustice John Lennon concentrated on freedom and liberty.

Protest music did not end with the death of John Lennon; his murder only symbolized the end of an era. John Lennon was not a leader in protest singing or a cultural revolution; he was only one *link in the chain* of musical troubadours and troublemakers from the original American colonists of the 17th century to the rockers and rappers of the 21st century. What followed the death of Lennon was a continuation of that tradition into the musical genres of punk, heavy metal and hip hop. Throughout the 80s, 90s, and 2000s, protest music flourished and continued to evolve into new forms of rhythm and rhyme with new messages of protest and dissent.

Conclusions:
Protest Traditions Popularized

Music has the power to cross borders,
to break military sieges and to establish
real dialogue.

Zack de la Rocha

American protest music is not only a reflection of people who have something to say, it is linked in history from the earliest days of Europeans and Africans on this continent to the contemporary musical troubadours and troublemakers of the current generation. The music of settlers, revolutionaries, migrants, slaves, abolitionists, soldiers, miners, unionists, Wobblies, okies, folkies, and rockers are all connected by their desire to attract outside support, promote solidarity, recruit new adherents to their ideas, reinforce their value system, point out issues and invoke solutions.

At the beginning of the American nation, singing protest songs was considered radical and revolutionary, while by the late 1960s and early 1970s, protest songs became not only standard on popular radio stations across America, but protest singers themselves were seen as American heroes. Slaves who sang an obvious protest song would have been punished or sold; abolitionists who spoke out against slavery were ostracized, persecuted and sometimes physically attacked; Wobblies were arrested and beaten for singing and speaking out for their rights; Joe Hill was probably executed for a murder he did not commit, because of the songs he wrote; Woody Guthrie was condemned because he sang for unionists and communists; and Pete Seeger was blacklisted for his union, communist and progressive connections.

But by the 1960s, American attitudes started to change. Bob Dylan emerged just as the 1960s began and he was not only idolized by American youth for his songs and political stances, he was accepted by mainstream America and its media as a cultural icon. His songs were more pointed and considerably more radical than most of what Joe, Woody, or Pete ever wrote or sang, but instead of being vilified and blacklisted he was admired and revered. Dylan has received multiple awards and honors including the Presidential Medal of Freedom, solely because of the songs he wrote. See the next page for a comprehensive listing of the awards and honors received by Bob Dylan.

One Academy Award: 2001 Best Original Song "Things Have Changed" from the film Wonder Boys

One Golden Globe Award: 2001 Best Original Song "Things Have Changed" from the film Wonder Boys

11 Grammy Awards:
1973 Album of the Year: Concert for Bangladesh
1980 Best Rock Male Vocal Performance: "Gotta Serve Somebody"
1990 Best Rock Performance by a Duo or Group with Vocal (with the Traveling Wilburys): Traveling Wilburys Vol. 1
1992 Lifetime Achievement Award
1995 Best Traditional Folk Album: World Gone Wrong
1998 Album of the Year: Time Out of Mind
1998 Best Contemporary Folk Album: Time Out of Mind
1998 Best Rock Vocal Male Performance: "Cold Irons Bound"
2002 Best Contemporary Folk Album: Love and Theft
2007 Best Male Solo Rock Performance: "Someday Baby"
2007 Best Contemporary Folk/Americana Album: Modern Times

Six songs/albums entered into the Grammy Hall of Fame
1994 "Blowin' in the Wind" 1963 Folk Single
1998 "Like a Rolling Stone" 1965 Rock Single
1999 Blonde on Blonde 1966 Rock Album
2002 "Mr. Tambourine Man" 1965 Rock Track
2002 Highway 61 Revisited 1965 Rock Album
2006 Bringing It All Back Home 1965 Rock Album

Rock and Roll Hall of Fame
1988 inducted Bob Dylan as Performer
Five songs by Bob Dylan were chosen as among the 500 songs that shaped rock and roll.
1963 "Blowin' in the Wind"
1963 "The Times They Are a-Changin'"
1965 "Like a Rolling Stone"
1965 "Subterranean Homesick Blues"
1975 "Tangled Up in Blue"

Other honors
1963 Recipient of the Tom Paine Award
1970 Recipient of Honorary PhD of Music, Princeton University, NJ
1982 Inducted into Songwriters Hall of Fame
1990 Honored by the Commandeur des Arts et des Lettres
1997 Honored by the Kennedy Center Honors
1997 Recipient of The Dorothy and Lillian Gish Prize

2000 Winner of the Polar Music Prize
2002 Inducted into the Nashville Songwriters Hall of Fame
2004 Recipient of Honorary PhD of Music, St. Andrews University, Scotland
2007 Winner of the Prince of Asturias Awards
2008 Winner of the Pulitzer Prize Special Citations and Awards
2009 Honored by the National Medal of Arts
2012 Presidential Medal of Freedom Recipient
2013 Recipient of the Officier de la Legion d'honneur

The rockers of the 1960s like Crosby, Stills and Nash and members of Jefferson Airplane made millions of dollars and were able to live opulent lifestyles because of the popularity of the protest songs they wrote and sang. While Lennon was harassed by the American government in the early 1970s because of a small drug arrest in London years earlier, he was loved by the record buying public and many in mainstream America. Once President Nixon's political power waned amidst Vietnam and Watergate, Lennon finally received his green card and permanent permission to stay in America.

By the 1970s protest singers were among the people Americans most admired and topical singing spread throughout pop culture. Rock concerts with themes of protest grew following Monterey and Woodstock into events like the *Festival for Peace, Concert for Bangladesh, Live Aid* and *Farm Aid*. Protest singing against racism and Vietnam continued in the 1970s with songs like Edwin Star's "War," Marvin Gaye's "What's Going On," Bob Marley's "Get Up, Stand Up," James Brown's "Say It Loud- I'm Black and Proud," Gil Scott-Heron's "The Revolution Will Not Be Televised" and Grandmaster Flash's "The Message."

The eighties and nineties continued the legacy of singing songs of protest. Rock legend Bruce Springsteen railed against the conditions of Vietnam War veterans with "Born in the USA" and police brutality with "American Skin (41 shots)." Other artists such as Billy Bragg wrote and sang songs for the improvement of working and living conditions of the world's industrial laborers with songs like "Great Leap Forwards." Punk legends Dead Kennedys also contributed to the genre with "Stars and Stripes of Corruption" while Rage Against the Machine performed their "Killing In The Name."

In 2006 singer-songwriter Neil Young (well-known for his collaboration with Crosby, Stills & Nash and solo performances) dedicated an entire album, called Living with War, to protest the war in

Iraq and the Presidency of George W. Bush. The first four songs on the album protested war, consumerism and government propaganda. Two other songs on the album that included clear condemnations of President George W. Bush were "Let's Impeach the President" and "Looking for a Leader."

Utah Phillips continued the legacy of singing union, IWW and Joe Hill songs until his death in 2008. In the nineties, Phillips joined up with Ani Defranco to perform new songs of protest. Defranco had been writing and performing her own songs of protest regarding sexuality, discrimination, consumerism and war with songs like "Self Evident." In 2012 Defranco released an entire album with themes of protest called Which Side Are You On to positive critical reviews.

In the 1990s and 2000s Hip Hop bands and artists continued the protest tradition in new forms of rhythm and melody. N.W.A. sang "Fuck the Police," Public Enemy chanted "Fight the Power," Jay Z released "Open Letter," Nas wrote "America" and 2Pac adapted Bruce Hornsby's "Changes" for a new generation. These troubadours and troublemakers sang songs protesting police brutality, economic injustice and racism.

From the seventeenth century to the twenty first century, troubadours and troublemakers have been singing songs of protest. Topical singing is a form of political expression that is as American as apple pie, baseball and the 4th of July. The subjects of the songs may have changed, but the spirit has continued unabated. The songs of settlers, revolutionaries, migrants, slaves, soldiers, abolitionists, miners, unionists, Wobblies, okies, folkies, rockers, and rappers have attracted outside support for their cause, promoted solidarity among their group, recruited new members to their cause, reinforced the value system of their participants, pointed out issues that need to be addressed and invoked possible solutions to the problems in society. By understanding the protest songs of the past and appreciating the protest songs of the present, we may be able to more willingly accept the protest songs of the future.

Post Script:

While writing this book, one of my favorite musicians passed away. Pete Seeger died January 28, 2013 at the age of 94. Throughout his life Pete Seeger fought against the establishment for the right to speak and sing freely. He fought for civil rights, peace and a clean environment. He was blacklisted by the music industry and indicted by the American government. In 1993 he was finally recognized with a Grammy, in 1994 he was awarded the National Medal of Arts from the National Endowment for the Arts and also received the Kennedy Center Honors. And in 1996 he was finally inducted into the *Rock and Roll Hall of Fame*.

Following his death in January, the outpouring of love and appreciation for his life, activism, and music was overwhelming in both traditional and social media. Written tributes and videos of his performances and interviews flooded YouTube, Facebook and other outlets. I personally think one of the best tributes was given by former NPR broadcaster Paul Brown: "If Pete Seeger didn't save the world, he certainly did change the lives of millions of people by leading them to sing, to take action and to at least consider his dream of what society could be." I believe that Pete Seeger was the greatest and most influential troubadour and troublemaker in the evolution of American protest music. I am glad I had the opportunity to meet him and shake his hand.

If there is a line in human literature that applies to Pete Seeger, it is the following: "How can I keep from singing?"

We will miss you Pete.
R.I.P.

Acknowledgments:

Thanks to all the Troubadours & Troublemakers that have paved the way for current and future singers, writers and collectors of American protest songs.

I would especially like to thank my former students for encouraging me to finish this project; my brother David Comtois for playing all those Beatles records when we were kids; my wife Maxine for her continuous support and contributions, including all the illustrations contained herein; my friend Dave McInnis and my Uncle Richard Arsenault for editing the early drafts of this work; my extended family for all their support over the years, especially the Roy family!; and my parents for giving me life, their unconditional love and consistent encouragement.

Thanks to everyone who took some time to assist in the editing process. Any errors that remain are my responsibility alone.

Additional thanks:

Robert Thomas, "Here's To the State of Barack Obama" (unrecorded) © 2013 by Robert Thomas. Used by Permission.

All Illustrations by J. Maxine Shaw

Author photo courtesy of Mike Dean

Cover photo by the author

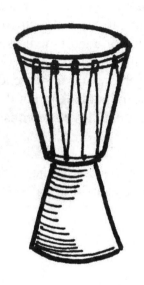

Appendix:
Slave Song List

Below is a comprehensive alphabetical listing of slave songs. Some of these are still being sung and recorded today. Many of these are segments of songs that have not been sung for years (and probably never recorded). Many titles are in the dialect of the original singers or those who compiled the songs. Much of this dialect is considered to be part of the Gullah language found mostly in South Carolina and Georgia. According to Alphonso Brown, an expert on Gullah culture: "There are no 'th' sounds in most African languages, and many blacks, even today, have difficulty pronouncing words like this, that, these, them and they. Dis, dat, dees, dem and dey are much easier." I have attempted to maintain the original spelling whenever I could in order to provide the dialect of the creators of this music. Some of this original spelling was changed when published and is now forever lost.

I have a couple of suggestions as you review these titles: First, pay attention to the overwhelming prevalence of songs with a religious theme. This attests to the importance of faith in African American communities. Secondly, note that many of these song titles are full of double entendre that could be interpreted in many ways. For example the song "Don't You Grieve After Me" is not only a message to family and loved ones not to cry when the singer dies, but also not to be sad when the singer escapes north to freedom.

A Balm In Gilead
Adam in the Garden Pinnin' Leaves
Ain't Goin' to Study War No Mo
Ain'y You Glad Got Good Religion
All God's Children Got Wings
A Little Talk wid Jesus Makes It Right
All God's Chillun Got Wings
All I Do, de Church Keep A-Grumblin'
Almost Over
Archangel, Open the Door
Aurore Brandaire
Away Down in Sunbury
Bell da Ring
Belle Layotte
The Blood-Strained Banders
Blow Your Trumpet, Gabriel
The Blind Man

Bound to Go
Brother Guide Me Home
Brother Moses Gone
Brudder Moses
Build A House in Paradise
By an' By
Calinda
Calvary
Canaan
Can't Stan' de Fier
Can't You Live Humble
Captain Holler Hurry
Caroline
Charleston Gals
Chilly Water
Children do Linger
Children We Shall Be Free

Choose You a Seat 'n' Set Dowm
Come Along, Moses
Come Go With Me
Come Here Lord!
Cott'n Pickin' Song
Couldn't Hear Nobody Pray
Crucifixion
Daniel Saw de Stone
Dark Was The Night
Dat Lonesome Stream
Day of Judgment
De Angel Roll de Stone Away
De Angels in Heab'n Gwineter
        Write My Name
Death Come to My House He
        Didn't Stay Long
Death's Gwinter Lay His Cold
        Icy Hands on Me
De Band o' Gideon
De Blind Man Stood on de Road an' Cried
Deep River
De Ol' Sheep Done Know de Road
Dear'e a Hand Witin' on de Wall
Dere's No Hidin' Place Down Dere
Dem Bones
Didn't My Lord Deliver Daniel
Didn't Old Pharaoh Get Los'?
Didn't You Hear?
Die in de Fiel'
Dives and Laz'us
Do Don't Touch-A My Garment, Good
        Lord, I'm Gwine Home
Done Foun' My Los' Sheep
Don't Be Weary, Traveler
Don't You Grieve After Me
Early in the Morning
Everywhere I Go My Lord
Every Hour in the Day
Ev'ry Time I Feel de Spirit
Fare Ye Well
Father Abraham
Follow The Drinking Gourd
Gimme dat Ol'-Time Religion
Gimme Yo'Han'
Git on Board, Little Chillen
Give Me Jesus
Give Up the World
Glory to that New-Born King

God Don't Like It
Go Down Moses
Go in the Wilderness
God Don't Like It
God Got Plenty O' Room
God Moves On the Water
God's a-Gwine ter Move All
        de Troubles Away
God's A-Gwinter Trouble de Water
Goin' to Shout All Over God's Heaven
The Gold Band
The Golden Altar
Good-bye
Good-bye, Brother
Good-bye, Mother
Good Morning Everybody
Good News, Chariot's Comin'!
Good News, Member
The Good Old Way
The Graveyard
Great Day
Got No Travellin' Shoes
Great Camp Meeting
Gwine Follow
Gwineter Ride Up in de Chariot Soon-a
        In de Mornin'
Gwine Up
Gwinter Sing All Along de Way
Hail, Mary
Hallelujah!
Haliela, Hallelu
Happy Morning
Hard Trials
Healin' Waters
Heave Away
Heaven Bell a-Ring
The Heaven Bells
Heaven, Heaven
Heav'n Boun' Soldier
Hell and Heaven
He's Jus' de Same Today
Hol' de Win'Don't Let It Blow
Hold Out to the End
Hold Your Light
Hinder Me Knot
Humble Yo'self de Bell Done Ring
Hunting for a City
Hunting for the Lord

The Hypocrite and the Concubine
I Am So Glad
I an' Satan Had a Race
I Can't Stand the Fire
I Can't Stay Behind
I Couldn't Hear Nobody Pray
I Done What Ya' Tol' Me to Do
I Don't Feel Weary
I Feel Like My Time Ain't Long
I Got a Home in-a Dat Rock
I Got Shoes
I Heard de Preachin' of de Word o' God
I Hear From Heaven Today
I Know de Lord's Laid His Hands on Me
I Know When I'm Going Home
I Feel Like My Time Ain't Long
If I Had My Way
If I Have My Ticket
I'm Gwine Up to Heab'n Anyhow
I'm a-Rolling Through
       an Unfriendly World
I'm a-Trouble in de Mind
I'm Crossing Jordan River
I'm Going Home
I'm Gwine to Alabamy
I'm In Trouble
In dat Great Gittin' Up Mornin'
In the Army of the Lord
In The Mansions Above
I Saw the Beam in my Sister's Eye
Israelites Shouting
I thank God I'm Free at Last
It's Getting' Late Over In the Evenin'
It's Me, O, Lord
I've Found Free Grace
I Want God's Heab'n to Be Mine
I Want to Die Easy When I Die
I Want to Die Like-a Lazarus Die
I Want to Go Home
I Want to Join the Band
I Wish I Been Dere
Jacob's ladder
Jehovah, Hallelujah
Jesus On the Waterside
Jesus, Won't You Come By-and-bye
Jimmy Bell's In Town
Jine 'em
Job, Job

John, John, Of the Holy Order
John the Angel Band
John the Revelator
John Saw the Holy Number
John Was A-Writin'
Jordan's Mills
Joshua Fit the Battle of Jericho
Jubilee
Just Now
Keep A-Inchin' Along
Keep Me from Sinking Down
King David
King Emanuel
Lay This Body Down
Lean On the Lord's Aide
Let God's Saints Come In
Let Me Ride
Listen to de Lambs
Little Black Train Is a-Comin'
Little Children, Then Won't
       You Be Glad?
Little David Play Your Harp
Lolotte
The Lonesome Valley
Long John
Look-a How Dey Done My Lord
Look What A Wonder Jesus Done
The Lord Delivered Daniel
Lord, I Want to Be a Christian
Lord, Make Me More Patient
Lord, Remember
Low Down the Chariot and Let Me Ride
Man Goin' Round
Many Thousan' Gone
Mary Had a Baby, Hey, Lord
Meet, O Lord
Members, Don't Git Weary
Michael Row the Boat Ashore
Moanin'
Mone, Member, Mone
Mos' Done Tollin' Here
Move, Members, Move
My Army Cross Over
My Body Rock 'Long Fever
My Father, How Long?
My God Aint No Lyin' Man
My Name's Been Written Down
My Lord's A-Waitin' All de Time

My Lord Says He's Gwinter
Rain Down Fire
My Lord, What a Morning
My Ship Is on de Ocean
My Soul's Been Anchored in de Lord
My Way's Cloudy
Musieu Bainjo
Never Said a Mumbalin' Word
Noah Hoist the Window
Noah, Noah
Nobody Knows the Trouble I See
No Man Can Hinder Me
No More Rain Fall For Wet You
Not Weary Yet
O Brothers, Don't Get Weary
O Daniel
O de Vinter
O'er the Crossing
O Ev'ry Time I Feel de Spirit
O, Gambler, Git Up Off o' Yo' Knees
Oh' Freedom
Oh, Hear Me Prayin'
Oh, Lawd, How Long?
Oh My God Them Taters
Oh, My Good Lord, Show Me de Way
Oh, Yes! Oh, Yes! Wait 'till I Git
On My Babe
Ol' Ark's A-Moverin'
The Old Ship of Zion
O Mother I believe
On to Glory
O Ride On, Jesus
O, Rocks Don't Fall on Me
O Shout Away
Over My Head
O, Wasn't Dat a Wide River?
O Yonder's My Ole Mother
Peter, Go Ring Dem Bells
Po' Mourner's Got a Home at las'
Poor Rosy
Praise, Member
Pray All de Member
Pray On
Precious Lord, Take My Hand
Rain Fall and Wet Becca Lawton
Reborn Again
Religion is a Fortune I Really do Believe
Religion So Sweet

Remon
The Resurrection Morn
Ride on, Moses
Rise, Mourner, Rise
Rise Up, Shepard an' Foller
Rock Chariot, I told You to Rock
Rock O' Jubilee
Rock O' My Soul
Roll de Ol' Chariot Along
Roll Jordan Roll
Round the Corn, Sally
Run, Nigger, Run
Run, Mary Run
Run To Jesus
Russia, Let That Moon Alone
Sabbath Has No End
Sail, O' Believer
Same Train
Samson
Satan's Camp A-fire
Set Down, Servant
Shall I Die
Shock Along, John
Shout All Over God's Heab'n
Shout for Joy
Shout On Children
Ship of Zion
Sinner Please
Sinner, Please Don't Let Dis Harves' Pass
Sinner Won't Die No More
The Sin-Sick Soul
Sittin' Down Beside the Lamb
The Social Band
Somebody's Knockin' at Yo'Do'
Somebody's Talking About Jesus
Sometimes I Feel Like a Motherless Child
Some Train
Soon One Mornin' Death Come Creepin'
Singin' Wid a Swaard in Ma Han'
Stan' Still Jordan
Steal Away to Jesus
Some Valiant Soldier
Stars Begin to Fall
Swing Low, Sweet Chariot
The Sun Will Never Go Down
Tell My Jesus Morning
There's a Meeting Here Tonight
These Are All My father's Children

This Is the Trouble of the World
This May Be Your Last Time
This Train
Tip Around My Bed Right Easy
'Tis Me, O Lord
Too Late
Tone de Bell Easy
To See God's Bleedin' Lam'
Travel On
Traveling Shoes
The Trouble of the World
Turn Sinner, Turn
Until I Reach-a Ma Home
Up on de Mountain
Wade in the Water, Children
Wai' Poor Daniel
Wake Up, Jacob
Wake Up Jonah
Walk about Elders
Walk in Jerusalem Jus' Like John
Walk, Mary, Down de Lane
Walk Together Children, Don't You Get Weary
Walt, Mr. Mackright
Wasn't That a Mighty Day
Water Boy, Where Are You Hidin'?
Way Bye and Bye
We Am Clim'in' Jacobs Ladder
Weary Traveler

Where Were You When They
       Crucified My Lord?
We Shall Be Free
We Will March Through the Valley
Woe Be Unto You
Wonder Where Is My Brother Gone
What a Trying Game
What Yo' Gwine to Do When Yo'
       Lamp Burn Down
When I Die
When I Fall on my Knees
When Jesus Met the Woman at the Well
When My Blood Runs Chilly and Col'
When We Do Meet Again
Where Shall I Be When de
       Firs' Trumpet Soun'
The White Marble Stone
Who Dat A-Comin'Ovah Yondah?
Who Is On the Lord's Side
Who'll Be a Witness for My Lord?
What Month Was Jesus Born In
When You Feel Like Moaning
Who will Deliver Po' Me
The Winter
Wrestle On, Jacob
You Go, I'll Go wid You
You Got a Right
You May Bury Me in de Eas'
You Mus' Hab Dat True religion
You Must Be Pure and Holy
'Zekiel Saw de Whee

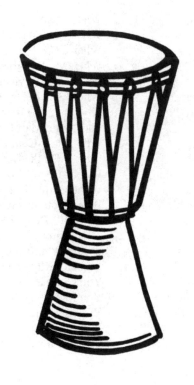

Selected Bibliography
Publications

E. Lawrence Abel, <u>Singing the New Nation: How Music Shaped the Confederacy 1861-1865</u>, Mechanicsburg, PA: Stackpole Books, 2000.

William M. Adler, <u>The Man Who Never Died: The Life, Times, and Legacy of Joe Hill, American Labor Icon</u>, New York: Bloomsbury, 2011.

Steven Ambrose, <u>Eisenhower: The President</u>, New York: Simon & Schuster, 1984.

William Francis Allen, <u>Slave Songs of the United States</u>, Bedford, MA: Applewood Books, 1867.

Michael Barone, <u>Our Country: The Shaping of America from Roosevelt to Reagan</u>, New York: The Free Press, 1990.

Stewart Bird, Dan Georgakas, and Deborah Shaffer, editors, <u>Solidarity Forever. An Oral History of the IWW</u>, Chicago: Lake View Press, 1985.

Taylor Branch, <u>Parting the Waters: America in the King Years, 1954-63</u>, New York: Simon & Schuster, Inc., 1988.

Richard Brazier, "The Story of the IWW's 'Little Red Songbook" <u>Labor History 9</u> (Winter 1968).

Paul Brissenden, <u>IWW: A Study of American Syndicalism</u>, New York: Columbia University, 1920.

Fred Bronson, <u>The Billboard Book of Number One Hits</u>, New York; Billboard Publications, 1988.

Alphonso Brown, <u>A Gullah Guide to Charleston: Walking Through Black History</u>, Charleston, SC: History Press, 2008, 2013.

Michael Brown, ed., <u>Politics and Anti-Politics of the Young</u>, Beverly Hills, CA: Glencoe Press, 1969.

Peter Brown and Steven Gaines, <u>The Love You Make: Beatles</u>, New York: Penguin Books, 1983.

Betsy Bowden, Performed Literature: Words and Music by Bob Dylan, Bloomington: Indiana University Press, 1982.

Joseph Bruchac, Poetry of Pop, Paradise CA: Dustbooks, 1973.
Mitchell Cohen & Dennis Hale, The New Student Left: An Anthology, Boston: Beacon Press, 1966, 1967.

Ray Coleman, Lennon, (New York: McGraw-Hill Book Company, 1984, 1986.

Steve Chapple & Reebee Garofalo, Rock & Roll Is Here To Pay, Chicago: Nelson Hall, 1977.

Ed Cray, Ramblin' Man: The Life and Times of Woody Guthrie, New York: W.W. Norton, 2004.

Ace Collins, Songs Sung Red White and Blue: The Stories Behind America's Best Loved Patriotic Songs, New York: Harper Collins, 2003.

Harold Courlander, Negro Folk Music U.S.A., New York: Dover Publications, 1963, 1992.

Richard Crawford, Americas Musical Life: A History, New York: WW Norton, 2001.

---. The Civil War Songbook: Complete Original Sheet Music for 37 Songs, New York: Dover Publications, Inc., 1977.

David Crosby with Carl Gottlieb, Long Time Gone: The Autobiography of David Crosby, New York: Doubleday, 1988.

Natalie Curtis-Burlin, Negro Folk Songs: The Hampton Series, Books I-IV Complete, Toronto Canada: General Publishing Group, 1918, 2001.

Robert F. Cushman, Cases in Constitutional Law: Sixth Edition, New Jersey: Prentice-Hall, Inc., 1984.

Peter Davies, The Truth about Kent State: A Challenge to the American Conscience, New York: Farrar Straus Giroux, 1973.

R. Serge Denisoff and David Fandray, " 'Hey, Hey Woody Guthrie I Wrote You A Song': The Political Side of Bob Dylan," Popular Music and Society 5 (1977).

R. Serge Denisoff, "The Proletarian Renascence: The Folkness of the Ideological Folk." Journal of American Folklore 82 (1969).

---. "'Take It Easy, But Take It' The Almanac Singers" Journal of American Folklore 83 (1970).

---. "Folk-Rock: Folk Music, Protest, or Commercialism?" Journal of Popular Culture 3 (1969).

---. Great Day Coming, Chicago: University of Illinois Press, 1971.

Robin Denselow, When the Music's Over: The Story of Political Pop, London: Faber and Faber, 1989.

John P. Diggins, The American Left in the Twentieth Century, New York: Harcourt, Brace, Jovanovich, Inc., 1973.

William Tulio Divale with James Joseph, I Lived Inside the Campus Revolution, New York: Cowles Book Company, 1970.

Robert Draper, Rolling Stone Magazine: The Uncensored History, New York: Harper Perennial, 1990, 1991.

W.E.B. Dubois, The Souls of Black Folk, New York, New York, Fawcett Publications, Inc., 1903, 1961.

Melvyn Dubofsky, We Shall Be All: A History of the Industrial Workers of the World, Chicago: Quandrangle Books, 1969.

David King Dunaway, How Can I Keep From Singing: Pete Seeger, New York: McGraw-Hill Book Co., 1981.

Bob Dylan, Chronicles Volume One, New York: Simon & Shuster, 2004.

---. Writings and Drawings, New York: Alfred A. Knopf, Inc., 1973.

---. Lyrics: 1962-2001, New York: Simon & Shuster, 2004.

Miles Mark Fisher, Negro Slave Songs in the United States, New York: Carol Publishing Group, 1953, 1981, 1990.

Philip Foner, History of the Labor Movement in the United States Volume 4: The Industrial Workers of the World 1905-1917, New York: International Publishers, 1965, 1997

Edith Fowke & Joe Glazer, <u>Songs of Work and Protest: 100 Favorite Songs of American Workers Complete Workers with Music and Historical Notes</u>, New York, Dover Publications, Inc., 1960, 1973

Simon Frith, <u>Sound Effects: Youth, Leisure, and the Politics of Rock'n'Roll</u>, New York: Pantheon Books, 1981.

Paul Fussell, <u>The Great War And Modern Memory</u>, London: Oxford University Press, 1975.

John S. Gambs, <u>The Decline of the IWW</u>, New York: Russell & Russell, 1932, 1966.

John A. Garraty, "Radicalism in the Great Depression" in Leon Borden ed., <u>Essays on Radicalism</u>, Austin: University Of Texas Press, 1972.

Gordon Hall Gerould, <u>The Ballad of Tradition</u>, New York: Oxford University Press, 1932, 1957

Joe Glazer, <u>Labor's Troubadour</u>, Urbana and Chicago: University of Illinois Press, 2001

Tom Glazer, <u>Songs of Peace, Freedom, and Protest</u>, New York: David McKay Company, Inc., 1970.

Albert Goldman, <u>The Lives of John Lennon</u>, New York: William Morrow and Company, 1988.

Michael Gray, <u>Song & Dance Man: The Art of Bob Dylan</u>, New York: Octagon Books, 1977.

Archie Green, David Roediger, Franklin Rosemont, and Salvatore Salerno, editors, <u>The Big Red Songbook</u>, Chicago: Charles H Kerr Publishing Company, 2007

Archie Green, <u>Only A Miner: Studies In Recorded Coal Mining Songs</u>, Chicago: University of Illinois Press, 1972.

---. <u>Wobblies, Pile Butts, and Other Heroes: Laborlore Explorations</u>, Urbana and Chicago: University of Illinois Press, 1993.

John Greenway, <u>American Folksongs of Protest</u>, New York: A.S. Barnes & Company, 1953, 1960.

Woody Guthrie, <u>Bound for Glory</u>, New York: Penguin Books, 1943, 1971.

---. <u>House of Earth</u>, New York: Harper Collins Publishers, 2013.

---. <u>Seeds of Man</u>, New York, E.P. Dutton & Co., Inc., 1976.

Wayne Hampton, <u>Guerrilla Minstrels</u>, Knoxville: University of Tennessee Press, 1986.

Bill Harry, <u>The Book of Lennon</u>, New York: Putnam Publishing Group, 1984.

David Hajdu, <u>Positively 4th Street: The Lives and Times of Joan Baez, Bob Dylan, Mimi Baez Farina and Richard Farina</u>, New York: Farrar, Straus and Giroux, 2001.

Clark D. Halker, <u>For Democracy, Workers, And God: Labor Song-Poems and Labor Protest, 1865-95</u>, Chicago: University of Illinois Press, 1991.

Charles Hamm, <u>Yesterdays: Popular Song in America</u>. New York: W.W. Norton & Company, 1979.

---. "Songs of the Civil War," Liner Notes to <u>Songs of the Civil War</u>, New World Records, NW 202-2.

James Haskins, <u>Black Music in America: A History Through Its People</u>, New York: Harper Collins, 1987.

Tom Hayden, <u>Reunion: A Memoir</u>, New York: Random House, 1988.

Abbie Hoffman, "Revolution For The Hell Of It," <u>The Best of Abbie Hoffman</u>, Daniel Simon ed., with the Author, New York: Four Walls Eight Windows, 1968, 1990.

Jerry Hopkins, <u>Festival: The Book of American Music Celebrations</u>, Toronto, Ontario: Macmillan Company, 1969.

Thomas Jefferson <u>Notes on the State of Virginia</u>, Chapel Hill: University of North Carolina Press, 1787, 1982.

Marty Jezer, <u>Dark Ages: Life in the United States 1945-1960</u>, Boston: South End Press, 1982.

James Weldon Johnson & J. Rosamond Johnson, <u>The Books of American Negro Spirituals</u>, Boston, MA: Da Capo Press, 1925, 1926, 1953.

Charles Kaiser, <u>1968 in America: Music, Politics, Chaos, Counterculture, and the Shaping of a Generation</u>, New York: Weidenfeld & Nicolson, 1988.

Joseph Kelner and James Munves, <u>The Kent State Coverup</u>, New York: Harper & Row Publishers, 1980.

Martin Luther King Jr. <u>Stride Toward Freedom: The Montgomery Story</u>, San Francisco: Harper & Row, 1958.

Joe Klein, <u>Woody Guthrie: A Life</u>, New York: Octagon Books, 1977.

Joyce L. Kornbluh, ed., <u>Rebel Voices: An Anthology</u>, Ann Arbor: The University of Michigan Press, 1964.

John Lennon, <u>Skywriting by Word of Mouth</u>, New York: Harper & Row Publishers, 1986.

Maryl Levine and John Naisbitt, <u>Right On: A Documentary on Student Protest</u>, New York: Bantam Books, 1970.

George H. Lewis, "The Pop Artist and His Product: Mixed-Up Confusion," <u>Journal of Popular Culture</u> 4 (1970).

John A Lomax and Alan Lomax, <u>American Ballads and Folk Songs</u>, New York: Dover Publications, Inc., 1934, 1994.

---. <u>Our Singing Country: Folk Songs and Ballads</u>, New York: Dover Publications, 1941, 2000.

Robbie Lieberman, <u>"My Song is My Weapon": People's Songs, American Communism, and the Politics of Culture 1930-1950</u>, Chicago: University of Illinois Press, 1989.

Norman Mailer, <u>Miami and The Siege of Chicago: An Informal History of the American Political Conventions of 1968</u>, London: Weidenfeld and Nicolson, 1968.

Joel Makower, ed., <u>Woodstock: The Oral History</u>, New York: Doubleday, 1989.

Linda Martin & Kerry Segrave, <u>Anti-Rock: The Opposition to RocknRoll</u>, New York, Da Capo Press, 1988, 1993.

Peter McCabe and Robert D. Schonfeld, John Lennon: For The Record, New York: Bantam Books, 1984.

Douglas Messerli, ed., Listen to the Mockingbird: American Folksongs and Popular Music Lyrics of the 19th Century, Los Angeles: Green Integer Books, 2005.

Wilfred Mellers, A Darker Shade of Pale: A Backdrop to Bob Dylan, New York: Oxford University Press, 1985.

Craig McGregor ed., Bob Dylan The Early Years: A Retrospective, New York: Da Capo Press, Inc., 1972, 1990.

Keith and Rusty McNeil, Civil War Songbook, Riverside California, WEM Records, 1999.

---. Colonial & Revolution Songbook, Riverside California, WEM Records, 1996.

---. Moving West Songbook, Riverside California, WEM Records, 2003.

James A. Michener, Kent State: What Happened and Why, New York: Random House, 1971.

Barry Miles, Ginsberg: A Biography, New York; Harper Perennial, 1989.

Juliet Haines Mofford, editor, Talkin' Union: The American Labor Movement, Perspectives on History Series, Carlisle, Massachusetts: Discovery Enterprises, Ltd., 1997.

Hugh Mooney, "Just Before Rock: Pop Music 1950-1953 Reconsidered." Popular Music and Society 3 (1974).

Richard B. Morris, ed., Encyclopedia of American History, Harper and Row, 1982.

William H. Nault, ed., The Americana Annual 1969: An Encyclopedia of the Events of 1968 Chicago: Field Enterprises Educational Corporation, 1969.

Richard Newman, Go Down, Moses: Celebrating the African-American Spiritual, New York: Clarkson Potter Publishers, 1998.

Philip Norman, Shout!: The Beatles in Their Generation, New York: Simon & Schuster, 1981.

Ronald J. Oakley, God's Country: America in the Fifties. New York: Dembner Books, 1986.

Mike Olszewski, "Lennon vs U.S." Lennon: A Decade Later the Legacy Continues, Masters of Rock, Vol. 1, No. 2, 1990, 32.

Richard H. Pells, Radical Visions and the American Dreams: Culture and Social Thought in the Depression Years, New York: Harper & Row, 1973.

Pat Perrin, ed., The Underground Railroad: Life on the Road to Freedom, Carlisle, MA: Discovery Enterprises Ltd., 1995, 1999.

Stephen K. Peoples, ed., Monterey International Pop Festival: liner notes.

Charles Perry, The Haight-Ashbury: A History, New York: Random House, 1984.

John Phillips with Jim Jerome, Papa John: An Autobiography, New York: Doubleday & Company, Inc., 1986.

Theodore Raph, ed., The American Song Treasury: 100 Favorites, New York: Dover Publications, Inc., 1964.

Jerome L. Rodnitzky, Minstrels of the Dawn: The Folk-Protest Singer as a Cultural Hero, Chicago: Nelson-Hall, 1976.

Shelly Romalis, Piston Packin' Mama: Aunt Molly Jackson and the Politics of Folksong, Urbana: University of Illinois Press, 1999.

Franklin Rosemont, Joe Hill: The IWW & the Making of a Revolutionary Workingclass Counterculture, Chicago: Charles H. Kerr Publishing Company, 2002, 2003.

Joel Rosenman, John Roberts and Robert Pilpel, Young Men With Unlimited Capital: The Behind-the-Scenes Story of Woodstock, New York: Bantam Books, 1974.

Richard A. Reuss, "Woody Guthrie and His Folk Tradition," Journal of American Folklore 83 (1970).

---. Songs of American Labor, Industrialization and the Urban Work Experience: A Discography, University of Michigan: Program on Workers Culture of Labor Studies Center, Institute of Labor and Industrial Relations, 1983

Stanley Richards, Great Rock Musicals, New York: Stein and Day Publishers, 1979, 1980.

Jerome L. Rodnitsky, "The Evolution of the American Protest Song," Journal of Popular Culture 3 (1969).

Theodore Rosak, The Making of the Counter Culture: Reflections on the Technocratic Society and its Youthful Opposition, New York: Doubleday & Company, Inc., 1968.

Barbara Rowes, Grace Slick: The Biography, Garden City, NY: Doubleday & Company, Inc., 1980.

Stanley Sadie, ed., The New Grove Dictionary of Music and Musicians, Volume II, Second Edition, London: Macmillan Publishers, 2001.

Salvatore Salerno, ed. Direct Action & Sabotage: Three Classic IWW Pamphlets from the 1910s, Chicago: Charles H. Kerr Publishing Company, 1997.

Robert Santelli, ed., American Roots Music, New York: Ginger Group Productions, 2001.

Anthony Scaduto, Bob Dylan: An Intimate Biography, New York: Grosset & Dunlap, 1971.

Eric von Schmidt & Jim Rooney, Baby, Let Me Follow You Down: The Illustrated Story of the Cambridge Folk Years, New York: Anchor Books, 1979.

Michael Schumaker, There But For Fortune: The Life of Phil Ochs, New York: Hyperion, 1996.

Pete Seeger & Rob Reiser, Carry It On: The Story of America's Working People in Song and Picture, Bethlehem, PA, A Sing Out Publication, 1985, 1991.

Pete Seeger, The Incomplete Folksinger, Lincoln: University of Nebraska Press, 1972, 1992.

---. <u>Where Have All The Flowers Gone: A Singer's Stories, Songs, Seeds, Robberies,</u> Bethlehem, PA: 1993.

Irwin Silber, compiled and edited, <u>Songs of the Civil War,</u> New York: Dover Publications Inc., 1960, 1988, 1995.

---. compiled and edited, <u>Songs of the American West,</u> New York: Dover Publications Inc., 1967, 1995.

Andrew Solt and Sam Egan, ed., <u>Imagine: John Lennon,</u> New York: Macmillan Publishing Company, 1988.

Howard Sounds, <u>Down the Highway: The Life of Bob Dylan,</u> New York: Grove Press, 2001.

Larry D. Spence, "Berkeley: What It Demonstrates," in Brown, ed., <u>The Politics and Anti-Politics of the Young</u>. Beverly Hills, CA: Glencoe Press, 1969.

Jon Michael Spencer, <u>Protest & Praise: Sacred Music of Black Religion</u>. Minneapolis: Fortress Press, 1990.

Bob Spitz, <u>Barefoot in Babylon: The Creation of the Woodstock Music Festival 1969,</u> New York: W.W. Norton & Company, 1979, 1989.

---. <u>Dylan: A Biography</u>. New York: W.W. Norton & Co., 1991.

David Sheff, interviewer, <u>All We Are Saying: The Last Major Interview with John Lennon and Yoko Ono,</u> New York: St. Martin's Griffin, 1981, 2000.

Robert Shelton, <u>No Direction Home: The Life and Music of Bob Dylan,</u> William Morrow and Company Inc., 1986.

Gibbs M. Smith, <u>Labor Martyr: Joe Hill,</u> New York: Grosset & Dunlap, 1969.

Geoffrey Stokes, "The Sixties," <u>Rock of Ages: The Rolling Stone History of Rock & Roll,</u> New York: Rolling Stone Press, 1986.

John Steinbeck, <u>The Grapes of Wrath,</u> New York: The Viking Press, 1939.

I. F. Stone, <u>The Killings At Kent State: How Murder Went Unpunished,</u> New York: Random House, 1970, 1971.

Joe Stuessy, <u>Rock and Roll: Its History and Stylistic Development,</u>
Englewood, New Jersey: Prentice Hall, 1990.

Walbrook D. Swank, ed., <u>Ballads of the North and South in the Civil War:</u>
<u>Civil War Heritage Series Volume VIII,</u> Mineral, VA: Burd Street Press,
1996.

Elizabeth Thomson and David Gutman, ed., <u>The Lennon Companion: Twenty-</u>
<u>five Years of Comment,</u> New York: Schirmer Books, 1987.

Howard Thurman, <u>Deep River and The Negro Spiritual Speaks of Life and</u>
<u>Death,</u> Richmond, Indiana: Friends United Press, 1975, 1999.

Derik Taylor, <u>It Was Twenty Years Ago Today,</u> New York: Simon & Sc, Inc.
1987.

Stuart Taylor and Richard Shuntick <u>Violence at Kent State: May 1 to 4, 1970,</u>
New York: College Notes & Texts Inc., 1971.

Irwin Unger and Debi Unger, <u>Turning Point: 1968,</u> New York: Charles
Scribner's Sons, 1988.

Various Editors, <u>The Report of the President's Commission on Campus</u>
<u>Unrest,</u> New York: Arno Press, 1970 (Pgs. 291-410).

Jacques Vassel, <u>Electric Children: Roots and Branches of Modern Folkrock,</u>
Translated by Paul Barnett. New York: Taplinger Publishing Company, 1976.

Michael Wadleigh and Bob Maurice <u>Woodstock: Three Days of Music, Peace</u>
<u>and Love,</u> Wadleigh-Maurice, Ltd. Production, Warner Brothers, 1970.

Bruce Watson, <u>Bread & Roses: Mills, Migrants, and the Struggle for the</u>
<u>American Dream,</u> New York: Penguin Group, 2005.

Robert Weir, <u>Beyond the Labor's Veil: The Culture of the Nights of Labor,</u>
University Park PA: The Pennsylvania State University Press, 1996

Jann Wenner, ed., <u>The Rolling Stone Interviews: 1967-1980,</u> New York:
Rolling Stone Press, 1981.

Jann Wenner, ed. <u>Rolling Stone Magazine</u>
    23 November 1967, pg. 7.
    11 May 1968, 1, pg. 22.

26 October 1968, pg. 24.
23 November 1968, 14.
23 July 1970, pgs. 20-22.
8 July 1971, pg. 10.
19 August 1971, pg. 19.
2 September 1971, pgs. 6, 8, 12.
17 February 1972, pgs. 6-10.
20 July 1972, pg. 48.

Newman J. White, American Negro Folk Songs, Hatboro, PA: Folklore Assoc., Inc., 1965.

Tom Wicker, A Time To Die, New York: Quadrangle, 1975.

Jon Wiener, Come Together: John Lennon In His Time, New York: Random House, 1984.

---. Gimme Some Truth: The John Lennon FBI Files, Berkeley: University of California Press, 1999.

Sean Wilentz and Greil Marcus, The Rose & The Briar: Death, Love and Liberty in the American Ballad, Doomed Lovers, Highway Shooters, A Nation Lost and Found, New York: WW Norton & Company, 2005.

Doris Willens, Lonesome Traveler: The Life of Lee Hays, New York: W.W. Norton & Company, 1988.

Donald E. Winters, Soul of the Wobblies: The I.W.W., Religion, and America in the Progressive Era, London: Greenwood Press, 1985.

John Work, American Negro Songs: 230 Folk Songs and Spirituals, Religious and Secular, Mineola, New York: Dover Pub., 1940, 1998.

Charles Wolfe and Kip Lornell, The Life and Legend of Leadbelly, New York: Harper Collins Publishers, 1992, 1994.

Ronald D. Cohen & Dave Samuelson, Songs for Political Action: Folkmusic, Topical Songs and the American Left, 1926-1953, (Book accompanying 10 cd set), Bear Family Records, Hambergen, Germany: 1996.

Milton Viorst, Fire in the Streets: America in the 1960's, New York: Simon and Schuster, 1979.

Israel Young, "Bob Dylan," East Village Other, October 1965.

Video Documentaries

Berkeley in the Sixties, a documentary directed by Mark Kitchel, Public Broadcasting System, 1990

Biography: Bob Dylan, A&E Television Networks, 2000

Eyes on the Prize II, America at the Racial Crossroads, Written, Produced, and Directed by Terry Kay Rockfeller, Thomas Ott, and Louis Massiah, (Blackside Inc., 1990), documentary on PBS

Festival: Joan Baez, Bob Dylan, Peter Paul & Mary, Donovan Filmed at the Newport Folk Festival, Patchke Productions, 1967

John Lennon: Live in New York City, Seghmet Production in association with Ono Films, 1985

Let Freedom Sing: How Music Inspired the Civil Rights Movement, Rhythm Mass Productions/Time Life, 2009

Long Time Comin', (Vidiots, Inc., 1990), Documentary Written, Produced, and Directed by Malcolm Leo, Malcolm Leo Production, 1990

Making Sense of the Sixties: Part One, Seeds of the Sixties, Part Two, We Can Change the World, Part Three, Breaking Boundaries, Testing Limits, and Part Five, Picking Up the Pieces, PBS, WETA/Varied Directions International, 1991

No Direction Home: Bob Dylan, A Martin Scorsese Picture, Spitfire Holdings Inc, 2005

The Other Side of the Mirror: Bob Dylan Live at the Newport Folk Festival, 1963-1965, Columbia Performance Series, MFL Productions, 2007

Pete Seeger: The Power of Song, Live Nation Worldwide, Inc., 2007

Phil Ochs: There But for Fortune, Kenneth Bowser, available on http://www.pbs.org/wnet/americanmasters/episodes/phil-ochs-there-but-for-fortune/watch-the-full-documentary/1962/ (accessed (September 19, 2013)

Woody Guthrie: This Machine Kills Fascists, Snapper Music 2005

Woody Guthrie; Ain't Got No Home, American Masters, PBS Home Video, Peter Franklin Productions, 2006

Audio Recordings

Any comprehensive music discography would be an entire book in itself. The records in this list are those that contain a song or songs that I refer to in the book and those that I suggest for further listening. Most of the discs listed here are still available.

Almanac Singers, Talking Union, Folkways FH 5285

Louis Armstrong, The Definitive Louis Armstrong: Ken Burns Jazz, Sony Music, CK 61440

The Beach Boys, Pet Sounds, Capital Records, 72435-26266-2-5

---. Sounds of Summer: The Very Best of the Beach Boys, Capital Records, 72435-82710-2-7

The Beatles, Abbey Road, Capital SN-16068

---. The Beatles (aka The White Album), Capital CDP 7 464442

---. Past Masters: Volume Two, Capitol CDP 7 900442

---. Rubber Soul, Capitol Records CDP 7 46440 2

---. Revolver, Capital records CDP 7 46441 2

Buffalo Springfield, Retrospective: The Best of Buffalo Springfield, Atco 38-105-2

The Byrds, The Byrds: Box Set, Columbia/Legacy C4K 46773

---. The Byrds- Original Singles: 1965-1976/Volume I, Columbia CK 37335

Chuck Berry, The Definitive Collection, Geffen Records, B0004417-02

Country Joe and the Fish, The Life and Times of Country Joe and the Fish, Vanguard VSD 27/28

---. Together, Vanguard VSD - 79277

Crosby, Stills, Nash, Crosby, Stills & Nash, Atlantic 19117-2

---. Crosby Stills & Nash: Box Set, Atlantic 782319-2

Crosby, Stills, Nash, & Young, Déjà Vu, Atlantic SD 19118-2.

---. 4 Way Street, Atlantic 7 82408-02

David Crosby, If I Could Only Remember My Name.... Atlantic 7203-2

Dick Dale, King of the Surf Guitar: The Best of Dick Dale & His Del-Tones, Rhino Records, R2-75756

The Doors, Morrison Hotel, Electra, R2 101173

---. Waiting for the Sun, Electra, R2 101191

Willie Dixon, Poet of the Blues, Columbia, CK65593

Bob Dylan, Another Side of Bob Dylan, Columbia CK 8993

---. Blond on Blond, Columbia, CGK 841

---. Bob Dylan, Columbia CK 8579

---. Bringing It All Back Home, Columbia CK 9128

---. The Freewheelin' Bob Dylan, Columbia CK 8786

---. Greatest Hits, CK 9463

---. Highway 61 Revisited, Columbia CK 9189

---. The Times They Are A-Changin' Columbia CK 8905

Elvis Presley, Elvis: 30 #1 Hits, RCA Records, RCA 07863068079-2

The Grateful Dead, The Grateful Dead, Warner Brothers 16892

Will Geer, A Tribute To Woody Guthrie, Warner Brothers 9-26036-2

Woody Guthrie, The Ash Recordings Volume 1-4, Smithsonian Folkways SF CD40100/01/02/03

---. Dustbowl Ballads, Folkways FH 5212

---. Library of Congress Recordings, Rounder CD 1041/2/3

Woody Guthrie and Huddie Ledbetter, Folkways: A Vision Shared: A Tribute to Woody Guthrie and Leadbelly, Folkways CK 44034

Jefferson Airplane, Crown of Creation, RCA LSP - 4058

---. Surrealistic Pillow, RCA/Legacy, 82876 50351 2

---. Volunteers, RCA 4238-2-R

---. The Worst of Jefferson Airplane, RCA 4459-2-R RE

Robert Johnson, King of the Delta Blues, Sony Music, CK65211

Huddie Ledbetter, The Legendary Leadbelly, Olympic Records 7103

John Lennon, Acoustic, Capitol Records, CDP 7243 8 74428 2 5

---. Imagine John Lennon: Music from the Original Motion Picture, Capital CDP 7 908032

---. The John Lennon Collection, Capital Records CDP 7 91516 2

---. Mind Games, Capitol SN-16068

---. Rock and Roll, Capital CDP7243 8 74329 2 5

---. Walls and Bridges, EMI Records CDP 7 46768 2

John Lennon/Plastic Ono Band, Imagine, Capital CDP 7 46641 2

---. Live Peace in Toronto 1969, EMI/Capital Records CDP 0777 7 90428 2 1

---. Plastic Ono Band, Capital SW-3372

---. Shaved Fish, Capital CDP 7 46642 2

John Lennon/Yoko Ono, Two Virgins, Tetragrammaton Records/Creative Sounds, ltd. 449818-2

---. Unfinished Music No. 2 Life With the Lions, Rykodisc RCD 10412

---. Wedding Album, Rykodisc RCD 10413

John Lennon & Yoko Ono/Plastic Ono Band, with Elephant's Memory, Some Time in New York City Capitol CDP 7 46782 2

MC5, Kick Out The Jams, Electra EKS-74042

N.W.A., Greatest Hits, Priority Records 0-4992-50561-2-9

Phil Ochs, All the News that's Fit to Sing, Warner Brothers Records, Inc. HNCD 4427

---. Greatest Hits, A&M Records Inc. ED CD 201

---. I Ain't Marching Anymore, Warner Brothers, HNCD 4422

---. Phil Ochs in Concert, Electra Entertainment R2 73501

---. Pleasure of the Harbor, Universal Music Enterprises CCM-137-2

---. Rehearsals For Retirement, Universal Music Enterprises, CCM-150-2

---. Tapes From California, Universal Music Enterprises CCM-138-2

Utah Phillips, We Have Fed You All A Thousand Years, Rounder Records PH 1076

Quicksilver Messenger Service, The Best of Quicksilver Messenger Service, Capitol Records CDL-57263

Gerome Ragni and James Rado, Hair: The American Tribal Love-Rock Musical, BMG Classics 1150-2-RC

Pete Seeger, American Favorite Ballads, Volume 1-5, Smithsonian Folkways Recordings MRC 520

---. American Industrial Ballads, Smithsonian Folkways SF CD 40058

---. Dangerous Songs, Columbia, CK 65262

---. God Bless the Grass, Sony Music Entertainment Inc. CK 65287

---. Greatest Hits, Columbia Records CK 9416

---. Headlines & Footnotes, A Collection of Topical Songs, Smithsonian Folkways SFW CD 40111

---. If I Had A Hammer, Songs of Hope and Struggle, Smithsonian Folkways SF CD 40096

Sly and the Family Stone, Anthology, Epic EGK 37071

Various Artists, 1969: The Original Motion Picture Soundtrack, PolyGram 837 362 2

Various Artists, The Best of Broadside 1962-1988: Anthems of the Underground, from the pages of Broadside Magazine, Smithsonian Recordings SFW CD 40130

Various Artists, Carry it On: Songs of American Working People, Flying Fish Records FF70104

Various Artists, Don't Mourn-Organize!: Songs of Labor Songwriter Joe Hill, Smithsonian Folkways SF 40026

Various Artists, The Encyclopedia of Early Blues Classics, Recording Artists Dejavu Retro R2CD 40-33

Various Artists, Hippie: Music from the 60s Generation, Warner Special Products OPCD7646

Various Artists, The Long Road to Freedom: An Anthology of Black Music, discs 1-5, Buddha Records 74465 997562

Various Artists, The Monterey International Pop Festival: Box Set, Rhino R2 70596

Various Artists, Nuggets: A Classic Collection from the Psychedelic Sixties, Rhino Records R2 75892

Various Artists, Only Rock'n Roll: 20 Pop Hits 1965-1969, Warner Special Products JCD-3126

Various Artists, Psychedelia: The Long Strange Trip, Sony Music DIDP086865

Various Artists, <u>Rebel Voices: Songs of the Industrial Workers of the World</u>, Flying Fish Records FF 70484

Various Artists, <u>Rock On!: The Rock 'n' Roll Greats</u>, N2K Publishing, (CD included with Carol King, <u>Rock On!: The Rock'n'roll Greats</u>, London, Caxton Editions, 2002)

Various Artists, <u>Say it Loud! A Celebration of Black Music In America, discs 1-6</u>, Rhino Entertainment Company R276660

Various Artists, <u>Sing For Freedom: The Story of the Civil Rights Movement Through its Songs</u>, Smithsonian Folkways CD SF40032

Various Artists, <u>Songs of Protest</u>, Rhino Records R2-70734

Various Artists, <u>Songs of the Working People From the American Revolution to the Civil War</u>, Flying Fish Records FF 70483

Various Artists, <u>The '60s Rock Experience</u> (volume 1-3 and Lost Gems) Rhino/Universal Music, Special Markets, DK 33466 / DK 33469 / DK33490 / DK33497

Various Artists, <u>'til we outnumber 'em</u>, Righteous Babe Records RBR019-D

Various Artists, <u>Woodstock: Three Days of Peace and Music 25th Anniversary Collection</u>, (4 cd set) Atlantic 82636-2

The Weavers, <u>The Weavers Greatest Hits</u>, Vanguard VCD- 15/16

Neil Young, <u>After The Gold Rush</u>, Reprise 2283-2

---. <u>Living With War</u>, Reprise Records 44335-2

Online Sources

Frederick Douglas, Narrative of the Life of Frederick Douglass, An American Slave, text maintained at:
http://sunsite.berkeley.edu/Literature/Douglass/Autobiography/02.html by the SunSITE Manager

Johnny Firecloud, "Nas Wants to Sell His CD at Wal-Mart," July 29th, 2008, on http://www.antiquiet.com/reviews/2008/07/nas-wants-to-sell-his-new-cd-at-wal-mart/ accessed (October 19, 2009).

Robert Fulford, "Racism, censorship, and words that sting," The National Post, May 11, 2002 (accessed October 20, 2009).

Warren Hinckle, "The Social History of the Hippies," Ramparts Magazine, March 1967. (Accessed on line December 2013) http://www.unz.org/Pub/Ramparts-1967mar-00005

Shaheem Reid, "Nas Explains Controversial Album Title, Denies Reports of Label Opposition" Oct 18, 2007, on http://www.mtv.com/news/articles/1572287/20071018/nas.jhtml (accessed October 19, 2009).

https://10protestsongs.wikispaces.com/American+Protest+Songs

http://ctl.du.edu/spirituals/freedom/civil.cfm

http://www.cyberhymnal.org/bio/r/o/o/root_gf.htm

http://en.wikipedia.org/wiki/List_of_awards_received_by_Bob_Dylan

http://www.folkarchive.de/breadrose.html

http://www.folkarchive.de/thetramp.html

http://www.folkarchive.de/hill.html

http://www.folkarchive.de/ragged.html

http://www.folkarchive.de/coffee.html

http://www.history.org/history/teaching/enewsletter/february03/worksongs.cfm

http://www.hobonickels.org/iwwsongs.htm#12

http://www.iww.org/history/icons/solidarity_forever/1

https://www.lds.org/topics/mountain-meadows-massacre?lang=eng

http://www.library.arizona.edu/exhibits/bisbee/docs/027.html#JOHN

http://www.marcus-brinkmann.de/slave-songs.html

https://www.marxists.org/history/ussr/sounds/lyrics/international.htm

http://www.mcgath.com/freesongs.html

http://memory.loc.gov/ammem/collections/voices/vfstitle.html

http://www.metrolyrics.com/i-dreamed-i-saw-phil-ochs-last-night-lyrics-billy-bragg.html (accessed September 23, 2013)

http://mudcat.org/detail_pf.cfm?messages__Message_ID=45775

http://murderpedia.org/male.H/h/hill-joe.htm

http://www.nationalgeographic.com/k19/disasters_detail2.html (access September 5, 2013)

http://www.negrosplrltuals.com/news-song/

http://www.pdmusic.org/civilwar2/62wwbtfb.txt

http://philochsthing.wordpress.com/tag/phil-ochs-celia-pomeroy/ (accessed September 5. 2013)

http://politicalfolkmusic.org/wordpress/richard-brazier/

http://www.pdmusic.org/work.html

http://www.songwritershalloffame.org/exhibits/C198

http://www.sing365.com/music/lyric.nsf/I-Dreamed-I-Saw-Phil-Ochs-Last-Night-lyrics-Billy-Bragg/E5401B54BD5F0E3F4825699A00253764 (accessed September 23, 2013)

http://web.cecs.pdx.edu/~trent/ochs/lyrics/i-dreamed-i-saw-phil-ochs.html (accessed September 23, 2013)

Song Index

Song Title	Page(s)
49 Bye-Byes	257
A Cry to Arms	82
A Hard Rain's A-Gonna Fall	195-197
The Abolitionist Song	59
Abraham, Martin and John	239
Age of Aquarius/Let the Sun Shine In	240
Alabama	185
All Hell Can't Stop Us	128
All I Really Want To Do	236
All I Want	162-163
All Quiet on the Potomac	68
All You Need Is Love	239, 274
Almost Cut My Hair	255
America	284
American Skin (41 shots)	283
America's Children	257
An Untitled Protest	246
Angela	272-273, 274, 278
Anti-Nigger Machine	48
Appetite for Destruction	48
Attica State	271-272, 273, 274, 278
Automation Song	214
Babylon is Fallen	77-78
Ball of Confusion	239
Ballad of the Carpenter	218-219
The Ballad of October 16	161
Ballad of William Worthy	214
Barbara Allen	11-12
Battle Cry of Freedom	85-86
Battle Hymn of	48
Black and Blue	47
Black Crow Blues	206
Blowing Down this Road	153
Blowing in the Wind	193-195, 200
The Boll Weevil	23-25
Bonnie Blue Flag	67, 83-85
Born in a Prison	274
Born in the USA	283
Bound for Glory	213

Bourgeois Blues	158, 176
Bracero	219
Bread and Roses	141-142
Bring On the Lucie (Freda People)	276
Brother Can You Spare a Dime	171, 214
Buffalo Skinner	30-32
Bury Me Not On The Lone Prairie	34
California As It Is	25
Cannons of Christianity	219-220
Casey Jones, the Union Scab	135. 163
Celia	214-215
The Century of the Common Man	166
Change is Gonna Come	185
Changes	284
The Charlestown Land Shark	20
Chicago/We Can Change the World	256-257
Chimes of Freedom	236
Coal Creek War (or Coal Creek Rebellion)	104-105
Coffee An'	135-136
Cold Turkey	274
Cold Water	60
Come Join the Nights of Labor Boys	115-116
Come Together	267, 274
Coming Around the Horn	27-28
Coming Into Los Angeles	250
The Commonwealth of Toil	128
Confederates Song	82
Convict Song	106
Cops of the World	220
Corrina, Corrina	197-198
The Cowboy's Dream	34-35
Cowboy's Life is a Dreary, Dreary Life	32-33
Coxey Army	111
Crazy Nigger	48
Crucifixion	221
Dance To The Music	251
The Days of Forty-nine	25
The Death of Emmitt Till (aka The Ballad of Emmett Till)	192-193
De Day ob Liberty's Comin'	75
Deportees	219
Dixie	67, 86-88
Do Re Mi	153, 219

Doctor Robert   262
The Dodger   108-109
Don't Call Me Nigger Whitey   48, 251
Don't Go Down in the Mine, Dad   102-103
Don't Think Twice, It's All Right   197
Down in Charleston Jail   80
Down on Penn's Farm   88-89
Draft Dodger Rag   216-217
Draft Morning   238
The Dream of the Miner's Child   103-104
Drill, Ye Tarriers, Drill   97
Drummer Boy of Shiloh   68-69
Dust Can't Kill Me   153
Dusty Old Dust   181
The Eight Hour Day   107-108
Eve of Destruction   235, 236
Every Man His Own Politician   16-17
Everybody's Been Burned   237
Everyday People   251
Fables of Faubus   185
The Farmer is the Man   22-23
Fight the Power   284
Follow the Drinking Gourd   45-46
For the Dear Old Flag I Die   70
For What It's Worth   243-244, 257
Fortunate Son   251
Forty-niners   25
Free America   12-13
Freedom   249
Freedom Day   185
Fresh Garbage   239
Fuck the Police   284
The Future America   98-99
Get Off the Track   60-61
Get Thee Behind Me   162
Get Together   238
Get Up, Stand Up   283
Give Me Some Truth   269
Give Peace a Chance   266-267, 274, 275
Give Us a Flag   80
Go Down Moses   43-45
Go Join Coxey's Army   111-112
God Bless America   153-154

Going Down the Road Feeling Bad	155
Goober Peas	82-83
Good Golly Miss Molly	232
Goodnight Irene	170
The Good Old Days of 50, '1 and '2	25
Great Balls of Fire	231
Great Day	166
The Great Dust Storm	152
Great Leap Forwards	283
Hail Columbia	15, 67
Handsome Johnny	249
Happy Xmas (War is Over)	269
Hard Times in Dixie	87-88
He Was a Friend of Mine	238, 242
Henry Wallace	166
Here's to the state of Barack Obama	227-228
Here's to the State of Mississippi	217, 227
Hey Jude	249, 262-264
Hi Nigger	48
Hills of West Virginia	218
Ho! For California	27
Hold the Fort	112-113
Hold the Line	181
Home, Sweet Home	66
Hound Dog	274
House of the Rising Sun	183, 206
The Hunters of Kentucky	19-20
I Ain't Got No Home In This World Anymore	153
I Ain't Marching Anymore	216, 223, 227
I Am A Walrus	262
I Don't Wanna Be Called Yo Niga	48
I Don't Believe You	206
I Don't Want to Be a Soldier	269
I Dreamed I Saw Joe Hill Last Night	227, 250
I Dreamed I Saw Phil Ochs Last Night	227
I Kill Therefore I Am	224
The Internationale	119-121
I Shall Be Free No. 10	205
I Want To Hold Your Hand	234, 262
I Want To Take You Higher	251
I'll Be All Right	185
I'll Overcome Someday	185
I'm a Rock and Roll Nigger	48

I've Got a Ballot 166
If I Had a Hammer 183, 184, 194, 213, 215, 237, 239
If We Will, We Can Be Free 116
I-Feel-Like-I'm-Fixin'-to-Die Rag 245-246, 250-251
Imagine 269, 273, 278
Immigration Man 257
In My Life 234
In the Heat of the Summer 217
In the Year 2525 240
Instant Karma 267-268
Iron Lady 218
Is there Anybody Here 220
It Ain't Me Babe 205
It Happens Each Day 237
It Takes a Lot to Laugh, It Takes a Train to Cry 207
It's All Over Now, Baby Blue 208
It's So Hard 273
Its Good News Week 236
The IWW Prison Song 128
Jefferson and Liberty 15-16
John Brown's Body (The John Brown Song) 71-75, 128
John Fremont 58
John Golden and The Lawrence Strike"
        (aka "A Little Talk With Golden") 140-141
John Henry 95-96
John Sinclair 272, 274, 277
Johnny B. Goode 273
Johnny Has Gone for a Soldier 14-15
Just After the Battle 66
Just Before The Battle Mother 69-70
Killing In The Name 283
King Alcohol 60
King Henry 47
Kingdom Coming (Year of Jericho) 76-77
The Klan 249
Knock on the Door 214-215
Labors Ninety Nine 106
Lady Friend 237
Landholders Victory 20
Last Night I Had the Strangest Dream 183
Last Will and Testament 146
Laugh at Me 235

Laughing	256
Lay Down Your Weary Tune	236
Let It Be	234
Let Me Be	235
Let the Sunshine In	250
Let's Impeach the President	284
The Liberty Ball	64
Life in California	25
Like A Rolling Stone	207-208
Links on The Chain	217-218
Little Red Rooster	47
Lonesome Death of Hattie Carol	203
The Long and Winding Road	234
Long Time Gone	247
Looking for a Leader	284
The Lousy Miner	26-27
Love City	251
Love Me Do	239
Love Me, I'm a Liberal	220
Love the One You're With	255
The Lowell Factory Girl	94-95
Luck of the Irish	272, 273, 274
Lucy In The Sky With Diamonds	262
Maggie's Farm	207
Many Thousands Gone	52-53, 192
Marching Song of the First Arkansas (Negro) Regiment	74-75
The March of Labor	114
Maryland, My Maryland	65-66
Masters of War	195
May Day Song	128
Memphis	273
The Message	283
Military Madness	256
The Mills Was Made of Marble	177
Mind Games	275-276
Mixed Up Confusion	198
More War News	161
Morning Dew	244-245
Mother	274
Motherless Child	249, 250
Mountain Meadows Massacre	30-31
Mourn Not the Dead	128

Mr. Block	136-137
Mr. Tambourine Man	205, 206, 208, 236
The MTA Song	182, 183
Music is Love	256
Music Lover	251
My Back Pages	205
My Country	61-62
The New Emancipation Song	63-64
New York City	270, 274
Nigger Be A Nigger	50-51
Nigger in the Cotton Patch	48
Nigger on the Woodpile	48
Nigger Rich	48
Nights of Labor	115
No Irish Need Apply	29-30
No More Songs	226
No Vietcong ever called me a Nigger	48
Norwegian Wood (This Bird Has Flown)	234
November	128
Nutopian National Anthem	276
O Tannenbaum	65
O'Cannan	42
Oh Freedom	53
Oh Happy Day	250
Oh, I'm a Good Old Rebel	89-90
Oh, It's Hard To Be A Nigger	50-51
Ohio	46-47, 255
Old Dan Tucker	60
Old Man River	181
Old Nigger	48
On To Washington	111
One More Parade	213, 216
Only a Miner	100-101
Only a Miner Killed in the Mine	102
Only A Pawn In Their Game	202-203
Only People	276
Open Letter	284
Outside a Small Circle of Friends	221
Oxford Town	195
Paint 'er Red	127-128
Parliament of England	17-18
Pat Works On the Railway	97
Patriotic Diggers	18-19

Peace Frog   239
People Got to Be Free   238
People's Party Song   110
Plop Goes the Missile   181
Poor Miner's Farewell   101-102
The Pope Smokes Dope   270
Power and Glory   213
Power to the People   268, 274
The Preacher and the Slave   135
Pride of Man   245
Prison Song   257
Psychodrama City   237
Purple Haze   252
Pushing Too Hard   236
Rainy Day Women #12 & 35   47
Real Niggaz   48
Real Niggaz Don't Die   48
Rebels   81-82
The Red Feast   128
The Red Flag   144-145
Renaissance Fair   237
Revolution   7, 262-264
The Revolution Will Not Be Televised   283
Rhode Island Algerines' Appeal to John Davis   20
The Rich Lady Over the Sea   13-14
Ringing of Revolution   220
Rock Around the Clock   190
Rocket 88   232
Roll Over Beethoven   232
Running in the Nigger Night   48
The Same Old Merry Go-Round   166
Santo Domingo   220
Say It Loud- I'm Black and Proud   283
School Days   232
Scissor Bill   137-139
Seeking the Elephant   25
Self Evident   284
She Loves You   234
She Said, She Said   262
Shew Fly Don't Bother Me   50
Signs   239
Sioux Indians   28-29
Sisters, O Sisters   272, 274

Sixteen Tons	171, 183, 214
Smoggy Old Smog	181
Solidarity Forever	128-130, 163, 252
Somebody to Love	246, 251
Somebody's Darling	66
Someday a Silent Guard	128
Song of Labor	99-100
The Song of the Rail	128
Southern Man	255-256
The Southern Soldier Boy	66
Spanish Harlem Incident	236
Stand	251
Star Spangled Banner	252
Stars and Stripes of Corruption	283
Step by Step	99
Storm the Fort	113
Straight Outta Compton	48
Strange Fruit	7
Strawberry Fields Forever	249, 262
Sunday Bloody Sunday	274
Superbird	245
Swing Low, Sweet Chariot	42-43, 250
Talkin' John Birch Paranoid Blues	198-199
Talkin' World War III Blues	195-197, 215
Talking Birmingham Jam	213, 217
Talking Cuba Crisis	215-216
Talking Union	162
Talking Vietnam	215
Ta-ra-ra Boom De-ay	134-135
Taxman	234-235
Tears for Johannesburg	185
Tenting on the Old Camp Ground	67-68
Terraplane Blues	47
That Sabo-Tabby Kitten.	125-126
That Was the President	218
That's What I Want to Hear	217
The Thresher	213-214
There But for Fortune	220-221
There is Power in a Union"	134
These Are the Days of Decision	218
They'll Be Paid for Bye and Bye	181
This Land is Your Land	153-154, 213
Ticky Tacky	180

Time of the Season	239-240
The Times They Are A-Changin'	200-201
To My Little Son	128
To My Old Brown Earth	181
To the Men of the North and West	78-79
Tom Dooley	182
Tomorrow Never Knows	262
Too Many Martyrs	213, 215
The Tramp	139-140
Tramp, Tramp, Tramp	79-80, 139
Triad	237-238
Turn, Turn, Turn	181, 236-237
Tutti Fruti	231, 233
Tzena, Tzena, Tzena	170
Up From Your Knees	126-127
The Union Maid	162
The Unknown Soldier	239
The Vacant Chair	66
Volunteers	251-252
The War is Over	222
Wallace Button/Goodbye Harry	166
Wallace Is The Man For Me	166
War	239, 283
War at 33 1/3	48
The Wayfaring Stranger	20
We Are Coming Father Abraham	70
We Can Be Together	252
We Can Win with Wallace	166
We Shall Overcome	185, 187, 250
We Wait Beneath the Furnace Blast	62-63
Welcome to the Terrordome	48
Well Well Well	268
We're All Water	274
What About Me	245
What Are Their Names	256
What's Going On	283
Whatever Gets You Thru the Night	277
What's Happening?!?!	237
What's That I Hear	215
When I Went Off to Prospect	26
When I'm Gone	221
When in Rome	221
Where Have All The Flowers Gone	183, 184, 213

Where the Frazer River Flows 133-134
Which Side Are You On? 162
White Boots Marching in a Yellow Land 222
White Rabbit 47, 246, 152
Why Do You Stand There in the Rain 161
William Butler Yeats Visits
        Lincoln Park & Escapes Unscathed 225
Wisconsin Immigrant 20-22
With A Little Help From My Friends 249
With God On Our Side 201-202, 205
Women is the Nigger of the World 48, 273-274, 278
Wooden Ships 251, 253-254
Woodstock 253
Workers of the World, Awaken! 133
The Workingman's Song 109-110
Working Class Hero 268
Workingmen, Unite! 131-132
The World Began in Eden
        But Ended in Los Angeles 226
Yankee Doodle 67
Yankee Doodle, Tell the Boss 166
You a Nigger Too I'm Black 48
You Don't Have To Cry 254

About the Author

Kevin Comtois has been teaching history and government since 1999. He has taught at Northern Essex Community College (NECC), Merrimack College, Quincy College and many other schools from kindergarten to college. Kevin earned his B.A. in Political Science from Westfield State College and his M.A. in American Civilization from the University of Massachusetts Boston. Kevin was a recipient of two National Endowment for the Humanities grants. One in 2005 to study the history of jazz at Washington University in St Louis MO and the second in 2008 to study the Industrial Revolution in Lowell MA. While serving as a high school social studies department chairman, Kevin designed a course on the history of American music. In 2011 Kevin created and taught an Honors Colloquium at NECC titled the *Social and Political History of American Music* while also participating in NECC's Speakers Bureau. He has been active in local politics since the 1990s, served as Chairman of the Tewksbury Board of Library Trustees in the early 2000s, served on the Tewksbury Historical Society Executive Board and continues as an amateur musician and writer. Kevin is currently teaching US History and American Government at the Academy of Notre Dame in Tyngsboro, MA and offers seven different audio-visual presentations on the history of American music to libraries and senior facilities in eastern Massachusetts and southern New Hampshire. Kevin lives with his wife Maxine in Massachusetts.

You can follow the author's teaching and speaking activities at:
www.kevincomtois.com

Contact the author at
kevin@kevincomtois.com

CPSIA information can be obtained
at www.ICGtesting.com
Printed in the USA
LVHW021547030821
694433LV00013B/995

9 781505 856200